songman

songman

The story of an
Aboriginal Elder
of Uluru

BOB RANDALL

ABC
Books

Published by ABC Books for the
AUSTRALIAN BROADCASTING CORPORATION
GPO Box 9994 Sydney NSW 2001

First published 2003

National Library of Australia
Cataloguing-in-Publication entry
Randall, Bob, 1934– .
  Songman : the story of an Aboriginal elder of Uluru.

  ISBN 0 7333 1262 4.

  1. Randall, Bob, 1934– . 2. Aborigines, Australian –
Northern Territory – Biography. 3. Aborigines, Australian –
Northern Territory – Removal. I. Newbury, Paul, 1940– .
II. Australian Broadcasting Corporation. III. Title.

305.89915092

Edited by Bruce Sims, Sue Wagner
Designed by Jane Cameron, Fisheye Design
Colour reproduction by Colorwize, Adelaide
Printed and bound by Griffin Press, Adelaide

5 4 3 2 1

This project has been assisted by the Aboriginal and Torres
Strait Islander Board of the Australia Council for the Arts,
the federal government's arts funding and advisory body.

Contents

Acknowledgments

I would like to thank the writers who worked with me over many months to produce my story. I met Aruna Byers in the United States while I was visiting there on a tour with the organisation Healing Touch. She arranged for me to return to the United States to talk on Aboriginal spirituality and during this visit offered to help me write my story. Aruna and I worked on this for many weeks. After I returned to Australia I applied for and received a grant from the Australia Council, and I was able to pay Aruna to go on with the work. She joined me in Alice Springs, to continue with the story in 1998. We completed the first draft in early 1999, before she left to continue her work overseas.

In April 1999, I met Barbara Lepani at the Aboriginal Philosophy Farm, a one-week program run by Jack Beetson of Tranby Aboriginal Cooperative College in Sydney. We spent the week discussing Aboriginal philosophy and I was struck by her ability to understand what I was trying to say. Barbara had previously been married to someone from the Trobriand Islands of Papua New Guinea and so had some understanding of the indigenous perspective and how it differed fundamentally from white culture. She had also been studying and practising Tibetan Buddhism for many years. She said she was amazed at the many similarities between the spiritual philosophy I was discussing with her, from an Aboriginal perspective, and that which she had learnt through Tibetan Buddhism. I knew nothing about Tibetan Buddhism, but my eldest son Alan had already made similar comments based on his own reading. A Tibetan lama, Loppon Ngawang Dhamchoe, had also visited me in Alice Springs, and had come with me to my country. We, too, had felt this similarity, and later I talked with him further.

I approached Barbara to help me find a publisher. Through her, I met my literary agent, Barbara Mobbs. After reading the draft prepared by Aruna and myself, both of them decided we needed to produce a new draft which brought out the spiritual philosophy of Aboriginal culture more fully. Barbara Lepani agreed to be my writer, and invited me to come and stay at her place at Stanwell Park, to work on the project together.

By late July 1999 I was able to wind up my affairs in Alice Springs, including retiring from my job with the Institute for Aboriginal Development, and come east to Stanwell Park. Barbara and I then started working on the book. During September, we visited my country in the Central Desert region, and in Arnhem Land, to help Barbara enter more fully into the world of my story. We completed the second draft of the book by Christmas 1999.

My literary agent Barbara Mobbs told me that the manuscript needed serious editing and I needed someone, hopefully with an interest in Aboriginal people, to bring the book into a form acceptable to publishers. At the Tranby College Philosophy Farm gathering in 2000 it was suggested to me by some people there that I contact Paul Newbury to help prepare my book for publication. I approached Paul and I was soon on the path to publication because of Paul's interest and qualifications in this area, especially since he was already published in the area of Aboriginal Studies. I spent a very pleasant time with Paul and Jan at their Bundanoon home and they also came to Mutitjulu in 2001 to spend some time with me there. I am extremely thankful to Paul who has worked assiduously to bring my book to publication, giving shape to my story, applying his editing skills and writing comprehensive notes to accompany the text.

I would also like to acknowledge the support and inspiration of my children and my wider Aboriginal family. They have nurtured me throughout my life and allowed me to find myself as an Aboriginal person. This book and the insights I have gained into our culture are my gift to them.

Bob Randall

Editor's Foreword

It has been my privilege to participate in the editing of this book, and to have helped in bringing it to publication. Bob Randall is a very special person, a *tjilpi* elder, or a person we would describe as a guru. This book is an integral part of Bob's vision, which is the teaching and sharing of Aboriginal culture, knowledge and spirituality with all Australians. As Bob points out more than once in his story, spirituality is the ultimate answer to reconciliation in this country, and he weaves Aboriginal spirituality throughout his story, as he says, 'like a Rainbow Snake'.

Bob Randall illustrates that web of religion and knowledge, that whole way of seeing that is the Aboriginal gift of spirituality. However, the concept of Aboriginal spirituality is not a given, immediately understood by other Australians. In weaving Aboriginal spirituality throughout his life story, Bob Randall gives us crucial insights into how this spiritual tradition is lived out in the lives of Aboriginal people and in their relationships with each other and with the land.

It has been the stated aim of the Council for Aboriginal Reconciliation[1] that reconciliation should mean 'a united Australia that respects this land of ours, values the Aboriginal and Torres Strait Islander heritage, and provides justice and equity for all'.

Bob Randall has given flesh to this statement, and his vision about the issue of reconciliation is an expression of hope of what we can achieve together. Bob is a builder of bridges between two divergent cultures. For those of us who find ourselves alienated from the land, or who are disinherited in that we are not engaged with the natural world, Bob provides the means of re-engagement in the Aboriginal philosophy of *kanyini*, the principle of connectedness through caring and responsibility that underpins Aboriginal life.

For those of us who belong to other world traditions of faith,

Bob Randall's story provides a bridge between our faith and Aboriginal spirituality. The promise of this could mean that many of us are able to look deeply into our own traditions to find anew those spiritual elements in harmony with our time and place. All we need to be is seekers after the truth.

We must aim for more than a grafting of our heritage onto an Aboriginal root. We must aim for a fusion, a synthesis of the old of this continent with the new of the recently arrived. The basic requirement of this mix is acceptance of the Aboriginal heritage as being uniquely appropriate to this continent, and to those of us who live here.

Bob's story, too, meets the need in reconciliation for us to acknowledge the truth of the events surrounding his life, of having like so many others been stolen as a child from his family and community, and of enduring the intense pain of this separation. All this in the context of nations of people forcibly separated from their spiritual base, the land itself. For the land, as Bob attests, is the basis of Aboriginal identity, of their wellbeing. In the words of eminent poet Judith Wright, until we acknowledge this history, 'we other Australians will never begin to heal the wounds we have inflicted on ourselves as well as on the people we have wronged.'[2]

In describing contemporary Aboriginal life, Bob Randall does not flinch from the truth in examining the problems that exist for Aboriginal people with alcohol and drug abuse, and the incidence of violence in Aboriginal communities. He makes the compelling argument that excessive drinking and drug use for Aboriginal people is part of their alienation from the land, and their need to regain a sense of fulfilment and belonging.

Bob Randall also points to the malaise of passive welfare dependency, which traps his people in frustration, alienation and despair. Reliance on welfare is debilitating to Aboriginal people and is a continuing part of their dispossession. Bob notes that regaining their sense of responsibility will lead to recovery for those Aboriginal people trapped in this system. In arguing for full Aboriginal participation in the economy, Bob agrees strongly with the notable Aboriginal spokesperson Noel Pearson.[3]

This book is essential reading for those who desire positive change in Australia in our relationships with our indigenous peoples, towards reconciliation. In *Edge of the Sacred*, David Tacey argues that spiritual change and revival is needed before our social and political life can move forward. Tacey says that 'the cure for our ecologically disastrous abuse of the earth and for our culturally debilitating racism is the spiritual renewal of consciousness.' This will not happen until we learn to respect the mystical bond between this land and its Indigenous inhabitants.[4]

Charles Perkins gave us great hope when he wrote of how an Australia, fully reconciled with her Aboriginal peoples, might appear:

My expectation of a good Australia is when white people would be proud to speak an Aboriginal language, when they realise that Aboriginal culture and all that goes with it, philosophy, art, language, morality and kinship, is all part of our heritage. And that's the most unbelievable thing of all, that it's all there waiting for us all. White people can inherit 40 000 or 60 000 years of culture, and all they have to do is reach out and ask for it.[5]

Paul Newbury

My Brown Skin Baby

Ya-weh, ya-weh
My brown-skin baby they take him away

As a young preacher I used to ride,
My quiet pony around the countryside,
In the native camp I'll never forget,
A young black mother, her cheeks all wet.

Between her sobs I heard her say,
'Police been take 'em my baby away,
From white man boss that baby I had,
Why he let 'em take baby away?'

Ya-weh, ya-weh,
My brown-skin baby they take him away.

To a children's home a baby came,
With new clothes on and a new name,
Day and night he would always cry,
'Mummy, mummy, why'd they take me away?'

Ya-weh, ya-weh,
My brown-skin baby they take him away.

The child grew up and had to go,
From the mission home that he loved so,
To find his mother he tried in vain,
Upon this earth he'd never see her again.

Ya-weh, yah-weh
My brown-skin baby they take him away

Map showing location of Speakers of Western Desert Dialects

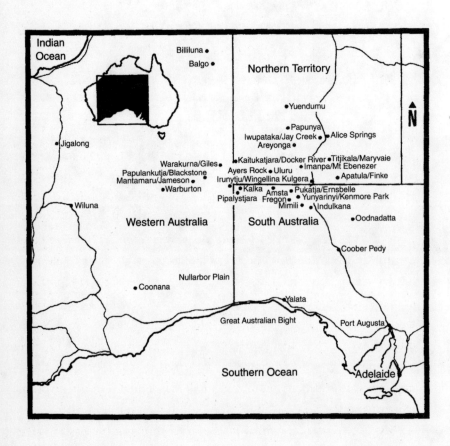

Tjukurrpa

our sacred relationship
to the land and all creation

My name is Bob Randall and I am *Anangu*, a *tjiḻpi* (elder) of the
Yankunytjatjara people, and one of the listed traditional owners of
Uluru, the great red rock which lies at the very heart of Australia,
in the central Western Desert region. I was born some sixty-five
years ago, at a place they now call Middleton Ponds on Tempe
Downs station, on the banks of the Palmer River, 200 kilometres
south-west of Alice Springs. But I did not know my true identity
until I was in my thirties. You see, I am one of the Stolen Generations.[1] Although my mother was Yankunytjatjara, and I lived
amongst her people in my early childhood, following a largely traditional way of life, my father was one of the white men who were
given grants over our land to run cattle and sheep stations. In those
days it was quite common for tribal Aboriginal women to have
babies from the white men who settled in outback Australia.

My Yankunytjatjara tribal land is a vast area on the eastern side
of Uluru. Our country is bounded to the west by the Petermann
Ranges and to the south by the loop of the Musgrave Ranges. It
stretches east to the Basedow Ranges and north to Lake Amadeus.
This desert landscape glows with the rich red ochre of the soils,
enlivened by the pale gold spinifex (*tjanpi*) grasses that are sharp
enough to cut the skin. Dotted across the red desert sands are the

acacia trees, home of the precious *maku* (witchetty grubs) and the hardy mulga trees from whose wood we shape our boomerangs and fighting sticks. So although this is a desert and water is scarce, it is not just sand. About thirty kilometres north-west of Uluru lies Kata Tjuta (place of many heads), with its domes of conglomerate rock separated by deep fissures. From a distance it looks like an ancient fortress, and lying within these sensuous folds of rock is the mysterious valley of the Whispering Wind. Here it is as if one can feel the very heartbeat of mother Earth, herself. On the other side of Uluru, going south, is another great dome of rock. We call this place Atila, the home of the Ice Men. This place is sacred dangerous, meaning that it can cause illness if approached without the proper spiritual authority.

A white man, William Gosse, named Uluru 'Ayer's Rock' after the then governor of South Australia. White men also named Kata Tjuta 'The Olgas', and Atila, 'Mt Connor'. But Uluru and these other great sacred sites go back to the time of creation, the *tjukurrpa*, to the Rainbow Serpent and the great ancestor creator beings who took the shape of many things to create the land and all the life forms we see today. Since 1985, when the land of Uluru was returned to its traditional owners, it has become Uluru again, and the Olgas once again have become known as Kata Tjuta, but on the maps Atila is still called Mt Conner and few people know the story of the Ice Men.

Uluru itself is majestic and awesome. Even white people feel this, and it has become one of the world's main tourist pilgrimage places. In the early morning, as the Sun rises to warm our other mother, the Earth, it glows molten red, then golden as the sun climbs high into the sky. During the day, the vast, brilliant blue, desert sky shimmers with heat, even in winter. At sunset, as the night rises from the eastern skyline, Uluru slowly changes its gown for its night dress, a deep purple dissolving into the beautiful blackness of the night. At this time my country is brilliant with stars, the campfires of our ancestors, the spirit people of the sky.

When I was a child I lived in a home without walls. These stars were the ceiling of my house and the earth was the floor. The horizon was just the entrance to another bedroom. Nothing separated me from the wind, the heat and the cold, or the sounds of the birds and insects that lived in my country. For seven precious years I lived like this, and through the stories told to me as we walked through country, or sat around the fire at night, this landscape and everything in it was my intimate family.

Many people around the world know us, the Yankunytjatjara and other people of the Western Desert, through our paintings. These paintings are all inspired by the vision of *tjukurrpa*, our sacred relationship to the land and all creation. *Tjukurrpa* is the Yankunytjatjara name for what white people call the Dreaming, or the Dreamtime. It is hard to describe the idea of *tjukurrpa* in English. We do not separate the material world of objects we see around us, with our ordinary eyes, and the sacred world of creative energy that we can learn to see with our inner eye. For us, these are always working together and we learn how to 'see' and 'hear' in this inner way from a young age. It took me a long time to understand that white people do not experience the world in this way. We work through 'feeling'. But we are not using this word feeling to mean ordinary emotions like anger, desire or jealousy, or our sense of physical touch. When we use the English word 'feeling' in this way we are talking more about what white people call intuitive awareness. We use this to feel out situations, to read people, and to talk to country.

Tjukurrpa is called 'Dreaming' because it joins the worlds of ordinary reality and creative forces, and because it is not just of this time and place. But it is not something we dream in our heads; it is our knowledge of creation itself: past, present and future. Once we drew our paintings on the sand as part of the ceremonies by which we passed on the deepest knowledge of the *tjukurrpa*. After the ceremonies these sand paintings were dissolved into space, scattered into the wind, the knowledge now part of us, informing every aspect of how we lived our lives, in our relationship to one another, to country and to the mysteries of creation itself. Now we paint on canvas and these paintings hang in art galleries, in the foyers of big office buildings and in many people's houses, all over the world. But few people know their real meaning.

There is such a gulf between the traditional Aboriginal way of understanding reality and the way white society seems to understand. For us, everything is intimately interconnected. But white people separate things out, even the relationship between their minds and their bodies, but especially between themselves and other people and nature. For example, they have one sort of doctor who fixes the body, and another sort of doctor who fixes the mind, and yet another sort of person who is responsible for spirit. And none of these sorts of people have anything to do with responsibility for country. This in turn is split up between people who use the land, like farmers, pastoralists and miners, or people who look after nature like environmentalists and national parks and wildlife rangers. This seems really crazy to our way of thinking and experiencing reality. So, on the one hand our paintings tell the story of people's relationship to country, to bush tucker (food), to waterholes and to people. But underpinning all of these are the deeper stories of our links to ancestral creation, the vibrating hum of existence that is recorded in the Dreaming tracks and in our sacred sites.

I want to write my story so that you will understand what I have learned about the *tjukurrpa* and our spirituality, that informs these paintings and has shaped my life and given me the strength to recover my Aboriginal identity, despite being stolen from my family at such a young age. Especially I want to tell you about the sacred principle of *kanyini*, unconditional love and responsibility to all things.

It was through my folk songs and poetry, as well as working with my people, that I found a way to communicate my feelings, and the feelings of my people, as we struggled to understand the nightmare which engulfed us. The government, the missionaries and the miners and cattle station owners spread across Australia and took everything from us: our land, our language, our ceremonies, our Law and even us, the children. In Aboriginal culture, our knowledge is kept alive and passed down through *inma*, the epic song cycles of the *tjukurrpa*, which are sung, danced and painted, vividly imprinting them in our minds and every cell of our being. Everything we were taught, we remembered. For example when a group of young boys are being taken along a Dreaming track through ceremony, at important points of the journey which might be as much as twenty kilometres apart, they will be told the story of that site by the ceremonial elders. At any one of those sites they might be asked about any aspect of the story or song cycle associated with that site. If any one of these boys does not get every detail correct, then the whole group will return to the beginning of the Dreaming track, and start the journey again. We had no books or tape recorders, so our minds were trained in this way to remember everything. Thus the songman of Aboriginal culture was historian, teacher and entertainer, and this continues in the modern world through those of us who, like me, have become songwriters and performers.

In my late twenties I had a job as a freight handler with the small aeroplanes which fly from Darwin to remote areas. I was in a plane flying high over the coast of Arnhem Land on the way to Croker Island, when the words of my song 'My Brown Skin Baby' came to me. I was sitting alone in the passenger area looking out the window and thinking about how beautiful everything looked. I just loved flying around when nothing had to be done. The waves of the Arufura Sea were gently caressing the sandy shore and the water shimmered as the plane soared away from the land. This scenery, brought alive by the clear blue sky, brought back memories of my boyhood at the Croker Island mission, when this ocean was my playground.

On this particular day I was also enjoying the sight of a reflection of the plane in the clouds. It had a rainbow around it, a symbol of great sacredness to my people. Suddenly someone whispered to me, 'I've got a song for you, write it down.' My eyes quickly swept the cabin looking for who it was that was giving me this message. But there was no one there. I knew then that a spirit was talking to me, not a human being. I sat quietly and waited for the words to come.

In a few moments the spirit of my mother appeared in the seat next to me. She said, 'Son, I want you to put this song down.' Tears began to form as I searched for something to write with, and they poured down my face as I wrote the words, 'My brown skin baby they take him away'. I wrote as fast as I could because the rest of the words and music seemed to come all at once. What I was writing brought back all the feelings of anger and frustration that I had hidden so well since I was taken from my family as a young child. I cried and cried. It had been bottled up in me for so long.

The pain that I carry is so deep that whenever I sing this song it takes me to hell and back. I now know that many others are hurting as deeply as I am. For more than thirty years I have sung this song all over the world. It doesn't matter where I am or who I am singing it to, everyone who hears it seems to be affected by it in the same way that I am. This song proved to be so powerful, it became one of the triggers for raising the whole issue of the experience of Aboriginal children who were stolen from their families.

Bill McKinnon, the policeman who stole me from my family, was called our police 'protector'. In those days we Aboriginal people were not citizens of this country, and we had no civil rights. Instead we were under the control of the government Protection Board. Because white people had passed the law that all mixed-race children were to be taken from their tribal mothers and placed in institutions to be brought up in the ways of the white man, it was these 'protectors' who ruled our lives. They had the power to ride into any Aboriginal camp or house and remove children. Consequently the word 'protection' has a bitter ring to Aboriginal people.

When you go back and read historical documents from this time, you discover white people had a great fear of intermarriage between races, and a great desire to defend the purity of the white race, which they regarded as vastly superior to any others. They had decided that the traditional Aboriginal people were destined for extinction, and they wanted to breed out mixed-race people, whom they regarded as a really big social problem[2]. I always wondered if my white father had tried to stop the police taking me away, but I was told that because of this law even he was powerless to prevent this.

The great mystical symbol which lies at the heart of all the Aboriginal nations is the Rainbow Serpent, and it appears in the stories of the many Aboriginal nations which comprise Australia. The snake is a very sacred and powerful cosmic symbol for my people. It is both male and female and is so sacred that many of the stories, especially among my people, may not be spoken about publicly. But it takes many forms and has many names, and each of these stories conveys deep truth to us about our lore. These stories are passed on to us through the sacred ceremonies that we call men's business and women's business. Men follow their path, learning from older men, and women follow their path, learning from older women. These ceremonial elders are the spiritual teachers of Aboriginal culture.

One of the stories I carried in my head, from my early childhood with my mother and her people, is the story of the snake (*kuniya*) people, and so the snake has always had a very special personal meaning for me. Because Uluru is so sacred to my people, there are many, many stories associated with its creation. Some of these stories are about the snake people, the *Kuniya* and the *Liru*, as well as the Rainbow Serpent, itself, known by the Yankunytjatjara as *Wanampi*. For example in one such story, *Kuniya* came from the east to Uluru. She carried her children, the eggs, on her head in a *coolamon*, the wooden carrying dish used traditionally by Aboriginal women. Because she was hungry and tired, she put the eggs down in a shelter on the north-eastern side of Uluru. The story that I carried with me throughout my childhood, and which grew from the story my mother had told me as a child, goes like this:

A long time ago my people lived on an island way in the north. Then the world started to become dangerous. The earth trembled and many volcanoes started to send fire into the sky. We called in all the meat eating birds and asked them to go out and find a safe place for us to move to. So they went out and searched far and wide, but everywhere there was destruction. Soon even the sea started to boil. So we called in our mother, the great Snake. She said, 'Quickly, climb onto my back and I will take you to a safe place.' So all the people quickly scrambled onto the back of the snake. My people, the Yankunytjatjara, were the first, and we climbed on behind the snake's head.

She urged us to hurry because she could feel her own body begin to cook. The snake then began to swim through the boiling sea. As she plunged through the sea, bits of her body broke off, carrying those people with them. These became the islands spread out towards Australia from Japan. Then the wedge-tailed eagle flew in and told the snake about a land he had found in the far south, where it was calm. By then only the head and shoulders of the snake, carrying the Yankunytjatjara people, were left. Everything else had fallen off into the boiling sea. The snake swam south, finding the northern end of Australia, then continuing down the coast till it came to a great bay. And this is where my people came to live. Uluru is the head of the mother snake that rescued us from that time of destruction and brought us south to where we live today.

When I studied geography during my years of schooling at the Croker Island mission, and learned about the map of the world and the shape of the islands that lie south from Japan, I would remember the snake story. I would draw the snake across the ocean, with the head at Uluru. Always my heart unconsciously drew me back to my origins.

Once you understand anything about Aboriginal culture, you begin to realise just how cruel the policy of taking mixed-race children from their Aboriginal families was. We are not like white people who think of themselves, primarily, as individuals. We are always family. Aboriginal people know one another through their family connections which also extend into their connection with their country. We are the descendants of our creation ancestor beings, and our country is our original mother. Another line of connection we have is through our totemic identity that is associated with our place of conception or birth. Our totems, whether birds or animals, are intimate members of our personal family. So to take us away to a world that was emotionally cold and hostile to us, even though it gave us food and shelter, was like spiritual death. It has left a wound in us that is so deep that it has dominated our lives. Many of us were crushed by our experience. Some of us found a way back to our Aboriginal ancestry and identity, and through this we discovered how much we had lost: language, ceremony and the closeness of family.

Although I suffered the great pain of being stolen from my Yankunytjatjara people, I was fortunate to be adopted by the Iwaidja people of Croker Island and the Gunwingku people of western Arnhem Land and the Gupapingu people of Galiwin'ku (Elcho Island) in eastern Arnhem Land. They shared with me their traditions and sacred lore and so kept alive my Aboriginal identity. As a mixed-race person living on the Mission, I was not encouraged to mix with full bloods (tribal Aborigines), but as I grew older I found a way to spend more and more time with them. As they taught me to be a hunter, they also taught me their lore. Even though their stories are different from those of the Yankunytjatjara, they share the same reverence for the ancestral time of creation, and the naturalness of life, and the secret Law of the Rainbow Serpent, known as Ngalyod in western Arnhem Land. Although I was never able to undertake the traditional initiations of my Yankunytjatjara people, through which the lore is passed on, I was able to receive a great deal of this learning through my extended families of eastern and western Arnhem Land. I am not just a man of the desert, but also of saltwater country, and in this I am doubly blessed.

As I grew into an adult, as well as being a community worker with my people, I have also lived in the world of the white man, working in hospitals, mining companies and universities. This has enabled me to become a translator between worlds, bringing the understanding of Aboriginal culture to the world of white doctors and nurses, lawyers, teachers and school children through my songs and stories, as well as my work. In this way I have been able to see how the Aboriginal spiritual philosophy of *kanyini* can help us find a way to live in tune with the *tjukurrpa* and with modern society.

My Yankunytjatjara family was drawn into the white man's world when Bill Liddle established his sheep station at Angas Downs in our tribal country. My family were involved in helping him care for his sheep, and looking after his house. It was the government system, at the time, to give station owners rations for the Aboriginal people who lived on their land. This was to compensate us for the loss of our traditional hunting game, chased away by the new animals, sheep and cattle. It was also meant to stop us killing the sheep and cattle for food, in the same way we had always hunted kangaroo, emus and other animals.

Station owners traded these rations with the Aborigines living on their land for labour and they also gave us parts of the bullocks that they didn't want for themselves. The ration system caused most Aborigines to settle down near stations instead of wandering around large areas looking for food. The rations consisted of flour, sugar and tea, and thus began our slide into dependency, acquiring with white man's food many of the problems which have beset my people ever since.[3]

At first my people didn't mind working for the station owners because the station was built on their land and they believed it was their responsibility, according to the Laws of *tjukurrpa*, to care for it. You see, Aboriginal people did not really understand this idea of 'owning' land. From our way of looking at things, the land owned us, it bestowed on us the responsibility for maintaining the sacred living energies of the *tjukurrpa*. We could not understand how white people could be so uncivilised as not also to feel this responsibility, once they lived in our *ngura*, our country.

I remember my childhood as a mixture of living at our camp on Angas Downs and travelling around with the livestock. When we travelled I learned what was good to eat and what was not. My family still hunted and ate bush food because this was an important part of our way of living. We ate meat from kangaroos, emus and the many varieties of lizards. We also ate honey ants and witchetty grubs. When we came upon these foods someone would catch them and feed them to us kids. We were also fed the local 'bush tucker', the fruits and vegetables that our parents found in the area.

My favourite bush food was the witchetty grub that we call *maku*. It is a white grub that lives in the roots of the acacia bush and in the river gum trees. *Maku* is oily and very nutritious. The closest way that I can describe how it tastes is to say that when it is cooked, it is like whole wheat bread with lots of butter and an egg on top. *Maku* is eaten raw or cooked and I like it both ways. When it was tested for nutritional value, the scientists found that one small grub about the size of my finger is equal in proteins, oils, minerals and vitamins to a steak as big as my hand. We had no idea they were so good for us. We liked them because they were easy to find and they tasted good. The mothers also used them as an ointment to treat wounds.

Recently I visited my family at Mutitjulu, the Aboriginal community who live next to Uluru. We went out with three of my aunties to look for my childhood delicacies, *maku* (witchetty grubs) and *tjala* (honey ants). We found both, as my aunties have a very keen eye for the signs that direct our attention to the mulga tree whose roots are their home. We followed the trail of the worker ant that feeds the ants that store the honey, and started digging deep into the ground. Eventually we found the tunnels, and sure enough, there were the ants with their swollen golden brown sacs of honey. My aunties carefully lifted them out with a small stick. Then we sat around, a cool breeze and the shade of the tree balancing the strong heat of the sun, as we sucked the honey from the sacs. It has a slightly caramelised flavour, compared with the bee honey most people are used to. Not far away we found an acacia tree that my aunties decided was a likely home for the *maku*. They dug down into the roots and broke off some of the pieces of root. And there in the roots were a number of big, fat *maku*. We made a fire and my aunties baked the maku in the hot sand beside the fire. Barbecued *maku* sure is delicious.

They felt so pleased with themselves that they started singing the song of the *maku* and this led them to stand up and start doing the *maku* dance. This experience was so precious to me. It flooded me with memories of my childhood, so very long ago, and filled me with tenderness for my people, still living their *tjukurrpa* despite the vast tourist industry which has grown up around them, bringing thousands of visitors each day to visit Uluru and Kata Tjuta.

As a child, I felt I had total freedom and I could go wherever I wanted at any time. There were always the eyes of so many aunties, uncles, mothers and fathers watching for my safety. Everybody was responsible for each other, that is *kanyini*. In this way, the *tjukurrpa* Law of *kanyini* informed every aspect of my universe.

When I was a young boy it could get just as cold as it does now, but we adjusted our body temperatures to keep warm by getting close to other people. On a really cold night we would invite the dogs to sleep with us. If the wind was blowing the mothers would pick a spot for us to camp that was in a low area among the sand hills, where the natural movement and direction of the wind could be directed away from us. If we were on flat country, they would make windbreaks out of tree branches and shape them like a horse-shoe, and put clumps of grass on top of them to create shadow or a shelter. Everyone in the family would then sleep close together inside this one walled area.

If we weren't using a shelter we would use a branch to sweep an area free of debris and sleep on the ground. It was really comfort-able. When the ground was hard we would just dig at it with a rock or a stick to soften it up. One of my favourite sleeping areas was in the dry sandy creek bed at Eyra Rock Hole, where there was a huge rock and a beautiful big gum tree.

All the elements of nature were part of our life experience. When it rained we got wet and when there was a flood we went to higher ground. We didn't worry about what happened to us. If a shelter was washed away we built another one when it was needed. Our actions were always determined by our needs. We didn't plan anything. We had no intention of staying in any one place permanently, so we didn't build permanent shelters. Everything material was very temporary. What was permanent was *tjukurrpa*. Even today I cannot get excited about architecture, even by grand buildings like the Sydney Opera House. I enjoy the different functions that buildings perform, but they always seem a physical scar on the landscape.

Some of my most vivid childhood memories are of times when we'd come across a certain plant and one of the mothers would tell us a story about that plant, sing us a song about it, and do the dance and the painting that was associated with it. The mothers would draw the stories on the ground with their finger or with a stick. Our hands were the only musical instruments we had then, so we clapped them on different parts of our bodies when the women were singing. Sometimes we would get a stick and hit it on the ground to keep time with the singing. There were no didgeridoos in the central Australian desert then. We were continually being given information about our environment through these creation stories of the *tjukurrpa*. This is how we grew up with the knowledge that everything in nature was part of our family.

They also taught us how to track for food. We learned how to judge the freshness of the tracks we found so that we would know if an animal was still around or if we were wasting our time looking for it. The land contours gave us information about foods that were available in a particular area. A certain kind of rock outcrop was home to echidnas and rock kangaroos. On the lower hills we could find plains kangaroos, wallabies and lizards. On the flatlands we could find honey ants in the mulga trees, *maku* in the acacia bushes and marsupials and reptiles. Hollow trees in the river beds were home to birds, possums and bush cats, and the big river red gum trees provided us with the other variety of *maku* and a white sugar that formed on their leaves during the winter months. After the rains we looked forward to finding grevillea flowers on the sand hills because they shared with us their beautiful sweet nectar.

Tjukurrpa gave us a strong sense of 'ours-ness'. Whenever I hear someone say, 'My way is the best', it seems so limiting to me. It is like saying, 'How little I am'. In the *ours-ness*, I see myself as an integrated part of the whole universe. In the *ours-ness*, I am related in many different ways to everything in front of me, around me and about me. Above, beneath and on every side. And I feel as if I am all of it.

We love and care for everyone in the same way, whether it is the smallest babies or the oldest people. We have no kings, queens, headmen or boss people who put themselves up as special and expect everyone to treat them differently. We don't pay special homage to certain ones because they are wiser or they have special gifts. We all give freely of our gifts and everything we have wherever and whenever it is required. Until the white lifestyle came in, there were no poor or homeless because those that were less fortunate would always be cared for. We were all bound by the Law of *kanyini* from the time of the *tjukurrpa*, the thread of connectedness, caring and responsibility that links *walytja* (family and kinship), *kurunpa* (spirit and soul in all things) and *ngura* (my 'country' or home). It was this that I lost when I was taken away, as happened to so many of my people.

We Were Warned

Chorus
We were warned by the crows,
We were warned by the eagle,
We were warned by the elders of the tribe,
We were warned by the emu,
and the big kangaroo,
They told us what would happen to our land.

As I sit alone at nights
And hear about land rights,
With troubles for the Aborigines;
How we've lost all we've had,
By the coming of white man,
All live now on empty promises.

Chorus

We were told of the future,
By the creatures of the land,
From results of destruction everywhere.
As we lived a life so gay,
Having love and peace each day,
Even when we met them on our shore.

Chorus

The stars up in the sky,
Sent messages from high,
From spirits of our race now long gone by.
The old men spoke of end,
But we trusted our new friend;
Now we see what has happened to our race.

Kanyini

the principle of connectedness that underpins Aboriginal life

Kanyini is the principle of connectedness through caring and responsibility that underpins Aboriginal life, linking four main areas of responsibility: *tjukurrpa* (philosophy, Law and religion), *ngura* (country), *walytja* (kinship and family) and *kurunpa* (spirit, soul and psyche).

There is us, as humans who have been given the Laws of *tjukur-rpa* to apply *kanyini* to all people. But this was never a restricting

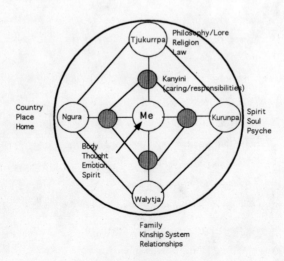

The Connectedness of Kanyini

thing because the term 'people' means all of us. Right throughout my life, old men would point to a forest of trees or a grove of trees or just one tree and refer to it as people: 'See that mob over there.' This way of talking could be referring to kangaroos, trees, hills or humans. Any of us could be 'that mob' or 'us mob' could include the totality of that. Throughout my life I discovered, from other Aboriginal groups with whom I have lived, that having that idea of connecting with all things was quite common through the different Aboriginal nations.[1]

Tjukurrpa is creation, the one time in the beginning when all things were created, and which we need to keep alive in the present. This includes not only the landforms and the original plants, insects, reptiles and birds, but also the social laws, the lore, which we have to live by. All this comes from *tjukurrpa*. This is the bigger consciousness of something that was and is the way to live, the way to live in harmony with all things. Living this is a matter of how we do things in the present. So when we think about time, it is only the now, the present, that is important. In each and every moment of 'now-ness' is where we live out the truth of the connectedness of *kanyini*.

Recently two psychologists flew out from Vienna to visit me to talk about the Dreaming. They explained that they were doing research on something they called 'lucid dreaming'. By that they seemed to mean people who can travel in their dreams. But as I explained to them, the Dreamtime,[2] the *tjukurrpa*, has nothing to do with dreaming. It is much bigger than that. It is our reality, not something we are dreaming about. It is very real. The creation period is not something that just existed in the past. To us it is also part of the present and will continue to exist in the future. When I look at a certain rock, it is not just a rock, it is my link to *tjukurrpa* and all the stories of creation that exist in that rock. Within a grain of sand I see me and the universe. Only our way of thinking, the thought that we are not an essential part of the universe, lessens our belonging, or our being part of what is, what has been, and what will always be. For me, I am part of the whole of *tjukurrpa*. It is the same when I hear the song of a bird, or find the tracks of an animal. When I tell *tjukurrpa* stories or sing the songs, I too am part of the past, present and future of all creation. Caring for the land by telling the stories, singing the songs and doing the dances and paintings is my responsibility. Separating me from that makes me weak.

My *ngura* (country) can be my tribal area or my house. It is also the idea that wherever I am at any moment of time, that is my 'country', my *ngura*, and it is my responsibility to get to know my country as intimately as possible. So wherever I go, the first thing I do is to get to know my *ngura*, and to make friends with all the birds and animals who live there. As a Yankunytjatjara I have special responsibilities as an 'owner' of different parts of my tribal country, and as a 'caretaker' of other parts. Through my mother's side, I am one of the traditional registered owners of Uluru, and a senior man (*tjilpi*) of my people there. My sisters are also senior elders and holders of women's ceremonial knowledge.

Walytja, our system of kinship, of family relationships, is how we express the connectedness of things through family. When you look at the Aboriginal family, there are many mothers and fathers, because there are four lines of relationship in our kinship system. One line is our physical bloodline. Another line is ceremony, the group of people who undertake ceremony together. Another line is the totemic line, linking all people who share the same totem. And finally there is the line that links all people who speak the same language. The whole tribal group is family, it's related, it's very big and if you break any part of that you are weaker. In modern times we also have the relationship that has developed from shared experience, such as all of us who were stolen, and are known as the Stolen Generations. Through our system of *walytja* we know how to relate to each other, our rights and responsibilities and where we can seek our wives. In Aboriginal society no one is a stranger. Everyone is family, everyone is brought within *walytja*. If our totem is, for example, a certain bird, then members of that bird family can communicate directly with us. We are of one mind, one family.

Kurunpa (spirit or soul) is the third aspect of our connectedness. Everything has *kurunpa*. I have got to be responsible for the strength in my spirit, the holiness has got to be mine. It is here right beside me always. We cannot move without each other. If *kurunpa* is weak and it is hanging back, it affects me physically. Our *kurunpa* is affected by everything we allow into our minds. For example, because under the Laws of *walytja* I am responsible for all my family, if I were to refuse to help because I wanted to keep money for myself, for something that I wanted, then my *kurunpa* would grieve. I would feel a sickness of spirit. A physical being without *kurunpa* will die.

Linking all these together is the principle of *kanyini*, the caring and responsibility for relationships on all levels. My understanding is that lots of lines of communication spread out from me and through me in every direction, just like a spider's web. That web is *kanyini*. The knowledge of this comes from *tjukurrpa* and it is what keeps *tjukurrpa* alive in the present. As you spread these lines out from you like a spider's web, they lead into the knowledge of so many things which benefit you, physically, mentally and spiritually.

So you see with the *tjukurrpa* Dreaming tracks, as the creator ancestor beings walked and created the topography around us, they did things and these could be like the little knobs on the spider's web. Those could become very significant or special or even sacred. Sacred joyously, or dangerously, to every person in that nation, like my people, the Yankunytjatjara. Most nations where I come from have their sacred sites, sites of significance and sites to be aware of. You work through the traditional owners of that line to find out what these sites are about and what you can and cannot do near them. Do you have to keep away from them or can you camp up close to them or can you swim in them? For example, if it is a waterhole and a place of ancestral creation, you will treat the site with great care, that is your responsibility; that is *kanyini*.

When white people came and made our land into sheep and cattle stations, we found it so much harder to fulfil our sacred responsibilities of *kanyini*. To them a waterhole was just a place to water their sheep and cattle. They did not understand its relationship to the *tjukurrpa* as a sacred place. As caretakers and owners of these sacred sites, our inability to meet our responsibilities of *kanyini* makes us sick, because it directly affects our *kurunpa*.

We can use this *kanyini*, this connectedness, through caring and responsibility in so many ways. That is why I like using the image of the spider's web. The spider knows, by the vibrations, when there is an insect hitting it, even right at the far end of the web, and whether it is safe to approach. These vibrations are coming and going with everything around us all the time. The spider also knows, by the vibrations, if there is something out there that is caught which is dangerous. So it knows not to go near it, or to circle around it and hope it breaks free. In this way the spider doesn't get himself killed by the rough actions of whatever it is that he has caught in his web. It is the same with us. We have to learn to feel the vibrations. And we can feel that with each other. A person can come to you and you can feel the vibration. Is it dangerous or is it not dangerous? And there are many other feelings between these extremes that allow you to make judgements as to whether to make friends, or something stronger than friendship, or to keep your distance because they could be dangerous for you. We should tune ourselves to that.

The *Tjukurrpa* Dreaming tracks crisscross all of this country, from east to west, and south to north, and every other direction from the middle of the continent. So you can see that these energy lines, all the way from Central Australia, are right across the continent. It is up to me to determine how long or short these energy lines are for me. I can have it long or short spiritually, long or short mentally or long or short physically. That is up to me and that affects me and my worldview of what is around me in every way that I exist.

What keeps the spirit (*kurunpa*) alive is the *kanyini*, the unconditional love and responsibility towards all things. This is so regardless of whether they are family members or other people and things, such as the spirit entities of the storm, earth and wind. They are just creator beings that are also people. What we have to do is to go beyond the action that could be really bad to get to the unconditional love. Go beyond the action and still love that person, including even my actions and to love myself. No conditions, no barriers. No saying I love you, *because*, or I love you, *if*. It is just, I love you.

Right from the *tjukurrpa* there were creator beings in the forms of whatever animal they chose for their spirit to be represented in. This was just a choice to do what they needed to have done. They could change anything. Spirits are not restricted. By showing that they could be humans, plants or animals, and by residing in the very landforms of country, we can see that all of life is connected into this single force, *tjukurrpa*. And this pervades all of time and space. Even today, our people see the spirits coming in all things, in birds and in the actions of animals. They are realities to a lot of our people, so they would pay special attention to the behaviour of certain birds. They can be referred to as messengers bringing good messages, or as bringing sad messages, or messages that people whom we have not seen for a while are coming.

From that time of the beginning when the land was featureless, the ancestor beings came out, and under the light of the stars, they started to move. As they moved across the landscape they developed their Dreaming tracks or song lines.[3] Every site has the story, the song, the dance and the painting. This is what you follow, the trail of these ancestor beings. And in every place where they did something, or if something happened while they were there, then that is the spot for ceremony and that site becomes very significant to that song line. Some ancestor beings didn't move very far at all, they were very localised. There are a number of stories around Uluru where the story is just in those particular areas. Others covered great distances, coming in to Uluru, or moving outwards, creating the *Tjukurrpa* Dreaming tracks. We Aboriginal people can find our way across country, because we learn to read country through these Dreaming tracks, passed on to us through stories and dances, particularly through ceremonial activities. There are different levels of ceremonial knowledge. Those at the highest level are our ceremonial elders and their knowledge is so deep that they are one with the ancestral beings. Today these ceremonies are still being performed in the Central Desert region and in Arnhem Land. For example, when young men are undertaking the Red Ochre ceremonies, the police will close the roads so that the uninitiated will not see them. This same thing happens in Arnhem Land. The ceremonial elders send a message down to the Land Council that ceremony is about to take place, and they close the road for a few days. During this time people can't use the road to come in, or to travel out. So the Land Council telephones around and lets people know so that they won't be caught out in their travel plans.

Although many of the anthropologists who collected our stories and wrote about them would have regarded themselves as having great respect for Aboriginal culture, even they did not seem to understand the meaning of secret/sacred. In white culture it seems that when people hear something is secret, they just become more determined to find out the secret and reveal it to others. When anthropologists first came to visit my people and talk with the elders about ceremonial knowledge, the elders did not understand this. They did not realise that this knowledge would be put in books for everyone to read and that in this way women could read about men's secret business and men could read about women's secret business. This is not our way. They also gave the *tjurungas*, the secret ceremonial objects that had been given to them in trust, to museums to be displayed.[4] To Aboriginal people these *tjurungas* are objects of great power, and without the right knowledge, they can bring destruction and suffering.

Thus it is obvious to us that most of the anthropologists who first worked with us did not ever understand the real meaning of this knowledge in the way we do. They just regarded it as something intellectual, to be talked about rather than to be lived. Even the way we use words is so different. For example, we use the English word 'business' to mean ceremonial activity, because from our way of thinking, this is our most important work and responsibility.

Ceremonial knowledge is secret because this knowledge only has meaning or power when it is spoken by a ceremonial elder to an initiate in such a way that it affects every aspect of his being. It must never be just conceptual. That is why it is always shared in special and powerful ceremonies, where the ancestral beings, themselves, come to us through the songs, dances and stories and transform us. Ceremonial elders are holders of the knowledge that is crucial for our survival. This is not just knowledge about country, but also about the attitude we need to cultivate and the mental discipline we need to develop to sustain this state of mind. As well as the ceremonial elders there are the *kadaitcha*, the Law enforcers. Another category is the healers, the *ngangkaries*, and yet another is the 'clever men and women', those who have command of the elements. These qualities are recognised as naturally occurring in young children, who are then chosen to learn along this path. Access to knowledge is always this: a combination of special talent and an attitude of maturity. A four-year-old who is concerned about others will be chosen ahead of a fourteen-year-old who is only concerned about himself.

In our culture we do not separate the spiritual or sacred from the practical. We learn the knowledge of country and the seasons through our sacred ceremonies, and we use this knowledge for hunting and survival, as well as to maintain the creative energies of the land through ceremony. That is why our relationship to our country and the *tjukurrpa* is so strong. But it is also why it is so hard to share it with just anybody.[5]

There are many snake stories associated with Uluru, and as well as *Wanampi*, the Rainbow Serpent, there are two other main snakes, *Kuniya* and *Liru*. The *Kuniya*, the python (carpet snake) people came from three directions. One group came from the east, westward from Waltanta and Paku-Paku. Another group came from the north, and a

23

third came from the south, from Yunanpa. Then they were attacked on the southern side by the leader of the *Liru*, the poison snake people, who had journeyed from the Petermann Ranges, and there was a big battle. Both sides used to kill and fight all the time. There are pockmarks on the rock from the holes made by the spearheads, which show their fight. The public area where people visit at Maggie Springs is the site of the fight where one of the ceremonial aunties fought a young *Liru* (poison snake) warrior.

A story about the Rainbow Serpent at Uluru, which is commonly known, is that of *Wanampi* at Maggie Springs. *Wanampi* is a spirit snake who shows all the many colours of the rainbow. He has a big head and beard, and enormous sharp teeth, and still lives there at Uluru. Traditionally we approached him with great caution in the caverns beneath the pool at Mutitjulu (Maggie Springs), which is high up on Uluru, because this is his home. We had to throw up meat, and light a fire stick, before we could drink at his waterhole. To some Aboriginal groups in different parts of Australia, the Rainbow Serpent is generally regarded as quite dangerous. This is because water is the sacred principle of life and without it we die. Up north, in Arnhem Land, the Rainbow Serpent can also come in the form of destructive floods and accompanied by thunder and lightning. We Aboriginal people see the elements as spirit beings, and much of our secret/sacred knowledge is about how to form proper relationships with these elements.

Growing up with my people in Central Australia and the Arnhem Land area, I have found that all my senses support each other. If I am not feeling so good in one sense, then the other senses can step in and carry its load. And that is that unconditional love again. What I know about my culture and my people is that we act this out in our lives. We practise *kanyini* by learning to restrict the 'mine-ness', and to develop a strong sense of 'ours-ness'. Also, by having so many mothers and fathers, sisters and brothers, and other relatives, including those who are not human beings, we experience our world as one of being completely surrounded by family, and so our system of *walytja* is very vast. You will commonly hear the saying of my people, 'the land is our mother' and it really is. From the land we get everything. We mature, are given our food and our water, and our mothers are symbols of that. The sister of that is the sun. Look how far your web can go when you start including the universe in your family circle. No one is a stranger, and the land itself is always reminding us of *tjukurrpa*. When we hear that particular bird sing, we remember the story connected to that bird, and we are reminded of that aspect of our lore. For example, here is a story about the butcher bird and the desert finch.

In the ancient times there was a community of birds. Within this community, you had all the different types of people, just like today. You had the caretakers, the elders and educators who looked after initiations, and the ceremonial leaders and songmen who led the dances and sang the songs. Like now, different birds were responsible for different things in the community's life. Those with the natural skills become the teachers. The ngangkaries *are people who are born with a natural skill in healing, but to develop this skill they learn under elders, who are also* ngangkaries, *about how to be of service to the community. The best singers in this desert community of birds were the butcher birds. So because of this they were always the songmen, the senior ceremonial leaders. So, if other birds wanted to learn how to sing, they would go to the butcher birds to learn. The nyii nyii, the desert zebra finch, could only make a tiny little noise, nyiit, nyiit. The parents of these nyii nyiis wanted their children to become good singers, so they decided to send them off to learn how to sing with the butcher birds.*

This went on for some time, until they began to notice that not all their children were coming home from their time with the butcher birds. At first they just thought they might have gone off somewhere else before coming home. But slowly they noticed that more and more of the children were missing, and these were always the plumpest ones. So they became suspicious, and decided they should secretly check up on the butcher bird. The adult nyii nyii are the same size as their children, but their beaks turn from black to red as they become adults. So the parents painted their beaks black, and sneaked into the back of the group of their children while they were learning to sing. At the end of the session, they heard the butcher bird ask one of their children to stay behind for extra lessons with the senior songman butcher bird. They hid behind so that they could watch what happened. After all the other children had left, suddenly the butcher bird songman killed the little nyii nyii, and then he and some other butcher birds ate him.

After this the nyii nyii realised that they should be content with the gifts they were born with, and not seek after those that belonged to other people. They also realised that it is very easy to be seduced by beauty, and that it is wise to find out the true face of all things.

When we think about the message of this story, the more we come to understand the true face of white culture, its worship of material things and its hard-heartedness, the more difficult it is for us. We have learned that the price we pay for learning the new 'songs' of the white man, is that it is very hard to go back to the inner world of the *tjukurrpa*. With Western education and new ways of living in towns, we are losing our language and culture. The deepest wisdom of the *tjukurrpa* has been shattered into fragments. Now, today, we are trying to recover these fragments so that we can keep this

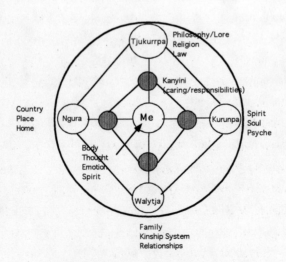

Disconnectedness and Loss of Kanyini

wisdom and pass it on to future generations of Aboriginal people, and perhaps to the world. This is not easy. Many Aboriginal educationalists find that the very way in which white culture constructs knowledge and how it is to be learned is completely foreign to Aboriginal culture. Perhaps this is why our children find it so hard to embrace modern schooling. It is not just that they do not see its relevance because of the lack of employment opportunities available to them, which is contradictory to the purposes of this education, but it is also because, in some way, it tears at our link with the *tjukurrpa*.

The Mala Story

The Mala Wallabies came from the northwest to perform ceremonies at Uluru. They travelled south through the Haasts Bluff area and arrived at Uluru on its northern side. They began the ceremonies, the men at one side, the women at another. When the women were not dancing, they gathered food for the whole group. The women's camp was on a small isolated area on the northeast side of Uluru, where one of their digging sticks can now be seen because it was transformed into stone.

While the dances were in progress, the Mala received an invitation to attend the ceremonies of the Wintalka men who were not very far away. The men sent their invitation to attend the ceremonies through Panpanpanala, the Bellbird. The Mala were already involved in their own celebrations and refused to stop them to go elsewhere. The Bellbird returned to the Wintalka calling 'Pak, pak' ('They can't come, they can't come').

When the Wintalka men heard that their invitation had been rejected, they decided to send a dingo-like creature called Mamu (evil spirit) to punish the Mala. This creature, called Kurrpanyngu, ran eastwards until he had picked up the Mala tracks and followed them south to Uluru. He crept up to where the Mala women were dancing. Kurrpanyngu peered over a projecting rock spur, but the women drove him off, and he continued around the base of the Rock to where the Mala men were sleeping. Lunpa the Kingfisher woman was with them and she called out a warning, but it was too late to prevent Kurrpanyngu from leaping into the camp. Where this happened Lunpa is transformed into a boulder looking up at the paw marks Kurrpanyngu left in the side of the cliff.

The surviving Mala ran south from Uluru in two groups. One group ran close to the northern part of the Musgrave Ranges to Utkiya and the other fled to the present site of the Mulga Park Homestead.

This is the *tjukurrpa* story of my totem as told to tourists visiting Uluru.

Stolen

When Constable McKinnon put me on a camel, I was so excited that I didn't realise I was being stolen, and was being taken so far away that I would never see my mother again. My aunty was with me and I just thought we were going for a ride. But the truth was that my aunty was being arrested for participating in the eating of a stolen cow. The truth dawned on me slowly as we got further and further away from my family, and their cries and wailing began to penetrate my mind. As we travelled towards Kings Canyon, along the Basedow Ranges, the land of Angas Downs with which I was familiar receded into the distance.

It was government policy at that time to remove mixed-race children like myself from our Aboriginal mothers, and bring us up in orphanages usually run by Christian missions. They wanted to convert us to Christianity, and the government did not want us to inherit our Aboriginal culture, which they regarded as primitive and without value. We were usually taken away by police who visited all the stations to enforce government policies and ensure that the white law was being obeyed. So this removal could occur at any age, from very young babies to older children, even teenagers.

I didn't know how old I was or in what year this occurred, in the white man's system of time. The only time I knew was the play of the seasons. But looking back from what I know now, it must have been about 1937. Bill McKinnon, the policeman who took me, was known to our people. He was involved in the murder of an uncle of mine outside a cave at Uluru where he had tried to hide from the pursuing police party. On this occasion, during his routine patrolling of the different stations around Central Australia, he rode into the homestead at Angas Downs, a vast property of spinifex grasses, saltbush and mulga and acacia trees which covers hundreds of square kilometres of Yankunytjatjara traditional land. My people were camped across from the homestead by the banks of the river that was running with water at that time, a rare occurrence. Because other children had already been stolen by the police, my family usually covered my lighter skin with ash from the fire. But on that fateful day I had been swimming.

That long journey northwards to Alice Springs, the nearest government town, took many, many days. During the day it was exciting to be riding a camel into new country, but when night came I began to wonder why my mothers weren't camping with us. As the sounds of the mothers' wailing crept back into my consciousness, I became terrified. I longed for the arms that held me and made me feel safe. I cried because I was now alone, and did not know what was happening to me.

I tried to pretend I was strong, like a hunter is strong in the way he faces all the challenges of the environment to get food. Yet in my heart I knew that I wasn't prepared for what lay ahead. The only kind memory I still have about that journey is my aunty trying to comfort me, pulling me close to her around the fire to keep me warm when we settled down, in the many nights of that ride into a world of confusion, violence and struggle. My world, that had once made me feel as big and free as the universe, would now become one which made me feel small and worthless, belonging nowhere.

Our journey ended at the Bungalow that was located at the old historic Telegraph Station, a few miles from the centre of town. This is the country of the Arrernte people, and southwards, behind

Alice, the MacDonnell Ranges rise as a spectacular spine of jagged rocks, in country we know as *Yeperenye*, the Caterpillar Dreaming. Children from all over Central Australia, speaking many different languages, were gathered at the Bungalow. There were some older Aboriginal women who helped to care for all the kids, and some of the mothers of local kids were allowed to come and go, because they contributed needed assistance in running the place. But for kids like me, who had been taken from far away, there was no one.

We, Central Australian Aboriginal people refer to the time between about 1850 and the 1930s, when I was taken away, as the killing time. It began in the 1860s with the first white expedition to the centre. In 1877 the Lutherans established Hermannsburg Mission, to convert us to Christianity and the ways of white men. Then in 1888 the town of Stuart, now known as Alice Springs, was established. The process of dispossessing Aboriginal people of their land and segregating them from white people gathered apace. In 1891 Aborigines were shot at Tempe Downs,[1] the area where I was born, as part of the continuing pattern of conflict over access to water and food sources, as well as white men's relationship with Aboriginal women. By 1915, as part of its policy of removing the mixed-race children resulting from these relationships, the government had established the Bungalow, the orphanage for 'half-caste' children to which I was taken. I stayed there for about two years, before I was sent to the Croker Island Methodist mission.

In 1928 the increasing conflict between Aboriginal people and white pastoralists resulted in the Coniston massacre.[2] The police and white pastoralists gathered together to punish the Aboriginal people responsible for the death of Fred Brooks, a knockabout bushman who worked as a station hand for Stafford Randall, owner of Coniston Station.

At this time Central Australia was in the grip of a severe drought which had forced Aboriginal people, desperate for water and food, to come closer to the stations where the supplies of water and food were more plentiful. Brooks was widely resented for taking Aboriginal women without honouring his commitments, and so breaking the Law of *kanyini*. Constable Murray, sent down to investigate the concerns of Randall about troublesome blacks, turned the hunt for the actual murderers into a punitive expedition that killed seventeen people. This was followed by a further raid to punish some Aboriginal people for attacking another white settler, leading to a total of thirty-five people being killed, including women and children. No one was ever punished for this massacre, despite a public inquiry.

In the Tempe Downs–Middleton Ponds area where I was born, there is also a report of Aboriginal men, in the early 1930s, being rounded up and killed for spearing some goats belonging to a station.[3] This story came out because one of the men escaped by hiding himself under the corpses of his friends, who had been told to dig a well for water, but were in fact digging their own grave. When a gold rush took place at The Granites[4] in 1932, the conflict between the two cultures became progressively worse. By 1937, shortly after the time when I was stolen and taken to the Bungalow at Alice Springs, the government had established curfews which sought to prevent Yankunytjatjara, Pitjantjatjara, Pintupi and Luritja people from coming into the town. Alice Springs was being developed as an oasis of white culture for white people in the middle of Aboriginal Australia. Even today, Alice Springs is like this.

The authorities estimated my age as seven or eight years when they took me, which means that I was born about 1934. Of course, this is whitefella time, as if history began with the birth of Christianity. For my people, time is ancient, stretching back to creation itself. When white people came to this land in 1788, they used their idea of 'terra nullius' (land not occupied), as if this land was empty of people and history. Aboriginal people were put in the same category as flora and fauna, and not regarded as human society. Europeans tended to think that everything began with their culture. However, even by white men's knowledge, they are discovering that we have been here at least 100 000 years.[5] We are the oldest continuing culture on the Earth, ancient just like this land which has nurtured us.

Later, when I was grown up and had managed to track down my family members, I found out from my sister, Junie, that when Constable Bill McKinnon took me away, the mothers began to wail and my Yankunytjatjara grandfather wanted to put a spear through that policeman. But everybody around jumped on him so that he couldn't do it. I was not the first child to be taken, and my grandfather was fed up. He was getting old and had already lost quite a few of his grandchildren. He said, 'We've lost too many kids already, and we never see them again.' Other children, my sister and a couple of brothers, had also been taken before me. Our mob loved all the children, no matter what colour they were.

At the Bungalow I was never told where I had come from, or why I had been taken from my family. They just tried to completely blot out my past. My world of the *tjukurrpa* and the sacred duty of *kanyini* which had sustained me, enveloping me and teaching me the caring responsibility of people to all things, was no longer around me. For the next many years of my life, I entered into the disconnected world of white men's 'dreaming', a terrible vision that sought to remove and 'save' mixed-race children from the Aboriginal way of life, in the name of civilisation and 'progress'. The establishment of the Aboriginal Protection Board, the work of the mission, and finally the welfare system, all took away our traditional Law of *kanyini* and recreated us as a dependent people.

Only much later, after years of confusion and struggle with this new world of the white man, did I come to understand that the English and other Europeans were driven by their strong belief in the utter superiority of, not only their culture, but their racial status. In this they were aided and abetted by the Christian missionaries who were convinced that only their ways were the true path to spiritual knowledge and that our ways were evil and must be destroyed. It was very confusing for people like me. On the one hand the missionaries told us about the love of Jesus and God, but on the other hand they themselves did not live this teaching. Instead the missionaries seemed to be hand in hand with the government to control every aspect of our lives, denying us the sacred duty of *kanyini*.

It took me a long time to make sense of this new world, but I eventually came to understand that the missionaries, although seemingly driven by the love of God for all people, were also puffed up with the pride of their own way of life, and their need, or perhaps what they saw as their spiritual duty, to 'save' other people from theirs. It is very painful to read the sort of things missionaries were saying about Aboriginal people at the time when white people came to settle in Australia, for example:

They [the Aborigines] are in the lowest state of social existence, all equally ignorant of the very humblest of the arts of civilisation, without clothing, habitations or agriculture, and when pressed for hunger, devour with eagerness, grubs, snakes, stinking whales and even vermin.[6]

Or, similarly, one John Harper, investigating the possibilities of establishing a mission station in the Bateman's Bay area of New South Wales, wrote in his journal:

It must be acknowledged that, altho' these tribes are uncontaminated by the whites, yet they are degraded as to Divine things, almost on a level with the brute. I could not find when speaking to my interpreter that they had any knowledge of a Supreme Being whatever. And in nothing, surely, does the blinding and perverting influence of a vitiating heart more strikingly appear, than in this failure among the Aborigines, of the knowledge of God. They are in a state of moral unfitness...[7]

This was the age of imperialism. At this time, all around the world, white men were seeking to take land and resources away from other peoples, and impose their government controls over them. At the Bungalow they broke us up into degrees of whiteness and blackness. During that time I also remember white scientists coming to the Bungalow to measure our skulls.[8] We later found out they were trying to prove that Aboriginal people were of lower intelligence, and were an earlier form of human evolution, by comparing the size of our skulls to those of white people.

Some of the children at the Bungalow were almost fully white. They called these quarter castes. There are a lot of Aboriginal Muslims in Alice Springs, because the Afghans who were brought to Australia to work with the camel trains, used for transport across the desert, married with our people. The Afghans were also frowned upon by the whites. It seemed the whites didn't like anyone who wasn't of English ancestry. They didn't even seem to like the Irish or Scots very much, yet they were like them, with similar ways. But they certainly didn't like the Chinese and the Afghans, and they despised the Aborigines. We mixed-race kids who were stolen away from our families found ourselves living in the atmosphere of that hatred every day. Although my people fought back, the white people had the guns, and that was that.

Instead of the wide open spaces of my desert home, we were housed in corrugated iron dormitories with rows and rows of bunk beds. After dinner we were bathed by the older women, put into clothing they called pyjamas, and then tucked into one of the iron beds between sheets. This was a horrible experience for me. I couldn't stand the feel of the cloth touching my skin. Out in the bush no one had clothes to wear and we were very happy without them. The wind and sun and rain kept us clean. We didn't waste water, and we certainly didn't spoil the sacred water by bathing in it with soap and other things. We were cleaned naturally when it rained, and if pools of water were left behind after the floods, we would swim in them.

I hated all these new things. When the lights went out I took off the pyjamas, climbed out of the bed and lay down on the cement floor, to get as close as I could get to the corrugated iron walls, so that I could listen to the familiar sounds of nature. It was the crickets singing me their lullabies that finally helped me go to sleep. At least some of my family were nearby, even if it was not my mothers and fathers.

During the day I was forced to wear clothes. I found them so uncomfortable that I kept taking them off and burying them or hiding them where no one could find them. I was constantly being smacked for getting rid of them and eventually they tied them on me so that I couldn't take them off. I really didn't like the feel of clothes and I still don't. The only reason I wear them today is because it is against the law not to wear them. At every opportunity I will gladly get out of them and wear as little as possible.

Coming from a non-disciplinary society, where all was explained through the stories of *tjukurrpa*, to one that ran only on discipline, was very hard on all of us kids. We were hit with a stick, a strap, a hand, or whatever they could get to beat us with. It was bewildering, painful and terrifying. Being forced to wear clothes was my first experience of this kind of discipline, but I soon learned that this was the way these people controlled things.

We were supposedly brought to the Bungalow to receive an education, which actually meant to learn how to live in the white man's world. One of the first things they taught us was the language of the bells and time. A bell rang to tell us to get up. A bell rang for us to go to school. A bell rang when school was over. A bell rang to go and eat. A bell rang to get ready for bed, and a bell rang when we were supposed to go to sleep. All my sense of personal responsibility, which comes with the idea of *kanyini*, was taken away. This was now taken over by people who were not family, and therefore outside my experience of people. I was introduced to a world of submission and control that sought to crush my spirit.

There were other languages to learn as well. I was Yankunytjatjara and spoke the native language of my family. At the Bungalow there were many Arrernte children, and Arrernte adults were working there. The Arrernte people are from around the area where Alice Springs was established. This meant that I had another Aboriginal language to learn, as well as English. I picked up some of the Arrernte language quickly, but English was much more difficult. I had to learn English by writing it and repeating it, sitting in a classroom with a slate pencil and slate board.

What I remember most about the Bungalow was the hardness and rigidity of being commanded to do things. I was punished for so many things that it felt like I could never do anything right. I kept thinking, 'What is happening to me?' When I looked around I couldn't understand why there were so many unhappy kids at this place. Lots of kids were constantly crying. Lots of kids were getting sick. Lots of kids were walking around like ghosts obeying orders and following rules and orders that were constantly being yelled at them. These people doing the yelling were not our uncles and aunties. They had no right to speak to us with such anger.

I tried to run away many times, and I would always head south like a homing pigeon. They would find me and bring me back and I would get smacked for running away. For some reason, I felt that those smacks were the price I had to pay, if I was ever going to see my family again.

They were crazy times while I was living at the Bungalow. Australia was at war with the Germans and then the Japanese, so there were a lot of soldiers around Alice Springs, on their way to Darwin for embarkation to either Europe or Asia. We enjoyed watching them march in parades and they taught us how to sniff petrol. It made our minds swoon and we forgot, for those moments, the pain of our lives. I remember playing with the other kids, sniffing petrol, and smashing windows. I loved the sound of smashing windows when I was a child. I used to like nothing better than to sneak away from the institution with the other boys and go into town to throw stones through windows, just to hear the beautiful sound of breaking glass. This was our way of releasing the frustration and anger we felt towards the strangers that had taken control of our lives. The whites in town didn't like us very much, but they certainly provided us with some good entertainment and therapy!

A small herd of donkeys roamed around the Bungalow area. When we could catch one, we would ride it. These donkeys were a catalyst for the many fights the Bungalow kids had with boys from the local community who thought they had exclusive rights to them.

When I finally realised that the life of freedom I had in the desert was over, I tried to make the best of things. I made friends with some of the other kids and that made it easier for me to accept my new situation. There was a group of us who became very close, and these relationships became a replacement for the families we had lost. At the Bungalow we played games together, like being rolled inside a truck tyre until it made us giddy. We wore tin cans on our feet while we ran around, to sound like horses. We discovered the game called marbles, but we used the seeds of the quandong (*mangata*) tree as marbles,[9] because we couldn't get the real glass ones. These activities provided us with a respite from our miserable existence.

I was forced to learn how to swim when the older boys threw me into the swimming hole. The first time they did it, I nearly drowned. Fortunately another boy was willing to jump in and pull me out. This incident made me realise the importance of being able to take care of myself. It reminded me of a frightening incident in my childhood when I had been swept away by a flash flood into the river where we camped near the Angas Downs homestead.

One of our biggest problems at the Bungalow was that we were constantly hungry. The Arrernte kids taught us where to find local bush tucker, and we made bark boomerangs so we could catch the small birds that came to drink at the waterhole. There were lots of all different kinds of birds then, and it was quite easy to get plenty to eat by throwing our boomerangs among them. When we caught some, we would build a fire and cook them on the spot in the way our mothers had taught us. We also supplemented our limited diet with *maku*, sugar from the gum tree leaves, pigweed and caterpillars. When the bush foods were limited, we made our way to the local dump and licked the empty jars we found there.

The Bungalow was very overcrowded and the school building was old and unsanitary. It had a very inadequate septic system with unsanitary water tanks, and it smelt really bad. Running through the water that overflowed from these tanks gave us sore feet. In spite of these deplorable conditions, the Bungalow became a tourist attraction. Visitors would come to stare at us just because we were brown. These visitors made loud comments about us as if they were looking at animals in a zoo. We would hear them say things like, 'They are much less intelligent than white children,' or 'Isn't it wonderful that they've been rescued from such a horrible existence?' They talked about us as if we had no feelings.

I was to learn more about what I had experienced at the Bungalow as a child, when much later I came back to Alice Springs in 1980, in search of my mother and the rest of my family. I now know that there were a lot of administrative problems due to a lack of qualified teachers and equipment. The government considered us inferior and did not maintain us according to white standards. The classes were much too overcrowded for real learning to take place. More than eighty kids were often packed into one small room. Our teachers really believed that Aboriginal kids had a low mentality and that we were naturally irresponsible, and more backward than white children. What they didn't understand was that our culture is group-oriented rather than individual-oriented and that competition was unknown to our way of life and made us feel really uncomfortable. Many of us tried to hide our abilities so that we would not stand out because of our accomplishments, which is the *Anangu* way.

One of my relatives told me he never learned to read or write at the Bungalow, not even his own name, and he was there for many years. He remembers a cane being used often in the classroom, and that it frightened kids out of learning. He also remembers that some kids had hearing problems and when they asked for something to be repeated they would get whacked for not listening.

It was also very interesting for me to learn about an evaluation made of learning levels at the Bungalow, when I was there in 1939. Despite the appalling conditions, and the commonly held belief that all the kids of our culture had low intelligence, the evaluation actually showed that the level of our school work at the Bungalow was only a year to a year and a half behind the work done by the white kids in Adelaide. Considering that all of us were being taught in a language that was not our native tongue, and that we were subjected to prejudice, cruelty from our teachers and horrible physical conditions, these results are really surprising. When some of the Bungalow kids were allowed to take the South Australia qualifying certificate examination, two out of ten passed. One of them, the late Joe Croft, was even given one of the two government scholarships allocated to Northern Territory kids to attend high school in Queensland. At that time there were no high schools in the Northern Territory.

One of the hardest things for me to accept was the way that the white teachers and caregivers tried to completely eliminate our Aboriginality. They continuously told us how much better we were than full-blooded Aborigines. The Arrernte women who worked in the home were constantly being ridiculed, as a way of convincing us that we were better than them and that we were being brought up to have a better way of life. They believed that these women were a bad influence on us, because they were uncomfortable with their pidgin English, their open discussion of sexual experiences, their *pituri* chewing, and their use of swearing, which was the language of abuse they had picked up from white people. They also considered them lazy. As a result of this brainwashing, many of the children at the institution started identifying themselves as half-caste rather than Aborigines and began treating full-blooded Aborigines as if they were inferior.

Growing up 'coloured' in a world of black and white has been a constant struggle for all Aborigines of mixed descent. Those of us who were taken away from our mothers as young children were taught that we were better than our Aboriginal families, but not good enough to be equal in white society. We were not allowed to speak our language or learn about the culture of our mothers. We were given a mediocre education because the Australian government believed that we were less intelligent than whites and could only be trained for menial work, like housekeeping and cattle mustering. We were brought up with minimal survival skills in a world that has never accepted us as equal.

The traumas we members of the Stolen Generations carry in our memories, and the identity questions we still live with, have been passed on to our children, creating a deep wound in the spirits of Aboriginal families right across Australia. Prime Minister Paul Keating[10], who was responsible for establishing the National Inquiry that exposed the extent of this suffering to Aboriginal people in Australia, was prepared to say:

It was we who did the dispossessing.
We took the traditional lands and smashed the traditional way of life.
We brought the diseases. The alcohol.
We committed the murders.
We took the children from their mothers.
We practised discrimination and exclusion.
It was our ignorance and our prejudice.
And our failure to imagine these things being done to us.
With some noble exceptions, we failed to make the most basic human response and enter into their hearts and minds.
We failed to ask: how would I feel if this were done to me?
As a consequence, we failed to see that what we were doing degraded all of us. . .
Imagine if ours was the oldest culture in the world and we were told that it was worthless . . .
Imagine if we had suffered the injustice and then were blamed for it . . .
Gradually we are learning how to see Australia through Aboriginal eyes, beginning to recognise the wisdom in their epic story.

When the new Coalition government came into power under John Howard in 1996, there followed a long debate in Australia about whether the government should formally apologise to the Stolen Generations, for the pain and psychological problems we suffered as a result of past government policy.[11] Finally, in 1999 as I was writing this story, after the intervention of a new Aboriginal senator elected to parliament, the government formally expressed its regret for our suffering, but there has been no apology.

I have always considered myself Aboriginal and I still do. Yet other Aborigines who were raised in the white system, including members of my own family, still reject their Aboriginal roots. It has not been easy to grow up in two worlds, but writing and singing my story songs have helped me release a lot of personal pain and frustration. I am grateful that these songs helped to focus public attention on the plight of the Stolen Generations, so that those who wanted to find and reunite with their Aboriginal families could get assistance in doing so.

When the government engaged the missionaries to take over the care of the children at the Bungalow, we were separated into groups. Each group was assigned to a religious denomination. The children who were to be Catholic were sent to Bathurst Island. Those who were to become Church of England were sent to Groote Eylandt and my group, the ones who were to become Methodists, were sent to Croker Island. Thus about forty of us were taken from Central Australia, north to the coast of tropical Arnhem Land, a distance of more than 1500 kilometres.

Quite a few of us were suffering from trachoma, an eye disease that we got from the dust, flies and wind of the desert. There were many old people who went blind from this disease. Much later, the specialist who looked at my eyes in Sydney predicted I would be blind in a matter of five years, but that's eighteen years ago and I'm okay. I do have weak eyes and they run to tears often, for instance when I'm in the movies and watching the bright light in one spot. That's why I don't like bright lights, because they hurt my eyes. This was a big problem for the desert people and the mothers used to wash the eyes of the kids with their breast milk to try and soothe our eyes. So because of this problem with trachoma, my group from the Centre stopped at a small Aboriginal reservation called Del-lisaville, near Darwin, so that we could have our eyes cared for. As soon as our eyes were better we were moved to a Methodist mission on Goulburn Island, to attend school there because there was no housing yet available for us on Croker Island. After six months on Goulburn Island, we were taken on a long boat journey to Croker island where we remained for the next six months, until the Japanese bombed Darwin in 1942.[12]

I was very fortunate that I was taken to a mission on Croker Island, rather than south to a city like Adelaide. Because the mission was just getting started when I arrived, we had to clear land to grow our own food. We quickly learned how to identify local bush foods and the seafoods that were edible. Some canned foods and flour and sugar were brought in, but we lived mostly from the land, and I was able to enjoy a more traditionally oriented way of life once again. Eventually some cottages and other buildings were built, but the cottages were just one room with floors made of sand. There were no toilets or running water.

One day a Japanese plane flew over the island and dipped its wing to wave to us kids looking up at it. We did not see aeroplanes very often, so we were very excited about seeing this one, and waved back. The missionaries were not happy about this at all. They beat us with sticks to get us to run and hide in the jungle. The mission decided the war had come too close, and that we should evacuate Croker Island. When the Japanese started bombing the city of Darwin, we were told we had to leave right away.

We then had to wait for a boat large enough to take the ninety-five children and our missionary caretakers from the island to the main coast. One of the churchwomen was pregnant and her baby was born while we waited for the boat to come. Eventually The *Larappan* arrived and took us all to Barclay Bay, a sandy beach opposite Goulburn Island. From that beach we rode and walked for two days until we reached Oenpelli, a Church of England mission fifty-two miles (84 kilometres) south of where we first landed. Two old lorries from Oenpelli met us at Barclay Bay and made several trips back and forth to the beach until all of us were taken to Oenpelli, but this took many days. The lorries had to cross many creeks and to plough along very rough bush tracks. They kept breaking down and having flat tyres, which wasn't surprising considering their poor condition and the kind of country they were travelling through. We had to get on and off the lorries every time there was a creek or a sand bog to cross. It seemed to me that we walked more than we rode.

The missionaries brought as much food with them as they could fit on the utility vehicles and the little ute that accompanied us, but that wasn't very much. The food supply was really low because of the war. Fortunately it was just after the wet season and there was lots of bush tucker around, so we lived off the food that we found around us. At sunset we'd make camp and sleep wherever we found a soft spot. Our first night was spent at Cooper Creek and, after a dinner of rice and syrup, we became food for the mosquitoes.

We stayed at Oenpelli for about a month. The mission area was surrounded by rugged hills and sat on the border of what is now known as Kakadu National Park. There was a big lagoon on the property, and we spent lots of time swimming in it, playing in an old canoe and searching for local bush foods. A crocodile once visited us, but he didn't stay around long.

The next leg of our journey was through the swampland, and here we learned about the natural foods: how to catch and eat long-neck turtles, file snakes, and the roots, stems and seeds of waterlilies and other local bush tucker. We were travelling through a cattle station, so we had plenty of meat to eat. Our caretakers decided we should stay in this area for a few days to replenish ourselves.

I will never forget Oenpelli because that's where we lost my cousin Charlie. He was only about four years old at the time. A bunch of boys were climbing on a poinciana tree and Charlie fell off. Later that day he started acting strangely and complaining that he felt ill. A doctor couldn't be reached because the radio wasn't working. By the next evening he was dead and we were all devastated. It was the first time we had to face the loss of one of our own, and a heavy cloud seemed to consume us as we left Oenpelli and continued south.

When we were told to move on, we walked to the East Alligator River and crossed the river on anything that would float. Some of our group went in canoes that had been left on the shore, but we made 44-gallon drums into rafts to get the vehicles across. There were crocodiles in the river but this didn't worry us. After crossing the river, we said goodbye to our Aboriginal friends who had accompanied us this far and continued walking until we were met by the Australian armed services. Since the Japanese had bombed Darwin, these men were preparing to defend Australia against them. They took us to a small town called Pine Creek where there were more Australian soldiers and a lot of American ones as well. The soldiers looked after us at Pine Creek and then took us further south to a place called Burdham that was located at the end of the railway line. Those soldiers were good to us. I remember that they gave us lots of money and kept us stocked up with food and chewing gum all the time.

When we reached Burdham we were transferred to a military convoy of trucks that took us to Alice Springs. I hadn't been on Croker Island very long, but it felt strange to be back in Alice. We didn't stay long because Alice had become a military town and they didn't think it was safe for us to be there.

A train took us from Alice to Adelaide and then we took another train to Melbourne where church people were waiting to look after us. They fed us at the railway station and gave us a chance to clean up a bit before continuing on to Sydney. We had never imagined that a town could be so big. Six weeks and two days after leaving Croker Island we arrived at our destination, Otford, a little village south of Sydney, on the southern border of the Royal National Park. We had travelled almost 5000 kilometres.

We were housed at a camping place that belonged to the church and lived there in little cottages for four years, for the duration of the war. At first we were very cold. Arnhem Land is a hot tropical climate, and our shorts and singlets were all that was needed there. But in Otford it was a different story. The climate was a lot colder and we didn't have any warm clothes to wear. We were totally dependent on the church for everything, and during the war there wasn't much money available to be spent on us. We were very happy when we received clothing that was donated by members of the church.

In Otford we learned very quickly how to live off the land because we had to eat whatever we could find. We ate possums, echidnas (spiny anteaters), goannas and lizards. We would also hang around in the bushes when visitors came for picnics, so that when they left we could go through the rubbish bins and eat their scraps.

There were a lot of fruit trees around and we didn't mind climbing over fences to shake the fruit off. Those of us who climbed over would collect as much as we could and pass the fruit over the fence to feed everyone else. We had no concept of privately owned fruit trees. We had grown up in open space and were used to eating whatever grew there. We thought that everything in nature was available for anyone who wanted it.

The owners of the trees we raided would often spot us and report us to the missionaries. The missionaries would then beat us with straps or sticks. They beat us for just about anything, but that didn't stop us from raiding people's yards for the fruit from their trees. If a beating had to be endured in order to have a full stomach, then so be it.

For us, living in the south of Australia was a no-win situation. We went to school with lots of white kids but the colour of our skin was not the only thing that was different. They wore uniforms but we didn't have any. They were privileged and we were underprivileged. They resented us, and would pick a fight whenever there was an opportunity to do so. If we performed better than they did at anything, such as exams or sports competitions, they would gang up on us and beat us up. We couldn't tell anybody about these beatings because we would get into trouble with the missionaries for fighting and they would beat us up too.

We were really fast runners and excelled at a lot of athletic games, because running was a big part of our way of life. Some of the animals which provided us with food moved really fast, and we had to run to catch them so we would have something to eat. As a result, we were very fast and our judgement was really good. I remember when we went to a nearby scouts' camp. The Aboriginal children from the mission were named the Rosella Troop, and we were given a small red and green ribbon that we pinned on our shoulders, on top of our ordinary clothes. We didn't have the proper scouts' uniforms or footwear like everyone else, but mostly I remember how really proud we were, marching as the Rosella Troop.

Once I won a race at a school carnival and a heap of white kids bribed me with a meat pie and took me to the back of the toilet area. They gathered around me in a circle and I was made to fight a whole group of them. I beat the first one easily and then they put two more against me. I beat them too, so they put four against me, then six and then eight, until there was no way I could win. The ugliest part of it was going home with my clothes torn and dirty, and being bruised and splattered with blood, and then getting beaten again at the mission for fighting. I was only nine years old, and my life felt like a living hell. I felt that no one outside of the group of friends I had from the reservation liked me and there was nothing I could do about it.

Some of the girls in our group made friends with the white kids, but I didn't. However, I learned to fight very well and to run very fast when the numbers were too big for me to beat. A lot of other Aboriginal kids were just like me, and we formed gangs and rebelled at the system. One of the ways we rebelled was to steal bread off the back of the baker's delivery van. One of us would jump into the back of the van and quickly break the loaves in half. The rest of us would hollow out the loaves as quickly as we could and then we'd put the shells back into the box where they came from.

There were some good times in the south. I enjoyed the beach and the rugby and cricket games we played against other schools. We spent hours watching the steam trains go by because the passengers would throw newspapers and food out the windows to us. I also remember being taken on a long train ride into Sydney to the zoo. That really was exciting. It was the same day that I got my very first pair of shoes. I wanted them so badly that it didn't matter that they were too tight. I was so proud of them.

Strangers were cruel to us on that journey. We heard lots of verbal abuse being directed our way. At the end of the day we were waiting to catch the ferry home and a group of us went into the toilet. There was a drunken white man in there. He swore at us and called us little black bastards. He scared the living daylights out of us. We ran out as fast as we could and told Mr Greentree, our teacher. We were really surprised because he went in to the toilet and stood up for us. We were amazed that a white person was sticking up for us; that someone outside of our Aboriginal group believed in us. That made the day perfect, even though my feet were wishing I had never taken those shoes.

There were other outings, too. Sometimes people would invite some of us kids over for dinner. The local policeman was particularly kind, and used to invite different pairs of children home to his place on weekends. At first we wondered if we were going to be the meal, but to our surprise they just wanted to share their meal with us. We were never too sure beforehand because of the things we had been told about white people at the mission. Once we realised that these white people were going to fill our stomachs instead of theirs we looked forward to these visits.

The way we were treated by white children in the south made such an impact on me that I remained wary of all white people for many years to come. My discomfort with whites strengthened my ties to the Aboriginal children in my group and solidified my identification as an Aboriginal person.

In 1946, after the war ended, we were shipped back to Croker Island on a huge ship, the *Reynella*. I was about twelve years old at that time and was very glad to be returning to my Croker Island home because I was really missing my Aboriginal family there. We were met by the elders to whom we had said goodbye some years before and they were glad to see us. However, after Otford, life at the mission was rather boring, lacking in excitement and challenge. It wasn't long became I became completely fascinated by the wild Timor ponies that roamed free on the island. The ponies bred up very well there because there were no animals in the area that were a threat to them. When we returned to the island they were every-where.

I couldn't stop thinking about how I could trap some of these ponies. Sometimes the older kids who were rounding up cattle on the plains would catch one or two of them. Sometimes I would chase them on foot around the plains twirling a length of rope in the hope of catching one and riding it home. No one in their right mind would do such a thing, but I was fearless in those days.

Some of the older kids had built a cattle yard at a place called Timor Springs, about twenty-four kilometres south of the mission station. They told us younger kids that a lot of ponies went to drink from this spring because the dry season had been longer than usual and most of the other watering places had dried up. When we heard about this, our imaginations ran wild. We envisioned ourselves catching all the horses we wanted and bringing them home. So we asked the white superintendent for permission to visit the spring and he let us go around three o'clock one Friday afternoon. That evening when we got to the yard we checked to make sure that all the rails of the yard were in place. Then we made camp under a bright moon and settled down for the night. At about two in the morning, I heard a voice whispering, 'Hey, there's something splashing water down at the waterhole.' Sure enough, there was the sound of animals splash-ing in the water. Quickly and quietly we went down to the yard and slipped the rail into the blocks. We had them!

The startled ponies became frightened and started snorting and circling when they picked up our scent. We heard loud galloping sounds as they raced through a lane of rails to the heavy holding yard. When the ponies ran into the yard, a couple of the boys who were hiding there locked them in. I ran up to the rail with a rope in my hand and announced, 'Whichever one the rope lands on is going to be mine.' I couldn't see anything because there was so much dust, so I just threw the loop in on top of the ponies and went back to our camp. At daylight we went down to the yard, and there was my rope around the neck of a little black stallion. Boy, was I excited. 'Wow! That's the prince of all ponies!' I said. And from that moment on I called him Prince.

The next day we filled the troughs with water and decided to go back to the mission to see if we could borrow a truck from the missionaries to cart our ponies home. The only thing we had to eat for that twenty-four kilometre journey was a little bit of leftover meat and we were very hungry. When we saw a cabbage palm tree not too far off the road it seemed to be the obvious answer to what to have for breakfast. A couple of the older guys got out their axes and cut it down and we split it open and had a good feed. Our first stop when we got back was at the superintendent's house, and he said, 'Okay, I'll send someone tomorrow to bring your ponies in.' We could hardly do our schoolwork while we waited for that truck to come back. After school we rushed down to the stockyards. The superintendent was standing there waiting for us. 'Did you boys cut that cabbage tree down?' he asked. 'Yes!' we said, really anxious to get to our ponies. 'We were hungry and we needed it for food.' 'Well, for that,' said the superintendent, 'I'm going to kill half your ponies.'

This was how he was planning to punish us for cutting down a tree for food! My head started to spin. My shock and disappointment at the loss we had to endure at the whim of this cruel white man was more than I could bear. The love I felt for the ponies was intermingled with the hate that I felt for this man. It seemed that anything that made us happy was destroyed by the cruelty of the missionaries. Thinking only of our poor ponies, I prayed that they wouldn't pick my black stallion to kill and feed to the pigs.

Eventually each of us was allowed to pick one pony for ourselves and the rest were put in a special yard while they waited to become pig food. I was very happy that Prince was not to be one of them. The superintendent told us, 'You boys will have to look after the ponies yourselves and you can't keep them on mission property. We don't want them mingling with our horses.' So we scrounged around for scraps of barbed wire and rails and built yards for our ponies. We also found troughs to water them with.

From this meagre beginning we started building a small herd of ponies. The mares had foals, and we also rode our ponies out to catch others. Eventually we had a herd of about twelve, and we used them to help round up cattle. The cattle must have wondered whether we were walking or riding because our ponies were the same size as they were. When we rode among them the old bulls and cows didn't want to move for us. We'd have to belt them. 'Come on,' we'd say, 'be frightened of me!' They didn't realise we meant business. So we'd muster them in and chase them around just for fun. This is how I spent my early teenage years.

Our pony herd continued to grow, but this was not without its challenges. One time I saw a herd of ponies on the plains and there was a chestnut one I liked the look of. I said to myself, 'That's a good little one. He looks like he's worth chasing.' I took off after him and just caught up with him when he hit the water. I threw the rope around his neck and pulled him towards me. Instead of pulling away like I expected, he came straight at me and got me on the leg with his teeth. I hit him with my fist and was surprised at how hard his head was. When I finally managed to separate his mouth from my leg, I wrapped the rope around his nose and tied it really tight so he couldn't bite me again. I held him close to me with his nose down until help came. I had a deep wound on my leg for many months after this incident.

Most of the mission kids learned how to ride on our ponies. We all rode bareback, with homemade bridles. One day at Mission Bay, Prince and his mare and foal were on the beach. I was walking along with a couple of mates when I saw my stallion galloping towards me, calling out in distress. We went over to him and tried to settle him down, and soon realised that the mare was missing. I said, 'The stallion and the foal are here. The croc that lives in that bay must have got the mare.' We tracked the hoofprints on the beach; sure enough, three horses had walked into the water and only the stallion and the foal had galloped out. I decided then and there to go after that croc.

The crocodile's name was Peg Leg because he had a swelling the size of a baseball on one of his feet and every time he walked on the beach you could see he had been there. He was huge and was well known for taking mission stock. We didn't feel personally threatened by him because he would just ignore us when we were swimming, or when Uncle Tim was fishing with his spear, even though we found cattle and horses with half their bodies missing. The Navy was once called in to get Peg Leg and stayed up all night without success. But now he was my 'Enemy Number One' for taking that mare and I was determined that his time was up, and that my pony was the last he would ever have for dinner.

One weekend a bullock was slaughtered to feed the mission and I asked the cook for the bullock's head. I put it in a hessian bag and hid it in a tree until it began to stink really bad and was full of worms and maggots. Then I talked another kid into helping me carry it down to the beach. We tied it to a stick and each of us carried one end of the stick with the bag dangling between us. Right after the sun went down we dragged the hessian bag with that stinking head in it along the beach. We just pulled it behind us as we walked in the water so the waves could take the smell out to Peg Leg. Then we dragged it up onto the sand about fifty metres from the waterline. I said to my friend, 'We'll hide behind the sand hills over there.'

The wind was blowing in from the ocean in an easterly direction. We waited quietly, and sure enough, it wasn't long before this big mound came out of the water and moved right up onto the beach towards the bag. It was a huge croc. He came closer and closer, and as soon as he got to the head I said, 'Now! Shine your light!'. My friend pointed the torch at Peg Leg and there was the huge croc with the whole head of the bullock in his mouth. My friend held his eyes with the torch and as he looked at us I walked up to him really fast and put my gun to his head. *'BANG!'* I had killed old Peg Leg! By eight o'clock that night we were back home. The generator was still going and the mission lights were still on. 'We got the croc,' we said, but no one believed us. They said, 'Tell us another big story.' 'Okay,' we said, 'tomorrow morning we'll take you down to the beach and show you.' I was about sixteen years old at the time.

The next morning when we went to the beach, there he was. Everyone could see we had really done it. The mission got a big truck and took old Peg Leg off the beach. They now had this huge crocodile skin and actually paid me for it. It wasn't much, but it was something. The payback for the taking of my mare meant much more to me than the money did.

My Pony Hookey

Chorus
Ride on, ride on, ride on
over hills and over plains,
Ride on, ride on, ride on
over hills and over plains,
Ride on, ride on, ride on
over hills and over plains,
On my faithful pony
Hookey from the hills.

On the coast of Arnhem Land,
On that island far away,
I spent my childhood
living on the hill.
My companion and my friend
that stayed on till the end,
Was my faithful pony,
Hookey was his name.

Chorus

Then to Darwin you must go,
were the words my father said
for schooling in that city far away.
Oh! my heart was filled with pain,
I could not hold back my tears
as he raised his head
and saw me sail away.

Chorus

Oh, but Hookey would not stay
on our island far away,
he swam and walked
for many nights and days.
Then one morning I awoke
to that once familiar sound.
It was my faithful pony,
Hookey from the hills.

Croker Island

My life on Croker Island was a blend of two cultures. Most of the missionaries and church workers were white, but there were some from Tonga and Fiji whom I could relate to more easily because of their dark skin and friendly ways. The other people on the reservation were black. They were the Iwaidja tribe of Aborigines who worked at the mission but would go to their own living places on the beach at sunset. They were forbidden to come near the mission after dark.

In the evenings and at weekends I spent time with them, and they adopted me into their family, so that I became an Arrapi, an Aboriginal person of this part of Arnhem Land. Through them I learned the traditional Aboriginal skills of hunting, and so I became an *angbadi*, recognised for my natural hunting ability, which laid the foundations of my leadership role as an elder today. I learned their language and the stories of their land. I was very surprised to discover that they were telling the same kinds of stories that I still remembered from my early childhood as a Yankunytjatjara in central Australia. At weekends they would take some of us for picnics and they taught us how to live from nature in the saltwater area.

I hated the way the Iwaidja people were treated by the missionaries, who had burned down their windbreaks and wet season houses and chased them away from where they had lived for many generations, so the mission could be built. Then they did everything they could to destroy the Iwaidja people's traditional lifestyle. A ration system was set up, but the people could only get the rations if they attended church. Medical care was provided, but only if someone was sick during open clinic hours. If there was an emergency at night, that was just too bad.

The missionaries' attitudes and behaviour towards the traditional people upset me to the depths of my soul. I knew these people were sharing everything they had with anyone who was interested and held nothing back. It seemed to me that these people were living examples of the teachings of Jesus, and it didn't make any sense that meanwhile those who were teaching about Jesus and love did not practise what they preached.

On the Croker Island reservation all of us kids became one big family. We were all Aborigines so we related to each other by using the skin system of our ancestors.[1] We referred to everyone by kinship terms and each person on the reservation had a place in the system. Everyone had a kinship name that was appropriate to our age. All the older kids were referred to as 'uncles' and 'aunties'. We called really close friends 'cous' (cousin) or 'brother'. A brother, of course, was the closest, and these close relationships continued to develop over time. The cottage mothers asked to be called 'mother', but it was very difficult for us to do this because they were white, and they did not behave like mothers. So we just called them by their names or by the term 'sister' in the same way that term would be used for an order of nuns.

We only went to school for half a day because the afternoons were for working in the gardens. We also had to take care of the chickens, the goats, the pigs and the cattle, as their numbers increased. I also remember playing with the other kids in the long grass. The older girls would tease us so that we would chase them. We had so much fun playing around with the girls that the goats often ran away.

The missionaries taught us how to live a Christian life. We learned their values of cleanliness, being well spoken, and having good manners. We were taught their system of time and we had to discipline ourselves to be on time. We were taught to dress in a certain way, speak in a certain way, and behave in a certain way that would make us more acceptable to white society. We also learned about the Christian ideas of integrity, honesty and the love of God. Every Sunday we were required to go to church and listen to the missionary preacher tell us about their God. At the time I couldn't relate much to what he was saying because it seemed that all the missionaries said one thing and did another. They kept talking about love, but I didn't experience love from any of them the way that I did from my Aboriginal family. Instead of telling us good things about our Aboriginal culture and ourselves, they did every-thing they could to get us to reject our Aboriginality. They would call us 'little chocolate babies', or say, 'You're not Aboriginal, you're coloured'. They repeatedly referred to the full-blood Aboriginal workers as dirty and told us that we weren't dirty like they were, because we were brown, not black. We were forbidden to speak our native languages or behave in any way that might be considered 'Aboriginal'. But the privileges of being white did not come with this teaching.

It was very confusing. The missionaries believed that they were called by God, and they were very responsible in the way they looked after us, the mixed-race kids in their care. We had good medical treatment and good teachers, and the 'cottage mothers' prepared our meals and looked after us with the help of the senior girls who were part of our group. All the older Aboriginal girls had to do domestic work and look after the smaller kids. However, these 'cottage mothers' were single women and they didn't touch and hug us, like our mothers did, so their care always lacked the natural lovingness of family, something I found among the Iwaidja people.

It seemed as though the missionaries only cared for themselves. They had the best food and they locked it up instead of sharing it the way our families would have done. They acted as though they could do nothing wrong and we could never do anything right. We could see them all the time as they moved around doing their jobs, but we weren't allowed to have anything to do with them. They were our bosses and they treated us like personal slaves. We didn't have to do really bad things to get into trouble. We just had to upset one of them. They made sure we were constantly being intimidated so they could control us.

None of us were allowed to do anything until we were given permission to do it. This made us feel worthless. When you feel that you are worthless, and whatever you do is wrong, it can sabotage the very purpose of your existence. You become afraid to do anything that you believe is right because it could be misconstrued as being wrong, and then you'll be punished for it. When everything you do is wrong, you just accept that you can't do anything at all without getting into trouble.

Once, when I was about thirteen years old, I was sitting on the stairway to my dormitory strumming the guitar when an old Aboriginal man walked by. He was struggling with the rations he had just collected from the storehouse about fifty metres away. I spoke to him in his language, 'Father, would you like me to help you carry your load?' So I helped him cart his stuff to where he wanted it, about a kilometre down towards the beach. When I came back, the missionary called me over to him. He then insisted I hand over the tobacco he assumed I had been given for helping the old man. I tried to tell him that my helping the old man had nothing to do with tobacco. That he was old and was struggling, and I just wanted to help him. This missionary said to me, 'You boys are not allowed to have anything to do with those full-blood Aboriginals in this community.'

The missionaries didn't like cheeky reservation kids. I was defiant and this often got me into serious trouble. There were older boys at the mission who would take things off of us younger ones. A lot of us got our ears clipped and were kicked and punched by someone bigger and stronger who wanted what we had. This made me fighting mad, and I never hesitated to fight them. Because of my willingness to fight, the other young boys saw me as a leader and from then on I always had a gang of followers. I took responsibility for their wellbeing and began to walk in front of them to make sure that they would not be hurt.

It seemed that I was always getting punished for something. I learned early on that if I started to cower and say I was sorry quickly when I was being verbally chastised, I wouldn't get a hiding. But I was too defiant to do this. I also knew that a hiding would stop when I started to cry, but I wouldn't cry and frequently ended up being severely beaten. There were times when I couldn't walk because of those beatings, but I still wouldn't cry. I didn't want to give in to my oppressors. I hated these people. Even today I grit my teeth when I think about those punishments.

I couldn't go to the cottage mothers for comfort because they were part of the punishment system. So I'd go to the trees and tell them how I felt, and somehow the pain seemed to lessen. There was something about the energy of those trees and the land on which I was living, that could take away the hurt in ways I could not explain. When I was older my Iwaidja brothers taught me about the way their people related to nature and that helped me understand more about my own relationship with trees. When I think back it seems that I was now beginning to understand that there was a caring, a loving energy, a beingness in spirit or something that I could communicate with, and if I was in a place of quiet listening, I would feel its presence. Was this the God whom the missionaries talked about? I used to feel good after being in this place, so I began to communicate with the feeling that was coming to me from the many life forms around me. I began to realise that the God that was being talked about was everywhere and in everything. Life was God in all things and it was only humans who were in the position of denying that, through our confused minds. Everything was already completely perfect, a dance of creation, a celebration of life itself in the land, in absolutely everything.

So I began to look for ways that I might become one with this perfection, with this dance of creation, this sense of God-ness. In this way the many things that other humans were doing to me that caused me pain and confusion lost their power. They seemed so temporary, because after the action was over, the greater bigness of creation was always there, and I wanted to be part of that bigness. One of the messages the trees gave me was, 'If you see the sunrise you've got another good day. Sing another song.' I started to appreciate every sunrise. I soon realised that when I sat on a high bank to watch the sunrise, I could walk to the sun.

My Aboriginal mothers had taught me that the earth mother and sun mother were sisters, so I knew that I could get comfort from both of these mothers. After the sun would rise there was a thin footpath she would throw out to me and I'd hear her say, 'Come, my son.' I'd go to her for a moment and she would embrace me and then send me back. This was the kind of relationship I had with the universe. Because I didn't understand this relationship, I wondered if the feelings I got from nature were from the same God that the missionaries were talking about.

As I grew into manhood, life took on new meaning as I began to explore my Aboriginal culture. I spent lots of time in the bush with my Iwaidja brothers, Jumbo and Dick Yamid and Charlie Ngalwamud. During these times I was totally free. We hunted together and they taught me about their country and their cultural traditions. I learned how to start a fire with sticks, how to use monkey vine to catch fish, how to make spears for fishing and which foods were good for eating and which ones could be used for medicine.

They also introduced me to their stories and ceremonies. I was very grateful for this because it helped me feel stronger about my Aboriginal identity. I was now part of their kinship system and these outings made our bonding stronger. The body markings which are part of the initiation ceremonies, which mark a man's journey into the knowledge of his people, were denied me because the missionaries would have spotted these cuts straight away, and punished me.

The only clothes we wore at the mission were the shorts that the church gave us. However, the old men, who became my grandfathers and *boonyi* (fathers) gave me the lore, as they shared their country with me, passing on to me their spirituality and ways of living with nature. With this I felt my spirit once again becoming bigger and bigger, filling the universe, and escaping the cramped space allocated to it in the white man's world.

On weekends we would go riding. There were wild pigs, ponies and water buffalo on the island. We had lots of fun chasing them on our ponies and actually caught some of the pigs. We sold them to the mission and they paid us sixpence a pound for them. It was good to have a break from tinned meat for dinner.

I was a really good student and just loved to read. At night I would create a tented area around my bed so that I could read by candlelight without any disruption from the cottage mothers. I read everything I could get my hands on but eventually got tired of reading paperback westerns and the labels on fruit tins and packing boxes. The one book that was always around was the Bible. I really enjoyed the stories about the Jewish people in the historical part. When I read the teachings of Christ and learned about his attitude of caring, this had a great impact on me. It just made so much sense. I am sure that reading the Bible so many times helped to plant the seeds of my present day spirituality.

Church never meant much to me, even though attendance was compulsory. Fortunately, I had the opportunity of listening to Aboriginal elders speak about spirituality, because some of the Aboriginal men with special powers, the ones anthropologists call 'men of high degree' or 'clever men', worked in the mission gardens. When we worked alongside them they would tell us about life, nature and the spiritual world. Old Sandy explained to me about the spirits and how they related to us. He taught me that everything is alive because of spirit. As an example he would point to a dead tree and say 'See that poor thing there, it's finished. Spirit bin leave 'em.' He also used to draw symbols of the spirits on the ground as he was telling me stories.

Another father, Yarmid, taught me how to see the tree spirits. He said, 'Look at them sideways because if you look straight at them, the spirits will hide.' I did it like he said and saw faces in the trees. They were smiling. I could tell they were really friendly spirits. As these old men taught me the language of nature I began to trust the feelings, energies and my own silent interpretation of the things I was picking up on a psychic level. Our intuition is developed when we act out what we feel to be true or what we are being told by the spirits. We believe that there are tree spirits, rock spirits and water spirits and that any of these spirits can talk to us. The elements are spiritual too. They give us practical knowledge. A storm will say, 'I'm coming, hide or you'll get wet. The lightning is flashing and the thunder is warning you to take shelter because I am coming. I don't know where I'm going to hit. The lightning may hit anywhere. It could hit you, so be ready.' All of my people were able to hear these messages.

I became so confident about my relationship with nature that I did crazy things like diving into crocodile-infested water in the middle of the night for no reason other than just wanting to have a swim. Another of my *boonyis*, Mick, made me a canoe and I would go everywhere in it no matter how rough or smooth the water was. I would paddle to the north-eastern point of the mission bay and sail back to the beach using a pillowcase as a sail. Many times the canoe would be tipped over by the big waves, and I would just tread water while I bailed it out and then climbed back in to continue my journey. Everyone would say, 'You're mad!'

There were two traditional ways of hunting crocodiles. At the end of the dry season, if we came across a crocodile in a lagoon that had been created when the waterways were drying out, one of us would walk into the muddy water carrying a harpoon and feel around with a foot to find the crocodile's back. Once he found the crocodile he would try to stick the harpoon into its back and then jump out of the water as fast as possible to avoid being hit by the tail. The crocodile would then start to spin and the hunter would pull the rope attached to a hook on the harpoon and drag the crocodile onto the shore where he could be hit on the head with an axe. The other traditional way to hunt crocs was to make a raft out of paperbark and dried pandanus tree trunks. We would then paddle onto a main waterway and look for a crocodile. If we couldn't see one in the water, we would look for its bubbles. When we found the bubbles, one of us would throw the harpoon about a metre away from the moving bubbles and hope he hit the crocodile's back. We would then paddle to shore as fast as possible and pull the croc in to shore with the rope so we could hit it with the axe. My brothers and I did it the easy way. We would go out with spotlights and harpoons, paddling our canoes while looking for the crocodiles, and then shoot them with rifles.

Boonyi Mick also taught me how to hunt for magpie geese. When we went out to the swamplands, he would be in front of me with a shotgun and we would crawl towards the flock of grazing geese on our bellies like a snake. We did this until we found a clump of reeds really close to the birds where we could load the shotgun. Sometimes we would end up right in the middle of them. We were only able to get two or three bullets to hunt with from the mission store, so every shot had to count. I had to watch Mick really closely because he could only communicate with me by hand signals. He had an uncanny way of knowing the right distance we needed to be from the birds to get the maximum number with each shot. Sometimes he would get as many as twenty birds with just one shot. My job was to chase down the ones that got injured by the pellets but weren't dead. I then had to grab them by the head and swing them around so their necks would break. After collecting all the birds we would carry them back to camp. We used reeds to tie their necks together in bundles and then threw them over our shoulders. The fleas from the birds really loved their new hosts, and we had to find a way of scratching ourselves while we walked. Even today, magpie geese are one of my favourite foods, which I look forward to whenever I return to visit family in Arnhem Land.

My reputation as an *angbadi* (successful hunter) was now well established. It wasn't only because I had better tracking skills than the other boys, I also had a smelling ability. I could follow anything by its smell. If the dogs weren't around I would run after the wild pigs this way. In addition, I had a special gift of perceiving things even before I left the house. I'd know where to go that day to get what I wanted. The other boys started to realise that I had this gift and it wasn't long before I had a strong following. There was another group of boys who were jealous of me because I was so successful, but the group that was following me knew they would get a good feed if they stayed with me. They said, 'Bob, you've got angels around you,' because the church was always talking about angels. The boys who were jealous would say, 'You've got the devil leading you.' One day someone hit me on the head with a hammer to get rid of the demons. It sent me spinning and my head ached for days, but I don't think it made any difference as far as the spirits were concerned.

One afternoon I was sitting in the classroom and for some reason, when I looked out the window, I had a vision of a big passenger ship pulling into the bay. I made a painting of it and said to the teacher, 'Teacher, this boat is going to come in the next few days.' She said, 'Don't be stupid, our bay is not big enough to have a boat that size come in here.' Even though she ridiculed me, I stuck the picture on the wall beside my desk because I liked looking at it. About three days later a big ship, exactly the same colour as my painting, pulled in. This ship was experiencing engine trouble and wanted to send a radio message to get a special part brought out to them.

I didn't think there was anything special about this kind of spirit message because I had learned about spiritual energies from my Aboriginal brothers and the tribal elders. They never thought it strange when they saw a boat on the horizon coming in after a weekend fishing trip and someone on the shore would know exactly what the person in the boat was bringing back to shore.

One of the ways they communicated with the spirit world was

to sing. When I asked about the songs they were singing, I was told, 'We sing these songs because of our relationship to the universe. The whole universe is part of us and you are part of that. You must consider everything as part of the family system.' The more I learned about their beliefs, the more I realised that these Aboriginal teachings were the same as the things that Jesus had said, which I read about in the Bible. I started to pay very close attention to everything around me, and eventually accepted that there was a consciousness of Oneness, of Godness. I began to find a way of bringing together the teachings of my Aboriginal people, and the teachings of the Bible.

I became aware that spirits were all around me. They can't be seen, but I can feel them. I always knew when my mother was near me, when her spirit used to come. She sent her spirit to comfort me even before she died. I could recognise that now, from my memories of how I used to feel at the Bungalow. Our mob did things like that and we always knew when this was happening.

It was very common to see spirit lights floating around on Croker Island. Boat captains have seen them, and have gone to shore to use the fire they assumed was the source of the light. When they got there they discovered that there was no fire. I once had a similar experience. I was walking on the beach with two other boys looking for fish. We saw a big man-size light that looked like a big fire was flaring up because people were throwing wood and grass on it. I actually saw a figure around that fire so didn't think much about it. I said, 'I'll go up there and ask them for a cup of tea.' When I got to the spot where the fire was, there was nothing there. I started feeling a bit strange and realised that I was in the presence of some spirits that had come back to the old campground where they used to live. I didn't know it, but this was the place where the missionaries had burned down Aboriginal houses.

Some kids were afraid of the lights and some weren't. I just accepted that they were there. My fathers used to talk to the spirits and the spirits would tell them who they were as human beings and why they were there. I found the spirits to be wonderful friends because they helped me all the time.

One night I went fishing on the beach because I wanted some fresh fish for breakfast. I was walking back to the mission carrying my torch, but it wasn't on. The stars were bright and the road was clear. All of a sudden this voice inside my head said, 'Shine your torch here.' I shone it in front of me, where my next two steps would have taken me, and there was a death adder (snake) looking right at me. I said 'Thank you,' stepped over the snake and just kept walking. This kind of thing happens all the time for my people. It's just a natural part of life.

One day a country music singer from Alice Springs named Herbie Lawton came to the reservation and sang for us. We really liked his music and his guitar. Some of the older boys studied the shape of that guitar and when Herbie left we made our own guitars out of big plywood tea chests. We stole the glue from the carpentry shop and were able to cut handles from the kapok trees. The guitar strings were wires taken from an American aeroplane that had crashed on the island during the war. We made about half a dozen guitars and we all learned how to play them. A lot of good guitar players started out by using those homemade guitars.

I started writing story songs about the experiences we were having on the reservation. Everyone enjoyed them and I was encouraged to sing whenever the opportunity arose. I had the most fun singing songs about everyone's romantic interests that they were trying to keep secret. I wouldn't put anyone's name in the songs, but we would all know who I was singing about and everyone would have a big laugh.

Sometimes we had access to the mission's two-way radio. We would use it for an evening of shared songs with the boys at the Goulburn Island Mission. We couldn't hear ourselves but the ones on the other end could hear the songs we sang and we could hear theirs. We really enjoyed these exchanges because it was a way to have contact with others through advanced technology.

Another way we boys entertained ourselves was to fight. There weren't enough of us to make up a rugby or football team so we were limited to sport activities that only needed a few people. Boxing was one of these. We'd all had lots of opportunities to fight when we were protecting ourselves from the white kids down south, so learning the techniques and skills of boxing was something in which we could see real value. One of the highlights of my boxing days was when my older brother Jim presented me with my very own pair of gloves. Jim and I met at the Bungalow and went to Croker Island together. He finished school before I did and became a hunter. He was the one who encouraged me to take up hunting, too. He would always make sure I had the things that I needed, and my first cowboy clothes from R.M. Williams were a gift from him. To this day we are the closest of friends. I call him Brother-Boy. He has continued to live in east Arnhem Land and I support him financially in his role as a senior ceremonial elder, as a way of fulfilling my responsibilities.

There were three girls on the reservation who played a very significant role in my life. They were not lovers, but they were a lot more important to me than ordinary friends. I called them 'the keepers'. Gladys, Polly and Violet were normal girls just a little bit older than I was, but there was something special about them. They seemed to have a sixth sense about everything that was happening to me and always showed up at significant times to give me some needed attention. It was as if they were my personal guardian angels. I have always been very affected by the moon, and on those nights when the moon was full I would have difficulty sleeping. The missionaries used to lock up the adolescent boys in our hut between 9 pm and 6 am, so that we could not visit the girls. I remember sitting at the window trying to get some cool air during one of those nights when along came one of the keepers to inquire if I was all right. It was the middle of the night and she would have been in big trouble if the missionaries knew she was out of her own bed. This is just one example of the kind of attention they gave me.

They were constantly doing things for me, and if I needed anything at all they always showed up to help.

Eventually I started noticing the girls in a more interested way and they started to notice me. Part of everyone's regular schedule was to look after the animals and work in the garden, but now we played new games together when we were out doing these chores. The older girls would flirt with us and when we chased them, they started to let us catch them. The grass was really high after the wet season and we could hide in it to have sex. It was great fun. We also played lots of games to get the attention of any girl who was the object of our affection. We were trained to be good trackers, so if we wanted someone to be our girlfriend we would track her and then walk on her footsteps. We had other secret methods, too, and we felt certain there was no way that the particular girl could resist our charms.

The missionaries did not like our sexual activity one bit. The punishments for having sex was to have our hair cut, get a strapping with the cane, and a penance of crushing big stones into little stones for making cement. None of this stopped us because we were really enjoying our sexual encounters and we were already very used to being punished. So they decided that the only way to keep us from having sex was to lock the more mature boys in a special cottage at night. Of course we weren't going to let that stop us from a rendezvous with our girlfriends. There were five girls to every one boy on the reservation and if we weren't looking for them, they would come looking for us.

We didn't realise that the missionaries thought sex was wrong. They didn't talk about it, but we knew that they were doing it too. Some of the missionaries had Aboriginal girlfriends as well as their white wives. They tried to sneak around when they visited them, but we were good trackers and knew everything that was going on at the mission. There were no sexual secrets as far as we were concerned. The aunties didn't care if we knew about their relationships with the missionaries and they were quite open about it. One particular aunty used to tell us whenever she had sex with the minister. All of those 'Thou shalt nots' he was preaching to us didn't seem to matter when aunty was around. He gave us a lot to laugh about because he was saying one thing and doing another. He just couldn't say no to aunty. She was pretty powerful with lovemaking, and doing it with him was good for her because it got her extra food.

After high school I was encouraged to stay on the reservation as a permanent resident. The islands were self-contained and those living there could have their own farms and live extremely well because there was no shortage of anything. By the age of seventeen years, I had become a very good stockman and hunter of buffalo and crocodiles. I hunted for the mission because I was one of the few boys willing to do it. Not many of us liked hunting. It was risky work and it was away from the comfort of the mission and all the girls. I was willing because I had just finished school and I liked money. The money was my incentive. I used it to buy western clothes from the R.M. Williams catalogue. They made cowboy outfits, boots, hats, trousers and beautiful silk shirts, and I had a taste for all that good stuff. I was willing to risk my life to buy these things.

In two hunting seasons I became a very successful hunter, and by mission standards was earning a great deal of money. My brothers and I would share what we made from selling crocodile and buffalo skins to the mission or selling baby crocs that we caught so they could be stuffed and made into souvenirs for the tourists.

At the end of every wet season, when it was dry enough, we'd go out to shoot buffalo. The church had a contract that allowed us to kill five hundred bulls. The skins were sent to dealers in Darwin, who used them to make leather. Hunting buffalo was done on horseback and on foot. On one occasion, we were shooting buffalo in the swampland on foot when Jack said, 'Let's go round and get a couple of bulls and skin them and drag the skins onto the hard ground.' We couldn't take the horses into the swamp because there was too much water, but we saw three buffalo bulls feeding out on the plain and were determined to get them. After we walked out there and shot at them until we thought they were dead, I started walking towards them and the skinners, Jack and Harry, were walking in front of me. Our guns were slung over our shoulders in case an emergency came up. As we got closer, one of the buffalo just got up and charged us. I happened to be the third in line, so I didn't see why my brothers were running. Then I saw that buffalo was really close and was heading right at me. I loaded my rifle as fast as I could manage it with my shaking hands, praying that the bullet I was going to use would not be a blank. When the gun was loaded the barrel was right next to the buffalo's head. The gun went off and that buffalo splashed mud all over me as he fell at my feet.

Jim rushed up and asked, 'Are you okay?' I was weak and shaky but glad to be alive. All I could say was 'Wow!' This was one of the times I knew without a doubt that something that wasn't human was looking after me. When I had the feeling that this something was watching me things always worked out right, even under the most difficult circumstances. I was often complimented on my bravery and my skills, but I knew that I was being protected by an invisible force that kept me safe, no matter what.

I will always remember these incidents; they reinforced my faith in the sort of God the Christian missionaries talked about. Later I began to wonder if it was Balil Balil's ceremonies that were making things work out the way they did. Balil Balil was one of the traditional owners of the land near Oenpelli. He was a very important part of our hunting staff. We called him 'the songman' because his job was to sing. At the end of every day we would hear his clapsticks and sometimes he would play a didgeridoo. He would start to sing when the sun went down. He sang all night until the morning star appeared in the sky.

Balil Balil sang for the safety of everyone there and also for the country. In this way he strengthened our relationship to the spirits of all the living things of that area. Not only did he make us feel safe, but I am sure that the many miracles that continued to occur were the result of his songs.

Balil Balil taught me about living in harmony with nature in that area of country. He also taught me about the plants and animals of the area and told me that I must obey Aboriginal Laws if I wanted to be strong. I could see the similarities of his teachings to what I had been reading about in the Bible. I called him grandfather. Slowly I was becoming a man, both through my hunting skills and through my growing knowledge of Aboriginal tradition and spirituality.

When I was nearly eighteen years old, I decided to marry Amy, an Anmatyerre girl from Alice Springs who I met on the reservation. She had started to look after me and wash my clothes. We had similar backgrounds. Both of us were taken to the Bungalow as children and then brought to Arnhem Land when it was time to attend school. We were about the same age and I enjoyed her company. She was a beautiful person. We started seeing each other as friends, and when my brother told me that a married person could get more money than the single guys were getting, I decided it would be a good thing for us to get married. I ordered an engagement ring from a catalogue and we became engaged. Two years later we had a typical church wedding and because we were being assimilated into the white system, we lived the mission way of a man having only one wife

By the time we were married, I was an extremely good hunter and was selling wild pigs, fish, crocodile skins and buffalo hides to the mission for extra cash. I was also being taught how to be a carpenter and decided to build a house for my family. I built a complete two-bedroom house using local timber and other supplies that were shipped in from the mainland. The mission told us that if we did the labour we only had to pay for the supplies that were brought in, and the cost of them was minimal.

Life was really good. Although I was living on the mission, I was also living the life of an Arrapi, an Aboriginal person of Croker

Island. I had found a way of being at peace with myself, even though I still carried the wounds of having been stolen away as a child from my family in Central Australia. I would go hunting with my brothers and come home to a nice house and a loving wife. Our first child had been conceived and we looked forward to the birth. After my house was complete I set up and ran the island's first fish and chips take-away business, catering to the others who were too lazy to catch and cook their own fish.

The Flying Doctor used to come to Croker Island mission regularly to check on the health of the people. It was also the practice that when anyone was having a baby, they were taken to the hospital in Darwin. So when it was time for the baby to be born, Amy and I went to the hospital in Darwin on the mission boat. When Alan was born we were both happy with our new son. I was really looking forward to teaching him all that I had learned about country from the Aboriginal elders. I silently made a promise to myself that I would never allow this child to be taken away from me.

However, this new found peace, with a successful life as an *angbadi* (great hunter) on Croker Island, was soon to be shattered, and I was once again forced to find my way in a completely different world. One day when my brothers and I had just returned from three successful weeks of crocodile hunting, I was banished from Croker Island.

When we got back to the reservation it was a regular work day so, like everyone else, we went to find out what our duties were for the day. But before we had come back there had been a fire at the mission, and one of the missionaries had been yelling at all the Aboriginal men for not helping with the fire break. I had been taught the traditional way of looking after country with patchwork burning by the Iwaidja people. In this system, lighting fires in small areas, starting at the highest point and working down towards the lowest, would clear undergrowth. This had been done on the island for as long as I could remember. When the new missionary superintendent had come in from Adelaide, he stopped the patch-work burning practice because he was afraid of bushfires. As a result, during the two wet seasons he had been there, the grass had grown so high that a rider on horseback had difficulty moving through it.

I knew nothing about the fire that the missionary was screaming about because we had just come in from hunting, but I had seen the damage, and it hadn't burned anything but the rubbish that was close to the houses. None of the houses were affected. It seemed as if someone had lit a fire down at the beach and the easterly wind had pushed it up to the long grass in our area. As I was walking in I said, 'Hey, a big fire was here. Who was the stupid person who made this six-foot fire break when the grass is at least sixteen feet (5 metres) high?' Everybody laughed, but little did I know that it was the missionary himself who had done that with his tractor.

Because we were in tune with nature we knew how to work with fire, but the missionaries did not have this same feeling so they did many stupid things. We can talk with the elements that we regard as spirit beings. We know the wind element just loves to play with the fire element. With this knowledge we know how to work with both fire and wind. Those of us who really develop this capacity can even learn how to shape the weather. Our weather magic does not consist of making it snow in the hot desert. It is not like that. Rather it enables us to be so in tune with the elements that create weather patterns that we can speak with them, using our inner voice. To do this we must cultivate the inner eye and ear and we must be able mentally to dissolve into the essence of the element, through the faculty of intuitive awareness. With this profound empathy, we can work *with* the elements, requesting them to respond to our needs. So while my mind was shaped by this way of living in the universe, that of the missionaries was shaped by their need to always be the boss.

When the missionary felt that his authority was being challenged, and he was made to look stupid in front of the other Aborigines, he shouted, 'You are just a cheeky blackfella. You can get yourself on the next boat out of Croker Island. We don't want people like you around here.' We had no rights and our lives were totally controlled by the whim of that missionary, despite the fact that we had built a house, and this was our community, with our Iwaidja family of brothers, sisters, fathers and grandfathers. Of course my wife and baby also had to leave with me, leaving the house and furniture I had built with my own hands. We were both only 19 years old, but fortunately I had a little bank account from my hunting business, and so we took our money and the few belongings we had, and left on the next boat to Darwin.

Let Me Loose

Chorus
Oh let me loose, get off me
And leave me as I am,
For my back is bended and low.
I try to stand with the load
That you have put on me.
Just get off now
And let me walk alone.

I stand on the corner of a big city street,
So alone with so many around.
I feel neglected and unwanted
As I stand on the corner.
Why can't I be accepted as I am?

Chorus

You have taken all I have
And all I ever want to be.
All I ask is for my will to be mine.
You've taken my wife and my children too.
Oh please, let me keep my spirit with me.

Chorus

People walking past me
Hurry on as they go
Always searching for the selfish desires.
Is there a way I can make them stop and listen to me?
Or are their ears now deafened to my cry?

Chorus

Darwin

Unlike Croker Island, Darwin was very much the place of white people and their ways. For the second time in my life, my *kanyini* connections had been shattered by forces beyond my control. Except for Amy and my baby son, Alan, I was alone again. I stepped off the boat onto the jetty not knowing exactly what was to happen next. I knew that I had to find a place for my family to live, some sort of employment, and to learn how to fit into the urban way of doing things. I asked a white man standing near me how to get up town. 'Grab a taxi,' he replied. 'How do I do that?' I asked. 'Go to the phone and ring them,' he mumbled as he turned to walk away. 'Can you help me?' I asked, 'I don't know how to use a phone.' So he rang up a taxi for me.

The taxi driver waited a while for us to hop in and then swore at us, 'Fuck you black bastards, what are you waiting for? Hurry up and get in the car.' Neither Amy or I knew how to open the taxi door and we were really taken aback at the abusive language he hurled at us. Here was another white man treating us like shit and he didn't even know us. I wanted to punch his head in and throw him in the harbour but controlled my emotions while he came around and opened the car door for us.

Everything here was brand new. There were no cars on the

reservation. There was only a truck with no doors that we hopped in and out of. The taxi took us to old Max. He was the old white fellow who sent our supplies out to the mission on a barge. We now had a base, so from there I began walking around the city of Darwin looking for more permanent accommodation and a job.

I decided to use the only connections I had, the church. I went to the church office that was headquarters for the Methodist Overseas Mission and asked if they could help me find a job. I also tried to locate some of the old missionaries who had left Croker Island and were now living in Darwin, and anyone else I could think of who could give me work or help us find a place to live. These were hard times, but I did get lucky and found a job as a gardener at the Darwin Hospital. I raked the gardens and levelled the soil to plant grass. I was to be thankful, again and again in my life, for the mission policy of teaching us so many practical skills, from gardening to building toilets.

One day I was walking up the street and saw an old missionary whom I knew walking towards me. He too had had a run-in with the then mission superintendent on Croker Island. I said, 'Hello, how are you?' and he replied, 'Hello, what are you doing here?' With a strong sense of the irony of life, I replied with a chuckle, 'Oh, I got kicked off Croker. The superintendent that kicked you off, kicked me off too.'

His wife was an Aboriginal woman and had been like a mother to my wife, so he invited us to come to live at their place, about twenty kilometres outside of the city. We now had a place to live. He then helped me buy a pushbike so I could ride those twenty kilometres from Nightcliff to Darwin Hospital and then back again every day. Now I could feed my wife and child.

Urban life was hard to get used to, but I could see that there was plenty of everything available in the city. There was food everywhere, and people seemed to have a lot of money. They were driving around in cars and I thought they all must have been millionaires.

For the first time I confronted one of the terrible consequences of mission life, the institutionalisation. I had come from a place where everyone told me what to do every minute of my life and here I realised that I had to quickly learn how to survive in the city. There was so much to learn because everything was so different.

I learned how to sit at a table in a restaurant and order a meal, and how to buy things. On the reservation everything that we could buy was on a big counter right behind the clerk. At shopping time, a big shuttered window was opened and we could see what was there and we chose what we wanted to buy. We then had to put our money on top of a smaller counter before telling the clerk what we wanted. In Darwin we had to order what we wanted first, and we didn't pay our money until the cost of everything was added up. And having a lot of money was another thing that took getting used to. On the reservation, I worked a whole week for three pounds (six dollars) and had a wife and child to look after on that small amount. Fortunately I was able to supplement this with what I earned from hunting, but this seemed like nothing compared to the fifty pounds a week I was getting in Darwin. A portion of these earnings went to rent, of course, but that wasn't much. Having all this money meant that I could now buy lots of food and look after many of my people. I could begin to recover *kanyini*.

That is Aboriginal thinking. We have never considered looking after other people a problem. It has always been part of our way of living. Anyone can come asking for money or for a ride or for food and we just give it to them. If we don't have it we'll say, 'Sorry, I've got nothing.' Everyone knows this is the truth because, if we have it, we'll give it.

I now had to start thinking for myself, instead of relying on the mission. I quickly made friends with other Aboriginal people in Darwin because as soon as I saw people of a similar colour I'd go and talk to them. There was no barrier there. We established relationships easily by asking, 'Where are your people from? What country is yours?' Then we would start to identify kinship connections that would allow us to communicate with each other, because for Aboriginal people, everyone is brought within family. Amongst the Yankunytjatjara, we call this *walytja*, and this system of making everyone family is one of the main ways we practise the spiritual discipline of *kanyini*.

One thing happened at the hospital where I was working that made me stand out. I was doing my gardening work and came across a wallet lying in the weeds. There was a great deal of money in it. Someone had obviously just been paid, but there was no name in the wallet. I took it to the people in charge of the hospital and they really were impressed by my honesty. They rang up the Methodist Church and complimented them on the way they raised their Aboriginal people. It had not occurred to me to do anything else but turn it in because it wasn't my money. The hospital administration offered me a promotion for being honest, and this is just one of the many ways in my life that I have seen how the practice of generosity and honesty brings rich rewards, often in quite unexpected and mysterious ways.

I started cleaning the wards and looking after patients for a slightly higher salary. Because of that one little deed I got one promotion after another. When a vacancy came up that paid more money, they offered me that position. I was a good worker because we'd learned how to work hard on the mission.

When I came to Darwin, I had some savings from the money I had earned hunting while I was on Croker Island. Having now found a way to support my family, I was able to use these savings to buy a house from a man I knew, who was flying the aeroplanes that took doctors to the reservations, which is part of the Royal Flying Doctor Service that is such a feature of outback Australia. He knew me from my time on the reservation and asked if I wanted to move into his house, because he had built another house and was about to move. The house he was vacating was huge and it was right next to the beach at East Point. It was formerly an army barracks, made of corrugated iron, and was surrounded by a small jungle. I liked it.

When I went to inspect it, I asked him how much he wanted for it and he said, '200 pounds.' I gave him that amount and moved the family in. In the 1940s and 1950s, houses were quite cheap in Darwin. Darwin was regarded as a really remote part of Australia. Apart from the public servants who were sent there and received heavily subsidised housing and hardship allowances, many of the people who came to live in Darwin were people seeking to escape the constraints of big city life, failed marriages or broken dreams. Here, although white people were in charge, Aboriginal people made up a considerable proportion of the population, and their period of colonisation had been much shorter than on the east coast where the traditional cultures and languages had been all but wiped out.

Over the next few years many more people started coming into Darwin from Croker Island. My wife's sister Dolly came and then her husband soon joined her. As soon as word got out that I had this beautiful big house right beside the beach, other family members came too. Lots of these people were using my house as a place to live until they could find employment and get their own place. My house also became a place where people could come to adjust to the urban lifestyle. This was typical Aboriginal living. Amy and I enjoyed the companionship. There were more women around to help care for the kids and share the housework and more men to hunt for food. I can now see that there was a higher power guiding things, because this arrangement was the beginning of the first Methodist halfway house in Darwin. I was finding a new way to practise *kanyini* in an urban setting and a new way to bring together the teachings of the Bible, which I had absorbed on Croker Island, and Aboriginal spiritual philosophy. The teachings Jesus gave in his Sermon on the Mount made a big impression on me. They gave much comfort to those of us who felt discriminated against and gave us the courage to feel we could overcome this, that we were blessed and that we should develop the heart of forgiveness and charity towards those who had harmed us. They were also completely in tune with our philosophy of *kanyini*. Although the missionaries had preached against Aboriginal culture as pagan and as something that should be abandoned, I was able to see from the actual teachings of Jesus in the Bible that this was not so.

I continued to seek a way to live my life, in all circumstances, in the spirit of these two spiritual traditions. However, the anger that I felt from being ordered off Croker Island reservation remained with me for a long time. At first I was so angry that I was ready to fight any man who had white skin. The white men in Darwin had a funny way of swearing at each other as a form of hearty greeting, but those of us from the reservation didn't understand this. To us swearing was a challenge to a fight. So when they said, 'Hi, you black bastard, how are you?' I heard these as fighting words and would hit them until they were on the ground. They didn't seem to understand what those words 'black bastard' meant to us.

When I was pulled into the hospital office and asked why I was fighting I would say, 'He swore at me. He threw out a challenge and ended up the worse for it.' That's how easy it was for me to fight. I was angry at the system and at the people whose skin colour represented that system. I think a lot of us were, and many still are. When I began to sing about the suffering of my people, this anger seemed to lessen. Also, as I read more and met white people who helped me, I gained a bigger picture of things. Over the years what was at first hot anger became channelled into social action and my sad anger turned into a wellspring of compassion, which could recognise the many forms of suffering that afflict people in our society, particularly those experienced by my fellow Aboriginal people.

A lot of the shopkeepers in Darwin in those days were Chinese. We could see that they were just like us in the way that they cared for family. They seemed also to care about other people and they shared with the Aboriginal people a sense of being excluded from the dominant white society. There was quite a lot of inter-marriage between Chinese and Aboriginal people. I felt comfortable shopping in their shops and some long-standing relationships began to develop. Although these days there are a lot of Chinese people in big cities like Sydney, in those days of the White Australia Policy, the Chinese were more concentrated in places like Darwin, and could trace their family connections back to migration during the gold rush in the 1880s. I called Darwin a 'fruit salad city', because people of so many cultures and nationalities got along well there. There was a large mixed-race community.

Among the mixed-race population, the so-called coloured population, those of us coming in from the reservation were considered to be the lowest of the low, because we didn't know city ways and we were very poor. However, in this caste system, the full bloods, the tribal Aboriginal people, were at the bottom because they were the furthest from understanding European ways, speaking English, and having access to material goods and European clothing. It was this caste system which made it difficult for many mixed-race Aboriginal people to identify with their Aboriginality. It meant embracing that part of their identity that would place them lowest in the social pecking order.

The way that some of us became accepted in this multicultural community was through our success at boxing. My wife's brother Johnny had become extremely good at this sport on Croker Island reservation. When we got to Darwin we discovered that there were competitions being held where boxers could win money. We agreed that I would become his trainer, and his training started at the Police Boys Club. Every day we ran and did push-ups on the beach. Johnny started winning these competitions and eventually won the local championship. A professional trainer asked if he could train him. I became the trainer's assistant. Johnny became a real celebrity and we decided it was time for him to try interstate competition. If a black man was good at sports or art, for example, his blackness immediately became less of an issue. Johnny's success encouraged other men coming in from Croker Island to take up the sport, and eventually we had winners in each of the divisions.

One day our big family went on a picnic out in the bush, about twenty-five kilometres from the city. The men in the group went into the bush to catch some birds for dinner. We were walking back to the camping area, with birds slung over our guns with their necks tied together, in the way we always carried them. We heard some magpie geese flying overhead and Johnny put a cartridge into his gun to be ready, but didn't fire it. He just put the gun back on his shoulder with the live cartridge still in the barrel. When we got back to camp he swung the gun off his shoulder and the geese slid down the barrel. This triggered the hammer and the gun shot him right in the chest. There was no way we could get him back to Darwin in time. By the time we got him to the hospital he had already left this earth. It was a tragic experience for all of us. I had learned to accept the loss of my original family, now tragedy struck again. We mission boys had become brothers to one another, and Johnny was a very close brother of mine. We did everything together. I was so devastated, it took me years to recover from this loss.

The family stayed in the house on the beach for about a year after that and then I bought another house in a Darwin suburb that was closer to the main city area. By now I had two more children: Johnny, whom I named after my lost mission brother, and my first daughter, Dorothea. During my first holiday break I decided to go back to Croker Island to visit my Aboriginal family. While I was there I made a cage for Alan's pony and brought him back to Darwin with me. All of the kids in the neighbourhood and the kids who came to visit just loved that pony, so I taught them how to ride.

I made friends with the man who drove a barge between the mainland and Croker Island and made a deal with him. If he would bring some of my other ponies to the mainland, I would give one of them to him for his daughter. He was happy to do this because the barge was usually empty on the way back and it was an easy thing for him to do. He brought me seven ponies and I gave him the one that I had promised his daughter. Another friend gave me a nice piece of land to keep them on and I set up a riding school. Lots of kids learned how to ride on those ponies. Many horses and ponies were roaming free around Darwin at that time, so I caught some of them and bred them with the other ponies until I had a herd of twenty. My horses and ponies were always available for charity events and some of the kids used them to enter competitions at the annual Darwin stock show. The ponies won a lot of ribbons. Alan rode his Timor pony in the barrel racing events at all the shows and he always won, even though he was challenged by the station owners who had really well-bred horses. The pony club and riding school was so popular that I was able to sell it when I later moved to Adelaide.

My attention began to turn to the education of my children, and about how to give them the depth of Aboriginal culture which I had received from my mother and her people in early childhood, and then later from my Iwaidja elders. I decided, during the dry season, to organise weekend 'survival training' out in the bush for boys between the ages of twelve and eighteen. I'd pick them up on Friday afternoons and they were not allowed to bring anything with them except a fishing line and a spear if they had one. They were there to learn how to live off the land. I taught them basic things about hunting, such as how to make spears, and then they went out to collect their food. On the days, when we got to our camping place late on Friday, the boys would end up going to bed hungry because it was too late to catch anything that night. I would wake up at sunrise to find some of them already out looking for their next meal. Some brought in magpie geese, others caught barramundi, some caught wild pigs and others got long-neck turtles. They were then taught the traditional way of making a fire to cook their catch, and how to share their food.

At night, I told them stories that I had been taught about the stars in the night sky, hunting stories about catching crocodiles, wild pigs and buffalo, and ghost stories about the spirit lights we used to see on Croker Island. It made me laugh to see the kids inch closer and closer together as the scary stories unfolded. In this way, although they were growing up in a white man's town like Darwin, they were also able to develop a relation to country as another expression of *kanyini*, and another way to nourish their spirit, their *kurunpa*. Not only is the natural environment a source of food, it is also the expression of *tjukurrpa*, the Dreaming, the energy of creation.

A lot of women who came to Darwin from the reservation were having relationships with men who were cruel to them. They were good at all the things that could be expected of a wife in European urban culture, because at the mission they had learned how to wash clothes, to cook and to look after lots of people. At the missions around Darwin, as the mission girls became older, they all took turns being cottage mothers to the younger children. They also held the Christian belief that they would serve one man for the rest of their life. When they committed themselves to a man, they thought it would be a permanent relationship and they expected from that man the same sort of love, integrity and truthfulness that they were willing to give. Instead, they frequently ended up with men who would beat them up and not be helpful to them at all. This was another terrible effect of the caste system. White men were drawn to mixed-race Aboriginal women for sexual companionship, as there were not many European women living in this part of Australia. However, all too often these men were torn between their sexual attraction to our women and their social shame about being connected to someone further down the caste system than themselves. This confusion would fuel their frustration and anger which, all too often, they took out on their women.

A lot of times these women would come to my house seeking help and I'd take them in and let them stay with us. If the men came after them, I would fight them if this was what it took to get them to stop flogging the women. As these women kept having more and more children, they would come with all of their kids and I'd still take them in. Amy would look after them. Amy's constant giving and caring was a great support to me and to all those who came to stay with us. Amy and I now had four children: Alan, Johnny, Dorothea and Anita, our youngest.

I worked at the hospital during the day and began going to night school, so that I could become better qualified to give advice to all the people who were coming to see me for help. I received a certificate in counselling. I was being stretched in every possible way because I was constantly helping all of these people in my own time and at my own expense. It was obvious that there needed to be some sort of structure set up to take care of everyone coming in from the reservation and I approached the Uniting Methodist Church to see if they would help. They agreed and hired me to set up the program.

It constantly upset me when I saw how Aboriginal people, the poorest people around, were being mistreated and abused by whites. So I started looking at the bigger picture to get a better understanding of what was actually happening. What I found made me furious. I discovered that white government workers were being paid the most money and were living in the best houses for minimal rent. Aboriginal people had to buy their furniture but the whites could rent theirs. These highly paid white people also had access to free rides in motor vehicles at the government's expense. This just wasn't fair. I felt that this sort of help should be given to those in the poorest group. I couldn't understand this unfair white system. The richest got everything for nothing and the poor were made to pay the highest price for everything.

I became more and more disturbed about the injustices that were being practised against my people. We were the real owners of the whole of Australia. We had been here for as long as 100 000 years and they had just taken our land from us. There had been no war declared against us, no treaty signed, and no agreements made with us. They just moved us to places away from our homelands so that they could steal our land. I saw these thieves now claiming to be the enforcers of a justice system that supposedly cared for us.

The longer I lived in Darwin, the more I learned about their 'not so just' system. I learned about the enormous salaries that white people were getting when they worked for government departments that were set up to help Aborigines, while my people lived like beggars on the reservations. I found out that even my own church, the caretakers and caregivers of my people, were stealing from us. They would buy food in bulk and then add exorbitant extra costs on top of the price they paid. The people on the reservation were paying four dollars for the same tin of milk that could be bought in Darwin or Queensland for one dollar.

They said that they were just adding surcharges for delivery, but the numbers didn't add up. The actual freight costs weren't that much. The missions bought things tax-free, so just adding the cost of freight could not have made things that much more expensive. There were no middle men. Everything went straight from the manufacturer to the purchaser. The cost of freight was the only other expense. It seemed to me that the church was just out to make big profits on all the goods they were buying on our behalf, in order to fund their missions.

When I was on the receiving end of this I didn't know that these things were going on. I'd just go up to the counter and pay the displayed price for what I wanted, because I wanted it. When I came into Darwin I couldn't believe that things were so cheap. I kept saying, over and over, 'This is mad, why is it so cheap here?' That led to a lot more questioning and that's how I discovered what was going on.

I had been proud of the church and the care they had given us on the reservation, even though I was angry about their racist attitude to us. It was hard to accept things the way they really were. Finding out that these things were happening within my own church made me start questioning society overall. When I began to understand more about how the white system was run, I decided it was a terrible system for Aboriginal people to live in. And that remains the case today. It is no accident that things have not got better for Aboriginal people, despite the huge sums of money which the government says it has allocated to Aboriginal services. Much of this money has gone to the senior staff levels in the administration of programs, for large salaries, travel allowances and subsidised housing almost exclusively occupied by non-Aboriginal people. It reminded me of life on Croker Island, where the first priority had been to build a large two-storey residence for the white missionaries, while we kids slept in small tin sheds with sand floors, and similar structures were used for the school and even the church.

Many of our people were poor because they just couldn't get the sort of job that could bring in a liveable wage. Sometimes this was because they didn't have a good enough education, but many of us were very well educated and were hard workers. I knew that many were qualified for jobs they were not getting. So I decided to attempt to change this situation by building up an organisation that had a social structure through which we could address the wrongs that were being done to our people and try to equalise society. In the early 1960s, the Aboriginal Development Foundation was established. I started the foundation with an Aboriginal woman named Vi Stanton, who had previously worked overseas with the Fijian people. We sold memberships for 50 cents or $1 and then began working towards achieving total control of our own affairs in every possible way. To help us, we recruited people who were knowledgeable about community development programs. I felt guided by something inside of me that kept saying, 'This has to be dealt with. This has to be faced.' *Kanyini* is not just loving kindness. It is also the courage to take self-responsibility. Increasingly I was finding ways to do this, despite the constraints of living in a white dominated society where the cards were stacked against me.

We learned how to work the system so we could get money. We ran programs after school and on weekends that celebrated our culture. I recruited all my family members from Arnhem Land to participate in indigenous cultural celebrations when they were held in Darwin. We started to do some of the ceremonies openly and in doing so, passed the teachings of these ceremonies on to the young people. It was great fun. As my life progressively gave me the opportunity to move back and forth between our ways and those of wealthier white people, the thing that I learned was that Aboriginal people laughed more often than white people did, and we were also able to cry for each other during the sad times. I think it is our wicked sense of humour and the open-hearted way we feel for one another that have kept us alive during the terrible impact of white culture on our people.

One time we had several tins of white paint that we had used for art class and everybody that came to do the ceremony, including my two sons and their friends, liberally put it all over their bodies, head to foot. They did the ceremony all that day and night, and when they went to wash off the paint, it wouldn't come off. It was permanent paint. We thought it was like the white ochre clay that we always used to paint our bodies. For weeks afterwards everyone who participated in the ceremony was still walking around in white paint. The kids decided to try using petrol to get it off and they got drunk on the fumes and started laughing and screaming and having water fights in the shower.

For many of us, this organisation helped us regain pride in our culture and we encouraged more of our mob to participate. What really shocked and saddened me, however, was that so many of my reservation friends and family refused to participate in any of the activities I was organising. They told me, 'We are "coloured people" not Aborigines.' It was as if a whole new race had been created because they did not want to be considered Aboriginal.

Throughout the 1960s, my skills as a political organiser continued to grow. As the spokesman of a recognised organisation I was now getting quoted in the newspaper when I said things about the system. I organised a conference, on behalf of the Larrakia people of the Darwin area, to discuss how we could get our land back. We did a sit-in on the only road between Nightcliff and Darwin, protesting about land rights. By the time the police came the sit-in was nearly five kilometres long. People wanted to run over us, but they were scared to because there were so many of us. This sit-in was very effective in supporting the Larrakia people, who were fighting to protect their land on the outskirts of Darwin from contractors who wanted to develop it.

The media became even more interested in what I had to say. They started printing my comments about the system and about the government. I continued to be involved in street demonstrations when anyone of authority visited Darwin. When Princess Anne visited Darwin in the late 1960s, another street demonstration was organised, with the help of the Communist Party, for the purpose of giving her a petition to take to the Queen. The petition told the Queen about the suffering Aboriginal people were still experiencing in a country that was part of her British Empire. My children marched with me, carrying placards in all of these street demonstrations, while the 'coloured people' watched from the sidelines. At that time the Communist Party and the Quakers were the only groups of white people willing to help us. The communists were disliked as much as we were, so we banded together.

The church started receiving threats from the head of the government welfare department. They were told that, if they didn't shut me up, they wouldn't get the money that was allocated to them. So I was called into the office of the administrator of the district and told to tone it down and to reduce the number of activities I was organising. I was also told not to talk about the heads of the departments who funded us to run our programs. At a staff meeting I said to my colleagues, 'What's the use of praying about it if we don't do anything about it?' I kept going, but eventually I had to leave my work at the Methodist Overseas Mission. Again and again in my life I have reached a point where I was forced to choose between submitting and toeing the line, or taking a sideways step.

When I was in my late twenties, I was given the opportunity to spend a few months in Canberra, as part of an intensive educational program. I became so well educated that when I returned to Darwin

I had a very hard time getting the type of job for which I was now qualified. This is a very common experience for Aboriginal people. I ended up doing odd jobs like driving a truck for a friend, working on a farm, helping another friend build a caravan park and working in a children's home.

Finally I got a job with the McRobertson–Miller Airways as a freight handler. It was during this time, as I was flying back from one of the island reservations, that the spirit of my mother gave me the song 'My Brown Skin Baby' and this was a major turning point in my life. I had been composing songs since I was a child on the reservation and had written a number of fun songs, but nothing really heavy or serious. This was my first serious song. When I arrived home, I proudly called all my friends and relatives together to share the song with them. The first time I sang it they walked out of the room. It was too painful. This same thing happened for years afterwards wherever I performed it.

It wasn't long after I received the song that I left the airline because I kept getting airsick. I went back to work at the hospital, but this time I was back working in the gardens again. At the same time I continued to help people from the reservation fit into the urban way of living, even though I was unable to get a paid job in welfare to do this sort of work. There were many Aboriginal people needing employment and assistance. When a law was passed that required equal salary be paid for equal work done by stockmen on the cattle stations, it actually worked against our people. The cattle station owners who had used our cheap labour to build up their stations preferred paying a single white man instead of a black man with a family. Previously they had tolerated groups of Aboriginal families co-existing with them on their cattle stations, because they paid the stockmen only in rations. This work had also suited our people. It enabled them to continue to live in their traditional country, and to perform the ceremonies of the Dreaming that keep the energy of creation alive. Because the work was seasonal, it also allowed them to mix a form of work that brought material support for livelihood with a more nomadic existence, and help fulfil our obligation to visit country for ceremony, and to take time out when mourning family members who had died.

A lot of our mob were now pushed off the cattle stations that had been set up on their family land, and they had to go elsewhere looking for jobs. Those lucky enough to live close to a city were pushed onto the social security welfare system, while others were living in the bush on the edge of starvation. You must remember that Aboriginal people no longer had free access to the resources that had supported them for millennia. Their traditional waterholes, which had attracted the native animals which they hunted, were now polluted by cattle and sheep using them. So I ended up helping these people too, because I could really feel their suffering and confusion.

I heard so many stories about the inequalities that my people were experiencing that it became very painful for me to listen. To ease the pain I began to compose songs that addressed some of the issues I was hearing about. I sang at barbecues, campfires and concerts. Whenever I sang 'My Brown Skin Baby' people were so disturbed that they would start to cry. Most of them had also been taken away and had grown up on a reservation. My children were only little, but they would ask, 'Why is everybody crying, Daddy?', and I would reply, 'It's our story, and hearing it is making them feel sad.' It's not an easy song for Aboriginal people to listen to.

I sang at a lot of social functions around Darwin. I sang for many fund-raising programs for the Police Boys Club and other organisations that helped the needy. These appearances gave me the opportunity also to introduce some of the other songs I had composed about the struggles of my people. Sometimes a group of us would just get together on the beach or in the bush and I'd get the guitar out and sing. People who had heard me before started asking me to sing 'My Brown Skin Baby'. It soon became a very well known and very well liked song in the city of Darwin.

Not too many people in Australia actually knew that there were so many children stolen from their families and relocated to other places. It wasn't common knowledge. And here I was singing the song that was saying that it happened. It made people curious about what I was telling them, and that led to bigger things. My original songs about the struggles of Aboriginal people began to be heard by a lot of white people and they started wondering if what I said was true. People came to Darwin to check it out, and then a couple of communist friends of mine who were film makers decided that the content of my songs would be good subject matter for a documentary. Eventually David Roberts, an Australian Broadcasting Commission research worker, came to Darwin in the late 1960s to hear the songs; he wanted to know where they were coming from. He wanted to know why was I composing such profound songs, weighted heavily against the system and the government. On enquiry, he found that all the story songs were true. This led to the production of two films based on my songs. One of them, *My Brown Skin Baby They Take Him Away*, telling the story of the Stolen Generations, was released internationally in the early 1970s, winning an award at the Cannes Film Festival. This aroused international interest in the plight of the Stolen Generations, as we had become known.

The ABC also made a second film, *The Mixed-Up Man*, about the identity crisis that those of us in the Stolen Generations were experiencing. We mixed-race people bore three major burdens. First, we were forcibly stolen from our mothers to prevent us identifying as Aboriginal, so we were all denied the normal human experience of a mother's love. This left us all with deep anxieties about love and abandonment. Second, although we were brought up in European ways, racial prejudice against people of other races or coloured skin prevented us from actually being accepted into European society. Third, our education was deliberately designed to wipe out our ability to speak our mother's language or understand her culture, or to have access to the ceremonial path of knowledge by which a young person becomes a man or woman in Aboriginal culture. So apart from problems of poverty, unemployment and access to housing, we mixed-race Aboriginal people struggled with these spiritual and psychological burdens which crippled so many of us.

A good thing that happened around this time was that I started hunting again, and this allowed me to spend time in country and feel my deep connectedness to all its family members; the birds, lizards, trees, waterways and other animals. This time I began leading hunting expeditions for white people who were not missionaries. I had been taught on the reservation that white people who were not missionaries were really bad people, and we couldn't trust them. So when I started taking white servicemen who lived in the area hunting, it was with a lot of fear and trepidation. I was therefore quite amazed when these ordinary whites opened their doors, and asked me to sit at their table and eat with them. The missionaries never did that. We had our place and they had their place and we very rarely got together in a trusting way. It was always 'We'll tell you what to do and when to do it,' and 'Do it or else'. That was their attitude. It had made us fear, dislike and be suspicious of all white people.

So it was a wonderful relief to find out that I could trust the white men that I went shooting with. I taught them how to hunt. These people didn't claim to be Christians or anything special, but they showed me the face of goodness in the ordinary white person, which I had rarely seen before. They were just ordinary folks and they were really good people. I was beginning to discover that there were good people, bad people and people in between in every race, and that I needed to get to know someone well before I could hope to establish a trusting relationship. At this time the Quakers (Society of Friends) began arranging public gatherings and they paid Aboriginal speakers to fly to Sydney and Melbourne to participate. They began ringing me up and sending me letters saying, 'Is it possible for you to come down and be part of a speaking group that will be talking to people around the southern states?' I started travelling to these meetings in the mid–1970s and did presentations with other prominent Aboriginal activists such as Paul Coe, Gary Foley, Gary Williams and Charles Perkins. My job was to open the session up with a song, then some of them would speak and then I'd do another song.

The Quakers organised many small groups for us to talk to in different towns and in all the major cities. They went out of their way to pick people to attend these meetings who could make a difference in getting the system to address the struggles of Aboriginal people. They invited people who held significant positions in organisations, companies or society in general. Then these people would help to create more meetings. The majority of these meetings were in Melbourne, Sydney and Adelaide. The audience was made up of whites and Aborigines. Anyone who was interested in Aboriginal issues could attend. The meetings were low-key, but the audiences always showed a powerful reaction to the presentations.

At this time in Australia's history, it was only the Quakers that helped us in this way. No other church was willing to do it, or else they didn't know how to do it. Possibly this was because of their heavy involvement in the system of removing Aboriginal children from their birth mothers to remote reservations, without any of the normal civil rights of citizens. It should be remembered that Aboriginal people did not get the rights to citizenship of Australia until the 1967 referendum. Some church people didn't even realise that there was a problem. They just went along with the status quo as though 'this is the way it is'.

Slowly this public awareness campaign of the Quakers and Aboriginal activists began to bear fruit. It reached a height with the establishment of the Aboriginal Tent Embassy on the lawn in front of Parliament House in Canberra, on Australia Day, 26 January 1972. Under this sustained political pressure, in 1976 the Federal government under Malcolm Fraser passed the first land rights legislation, affecting people in the Northern Territory where the Commonwealth had jurisdiction.

At these speaking group gatherings I could only present my message to the general public as a composer, singer and performer. The Federal Council for the Advancement of Aboriginal and Torres Straight Islanders (FCAATSI) started arranging conferences all over the south. Aborigines from every state were represented and I was asked to become the Northern Territory representative. I happily accepted, but I realised that to be a good public speaker I had to go back to school and get a good command of English.

At the same time, the hospital started to get upset about my political activities. I was taking too much time off to travel to meetings. They told me that I had to choose between working at the hospital and being involved in Aboriginal issues. I knew that I had to keep on helping my people in any way that I could, so I left the hospital and got another job with the Uniting Church Mission. On this occasion, I was hired as a purchasing agent.

When the Labor Party was elected into power in 1972, they started allocating money to Aborigines for education. An organisation called the Task Force was formed for the purpose of sponsoring people to get higher education. The church agreed that I should go to college in Adelaide, so Amy and I moved south with our four children. I was very grateful for this opportunity. I was now able to improve my English skills so that I could begin speaking publicly about the experiences of my people and the mistreatment we were getting under the white system. *Kanyini* was taking me further and further into the world of social action.

Angas Downs

My days in life of searching
Have now come to an end
For I have found the home I love,
Back there at Angas Downs.

Angas Downs, my peoples' home,
I had no choice to leave,
Taken from my people, taken far away.
Now after many years have gone
I now have found my home
The home and my country is there at Angas Downs.

Now my search is over
The tears will slowly cease.
I listen to my people talk of times gone by,
The hard times and the good ones,
By those who still remain.
How I love the green and brown
Of my home of Angas Downs.

Angas Downs, the place I love,
Angas Downs my home.
How I love the people who come
From Angas Downs.

You'll never know the heartaches,
You'll never know the pain
Of many years of suffering,
Of strange lands far away.
Instead of dreams were nightmares,
Instead of laughter, tears,
But now those tears are running dry.
I'm back on Angas Downs.

Angas Downs, the place I love,
Angas Downs my home.
How I love those people who come
From Angas Downs.

Ngura

my search for country

One of my fathers used to pester me to take him home to his country, and I'd say, 'Well, a bit later, Old Man, hang on, a little bit later. I've got work to do.' He'd say, 'Oh, but you've got to take me, you said you'd take me.' And I'd say, 'But I've got to take a week off to do that, we've got a long way to travel.' Eventually I said, 'Okay, I'll take you out this weekend.'

So my brothers and I picked him up on a Friday and we drove out, heading towards Arnhem Land. He was feeling slow and miserable when we left Darwin, but as we neared the East Alligator River we could see the spirit starting to come back into him. Just knowing he was going there was enough to make him stronger.

And when we entered the reservation, heading towards the coast where his country is, *boom!* He changed before my eyes. He was getting younger. I couldn't believe it. He was almost jumping out of the car to do jobs like clearing the track himself, instead of telling me to do them.

And when we went into the country, it was amazing. Here was a man who'd lost twenty years in the four-hour drive from Darwin to his country. He was so different. Even the tone of his voice had become strong.

He had us stop near a special site and began speaking to the ancestral spirits there, before taking my brothers and myself in to show us around. Now he could pass the knowledge down to us. It was hard to believe that this man was the same sick old man who had seemed ready to die. Now that he was back where he wanted to be, back to his country, his spirit returned and he looked as if he could live another hundred years.

Many non-Aboriginal people are fascinated by the deep spiritual relationship we Aboriginal people have for our country. It is the fourth dimension of our identity, like our hand is to our body. Every year more and more non-Aboriginal people visit outback Australia. They come from the cities of Australia, and increasingly they come from the cities of Europe, America and Asia. Many are in search of a rekindling of their spirit, especially its link with land. Perhaps they are drawn here because they know the earth herself is troubled with the destruction of forests and waterways. Perhaps it is here in Australia that, because of our *tjukurrpa* which stretches back unbroken for millennia, the voice of the earth reaches us so powerfully that even those with untrained eyes and ears begin to hear her voice.

In many ways, through my life at Croker Island and particularly my life as a hunter and my introduction to the ceremonial path of knowledge of Arnhem Land, Arnhem Land had also become *ngura* to me. It had become country. But yet memories of my mother and the desert had continued to haunt me. When I was forced to leave Croker Island and make my life in Darwin, I began to dream of finding my original family and the *ngura* of my birth.

At the mission, when thoughts of my family arose I kept them to myself, because these thoughts made me feel sad. However when I got older, I felt more able to handle these emotions. I had overheard someone say that all the records of our families and where we came from were in the mission office, so I went to the superintendent and asked him to give me my records. The welfare card he handed me had very little on it besides the name Bob Randall. It said: 'father unknown, mother unknown, tribe unknown, country unknown'.

That was it; all they had on that card was my name, a number, and my birthday.

It wasn't my real birthday, however. On Croker, they didn't know when that was, so they just gave me one. Someone must have realised that we would need to have birthdays, so one day we were asked to line up and the missionaries looked us over and said, 'How old do you think you are now?' We each made a guess, and then they reviewed our lives with us, going back to events like the end of the war, when we left the Bungalow, how long we had been there, and things like that. This review happened when we were back at Croker after the war. That is how I learned how old I was. By then they thought I was twelve years old.

Amy's Aunty Melba in Darwin had seen her and recognised her as her niece, and told her where she could find her mother. So we decided to begin our search for our families, by looking for Amy's relatives. On our first holiday break we packed up the family and headed south. We didn't have much money, so we camped in the bush wherever we found ourselves at sunset and lived off of the land. My hunting skills and knowledge of bush tucker enabled me to feed myself, my wife, and our four hungry children while we were on the road. I also caught pigeons, lizards, and kangaroos to give as gifts to the Aboriginal people we would be meeting on the cattle stations.

I intuitively knew that I had come from the south or west of Alice Springs, but I didn't know where. I didn't know who my family members were. Amy and I headed towards Alice Springs, visiting every cattle station we passed, asking if anyone could help us find my parents. I looked at a map and whenever I saw a cattle station we'd go there and ask the station owners, 'Where are the Aboriginal people?' and they would direct us to the Aboriginal camping area. We'd go there and speak to the elders. I told them, 'I'm looking for my parents, because I was taken away from them as a child.'

By the time we got to Katherine, only a few hundred kilometres south of Darwin, women started claiming me as their son, and then a whole lot of women would start to wail. In our system, there's more than one mother for every child, and these women were wailing to support the woman who thought her son had returned. Each time this happened, it was a very emotional experience for everyone concerned. After a few times I began to realise how many children had been taken. Previously I'd had no idea that this had happened to so many people.

Amy and I continued travelling south, stopping at every cattle station, until my holidays ran out and we had to return to Darwin. I was forced to accept that my search would take a long time.

Eventually we found Amy's mother at Aileron. Her family were still trying to live a traditional way of life, but they no longer had their land where they could move from one waterhole to another, or access to hunting resources that had previously sustained this way of life. Aboriginal people had become like ghosts, floating on the edges of white men's cattle stations. The seasonal work which Aboriginal men had been able to get on the stations was also becoming more scarce, due to the new legislative requirements to pay them the same wages as white men. Some of the women could get work as housekeepers for the station owners or at local hotels, but this required them to be dressed in European clothes, which required a lifestyle with ready access to water for washing clothes, and money to buy such clothes. Consequently Aboriginal people, once proud nomads, masters of an open, free way of life, now appeared as dust-encrusted, broken people, dressed in rags, trying to create their camps with the discarded remnants of modern living, like sheets of corrugated iron, tin drums and plastic.

We could see that there were a lot of very bad cases of trachoma, an eye infection that is associated with dust, and some, like Amy's stepfather Paddy, were blind from the disease. The camp, which Amy's family had established with bush materials, bits of tin and plastic, had no water nearby. The women had to roll 44-gallon drums to a bore hole almost a kilometre away to get the camp's daily water supply, and then they rolled the full drums back. They were forbidden to camp closer, in case they frightened the stock that drank at the bore hole. There were a lot of children running around because there was no school for them to attend. Traditionally, these children would have been working with their mothers, collecting bush tucker in tune with their nomadic pattern of wandering, which was tied to the seasons and the different foods that were found in various country at different times. It was this knowledge that was an important part of ceremonial learning.

Amy and I wanted to do something for these people. It seemed to us that if they could no longer enjoy their fully traditional way of life, then they had the right now to enjoy some of the benefits of the Western way of life. After all, it was Aboriginal land that white people were using to build their wealth, in the form of cattle and sheep stations and mines.

Amy, the children and I continued visiting her family in Aileron whenever we travelled south, and over time we were able to get to know them and feel connected to them. Our children started to establish close relationships with other members of the family. For the first time they knew they had a lot of grandparents. These visits also gave them the opportunity to learn how other Aborigines were living. They quickly learned to ride donkeys and steer them with sticks. They learned about the bush tucker of the desert area, and our sons Alan and Johnny would go kangaroo hunting with the men. This helped them identify themselves as Aborigines of the Anmatyerre nation. They liked having lots of brothers, sisters, uncles and aunties and the many grandparents who told them stories about the country around Aileron and Ti Tree.

On our third visit we talked Amy's parents and sister into coming to Darwin to see how we lived. Amy was able to persuade her mother to come by telling her she could also visit her sister Dolly and Dolly's children. Dolly was another member of the Stolen Generations.

Their first visit was as much of a culture shock to them as our first visit to Aileron was to us. They loved eating their meals while sitting on the polished floor instead of with us at the dining table. They preferred to sleep outside instead of in the beds we offered them, which reminded me of my first experience with beds. When we took them to the ocean, they were very hesitant to approach the salt water as the waves rolled up onto the beach. They couldn't get over how much water there was in front of them. Amy's sister Beryl came up from Aileron later and lived with us for a while. She fitted in quite well, and was another mother for the kids.

On our fourth visit to Aileron we were accompanied by a film crew from the Australian Broadcasting Commission, and Amy's cousin Flo. Amy had received a letter from her mother asking about her sister Ruby's daughter Flo. When she got the letter she realised that this was the same Flo who was her friend from Croker Island. When Flo agreed to go to Aileron to meet her mother, it was about the same time I was approached by the ABC to do a film documentary based on my song 'My Brown Skin Baby'. David Roberts, the film's researcher and producer, thought it would be a great opportunity to film the first meeting of a mother and her daughter who had been taken away.

The film crew flew to Alice Springs and they were scheduled to meet us at the homestead under a really big shade tree near Amy's parent's camp. David drove down with Amy, Flo and myself so that he could get to know the country. He was very interested in the way Aborigines communicate with each other without telephones, and on this occasion he was given a demonstration. We drove onto the property, and as we approached the big tree we could see that a lot of family members were gathered under it. We said, 'Ah, the film crew has everyone set up for the filming.' But when we got closer we realised that the film crew wasn't there. We asked the family where the film crew was, and they weren't aware that a film crew was expected to be there. They had not been told that we were coming, but they were out there waiting for us. David asked them why they were waiting under the tree and one of them replied, 'When Bob left Darwin to come and visit us we knew he was coming and where he wanted us to meet him.' The film crew's hired car had broken down, and when they finally did appear a couple of hours later the introductions of mother and daughter had to be made all over again.

This film, which aroused much controversy in the early 1970s, was shown on national and international television, and won a bronze award at the Cannes Film Festival. For the first time people began to understand the agony of mixed-race Aboriginal people and how our experiences have shaped many of the problems confronting Aboriginal families today. After twenty years, as other songs joined my songs, and more and more people spoke out, the Federal Government was forced to establish the inquiry in 1995. *Bringing Them Home*, the report from the inquiry, revealed the full horror of what children like me, and our families, had suffered.

Many white people who saw the film *Brown Skin Baby* became angry because they realised that they had been supporting a system that they didn't agree with. Several of the leaders of my church were very disturbed. They just saw themselves as caregivers. The Australian government told them that we were neglected, dumped and unwanted orphans and they had believed that. Many beautiful people had joined mission organisations as volunteers to help look after us, because they thought we were in desperate need.

The film also made people aware of the very primitive conditions Aboriginal people were still living in. They saw that there were places where Aborigines still had no running water, no houses, and no comfortable sleeping places. They were living in these terrible conditions in the middle of an affluent society, where the government was boasting that all Australians were equal. They were telling the world that we were all 'mates' and no one was disadvantaged. The whites in the system may have believed what they were saying, but in truth the government was very cruel to anyone who was not part of the system.

The film showed how Amy's family, the Anmatyerre people, were living on their land that had been turned into a cattle station. The cattle station owners were 'sort of' looking after them, because they were living there and working for them, but the level of care they were getting was deplorable. After the film appeared, the government sent in people who were concerned and interested, and an area of land near Ti Tree Station was allocated to the Anmatyerre people. The new site had water available so they no longer had to walk such a long way for water. The people were given houses, a little clinic and a women's shelter with a community room. Slowly but surely things improved, and there is a growing community there now. All the families have three bedroom houses if they need them.

The Lutheran Church also became involved with this community because of Eric, the Lutheran minister, who was in the film. Public opinion helped push things along so the people could live on their own land in a more comfortable and more equal way. They were now able to become part of society. They could buy things, make and sell artefacts, and if people wanted to develop a business nearby, they were available to be hired as labourers. The sad thing for me was that the elders, who had lived without these improvements for so long, were dying just as things began to get better. In those days we didn't foresee the problem that alcohol would become.

After living most of her life in European housing in Darwin, Flo found the camp conditions so physically confronting that she could not handle the situation and never returned to visit her people again. I had the idea of getting a committee together in Darwin so that as a group we could apply for some money to help make needed changes at these camps. One thing I realised during my visits to Aileron was that the family had very little money coming in, once the mustering season ended. The whole family barely survived on the small amount of money that some of the girls earned cleaning the local hotel. I could not understand why all the elders were not getting their pensions and other benefits. I went to the Department of Social Security in Alice Springs and spoke to one of the Aboriginal men working there. He was also surprised when I told him about this large group of people, who were not getting any of the benefits due them. As a result of that inquiry, social security workers went to Aileron and were able to identify who was entitled to these benefits, and for the first time Aileron people were put on the benefits list. I was able to assist them because I could read and write and knew what they were entitled to.

The older men of Aileron welcomed me into the family and started to share stories and songs of their country with me, which I have passed on to my children. The children can now go back to live on their mother's traditional land, and one of my daughters has recently decided to do this. Although she has a Western education, she has been drawn back to discover her traditional roots, and to undertake the path of ceremonial knowledge which will enable her to paint and learn her mother's language.

We continued to spend all of our holiday time searching for my family and it was a painful process. There were so many false leads, and so many parents who claimed me as their son. Two things had remained in my head since I was taken away. One was a mental picture of the land at Angas Downs, and the other was my mother's name. All of the women who thought they were my mother didn't have the name that I knew my mother carried. Her name was Thungawa. I was told that she was given the English name of Nellie, but the person who told me that wasn't certain of it, because in our family system we don't call each other by given names. We refer to family members as mother, aunty, granny, father, brother, and so on.

Amy's family was a big help to me because they said, 'Ah, your name is Randall. There's a station owner named Randall Stafford around here. Might be that's your family.' In fact, the superintendent of Croker Island had also told me he thought I was the son of someone named Randall Stafford. It seemed logical, because my name was Randall and the government could have added the name Bob when I arrived at the Bungalow. They were giving all Aborigines English names at that time, and who knows where they might have got these names from?

Randall Stafford lived west of Aileron at a place called Coniston, the site of the infamous Coniston Massacre, with which he had been involved. He was a white man who did have an Aboriginal wife, and a child who had been taken away. I met his wife and other members of her family, and they too thought that I was their missing child. We went to where the old Coniston Station used to be, to see if I remembered anything about the land there, but there wasn't much of the station left and the land was very different from the pictures in my head. It was too flat. I drew a picture on the ground of what I remembered about my home country, but nobody with us recognised the place that I had drawn. We continued to visit all the other cattle stations in that area, and took a look at another place where the people who thought I was Randall Stafford's son said I might have lived.

I thought that I could very well be Randall Stafford's son, but the place where they lived was very different from the land that I remembered. However, they fitted me into their skin system (another line of relationship that runs parallel to the biological relationship system), and to this day I consider them my Walpiri family. But the Walpiri live in the west and I still had some reservations about them being my biological family, because I had an inner feeling that I had to keep going south.

It was only after I had left Darwin and moved to Adelaide to further my education that I got the lead which would take me to my original family. By this time I was in my late thirties, when I received a letter from Lily, who was one of my closest friends from Croker Island. Lily and I had both felt like we could be related, but there was no way to substantiate it. When Lily left the mission, she went down south to do a nurses' training program and ended up living in Alice Springs. She wrote me a letter from Alice that said, 'I have found out that we are brother and sister. Your brother Milton Liddle in Alice Springs has all of our family history.' I now knew that I might eventually find my real biological family. It also confirmed that inner feeling I had about my sister. I always liked her and she had looked out for me as an older sister would, but I had no idea that we had the same mother. Of course, who would have thought that when her last name was Kunoff and mine was Randall? I discovered that the Kunoff line had strong links to the Utopia community, and that is why, today, I have a kinship line with this community. That is how Aboriginal kinship systems work. There is the thread of the biological connection and then this extends sideways through the sisters and brothers, who are equally our mothers and fathers.

Unfortunately, Lily didn't tell me who the other members of the family were, because when I came to Alice Springs a few years later looking for Milton, I walked right past my sister Junie without knowing that she was one of people I was looking for. Our mothers were sisters, and therefore mothers to both of us, and we shared the same father. She later told me that she recognised me straight away and even said hello but I just ignored her. I don't know whether I didn't hear her, or didn't respond because I didn't know who she was. Maybe I just had other things on my mind at the time.

When I met Milton he told me, 'You are my younger brother. I remember when you were taken away. Lily, Alfie, Teddy and Tommy were also taken from our family.' He told me that our father used to look after lots of kids and we all grew up as brothers and sisters, even those who were not biologically connected. I don't think Bill Liddle was the father of all the mixed-blood kids at Angas Downs, because there were other white men around and the Aboriginal women also had children with them. So I don't know for sure whether Bill was my biological father, but his attitude to the children associated with the Aboriginal people who lived on Angas Downs showed how much he had integrated into the Aboriginal way of life. My family line remains anchored firmly in my Aboriginal heritage, while my European heritage remains somewhat hazy.

According to a German publication called *The Wind of Change in Central Australia*[1] published in 1965, Bill Liddle had children with five wives. His first wife Mary had four children, Hilda, Milton, Harold and Arthur and the other wives had one child each. The other wives were my Yankunytjatjara mothers, who were sisters. I do not know who supplied this genealogy to the author, but those of us who were taken away as young children were not listed.

I accepted that Milton was my brother when he said so. Milton told me about the rest of the Liddle side of the family and what it was like when I was taken away. I was amazed at how large this family of mine was. Milton had six children, Harold had ten, Hilda had four, and Arthur had three. By the time I showed up there were quite a few grandchildren as well. Milton introduced me to other members of the Liddle family and then he told me where to look for the Yankunytjatjara side of my family.

Old Bill Liddle had sold Angas Downs to Milton and Arthur because Harold preferred to live in Alice Springs, and Hilda had married and moved to Adelaide where she died of cancer at a young age. After selling the property to his sons, Bill Liddle lived in Alice Springs with my sister Junie until he died in the Alice Springs hospital in 1960. He had wanted Angas Downs to stay in the family, but this was not to be. After Milton died, Arthur offered to sell it to me, but I had had my fill of mustering cattle on Croker Island and wanted to remain working in education. The property was eventually taken over by the bank because of some financial problems.

When Bill Liddle died, all the Aboriginal people who lived on Angas Downs left the property. This is our custom when we lose a close family member and it was a statement of their respect for him. The one thing they most admired about him was his willingness to give all of his mixed-blood children the Liddle name. It didn't matter what other whites thought. I was probably named Randall Liddle, but this identity was lost to me when I was taken away.

The way in which many Aboriginal women had children with white men, and the way in which this led to large inclusive family groups, says a lot about our tradition of kinship, marriage and sex. On Croker Island, despite the attitude of the white missionaries, we kids had a very open and joyful attitude about sex. We Aboriginal people live so close to the rhythm of nature that sexuality, to us, seems very natural. It is the 'love magic' of the universe. Although we recognise that human sexual union is linked to bearing children, we think that this only prepares the physical possibility for the spirit child to be drawn into our world. The voice of the spirit child speaks to us through our intuitive awareness, often in dreams or visions, or through contact with sacred sites. We Yankunytjatjara people derive our skin system (kinship group) not only from our biological parents, but also from our 'conception site', the country where our mother first feels our presence in her womb. However, the whole area of growing the child and giving birth is sacred women's business, so I can't talk about that side any further.

In our traditional culture, men and women may have more than one wife or husband. My wife's sisters are all my wives, while my brothers can be husband to my wife. In our traditional culture it was also normal for a man to offer his wife to another as 'brother', as a gesture of hospitality and inclusiveness. But this was never forced on their wives, because they felt the same obligation of hospitality through this custom. Similarly a woman could ask one of her brother-in-law 'husbands' for his child, and he was free to say no. This has happened to me many times, and I have always felt free to say no, without any embarrassment to either side.

During the early years of dispossession, when the establishment of cattle stations was disrupting our traditional way of life and access to food sources, men would offer their wives to the white men within this system of reciprocal hospitality. A man accepting this offer would be expected to return such a gesture by offering food. Traditionally this was from his hunting, and it became transferred to the white man's access to rations or other supplies. So in our culture there was no shame in these exchanges. We just incorporated these new white people, with their superior wealth and weapons, into our system of *kanyini*. It is true that many white men did not understand this, and so did not fulfil their reciprocal obligations, causing such events as that which led to the Coniston

Massacre. However, Bill Liddell did, and that is why we respected him and why today the many children who are descended from him, from a number of different women, all recognise each other as brothers and sisters. We do not distinguish between the children of his Arrernte wife, whom he married whitefella way, from the children of his Yankunytjatjara 'wives'.

When I met Milton I was on leave from my job at Darwin Hospital, and had to go back to Darwin when my leave time ran out. A few more years passed before I was able to save up enough leave to head down south again. It wasn't until many years later, on my fourth or fifth trip to Alice, that Milton introduced me to my sister Junie. She turned out to be the most valuable person to my search, because she took me out to Angas Downs. It was hard to believe that I was finally going to see the place where I was born.

We loaded up our camping gear and Junie, Arthur's wife, Bessie, and I headed south from Alice Springs. As soon as we turned onto one particular track in the bush, it felt as though I was home. I could see the red sand hills and the big casuarina trees and they were all familiar to me. I had the feeling that I had been here before, but I still wasn't sure if this was the home that I dreamed about. I was looking for two hills that met each other like a woman's breasts, with a creek running through them. It was the place where we used to camp, and I couldn't forget that creek because I was nearly washed away in it during a flash flood when I was a young boy. We kept driving along and, when we drove around one particular corner, I said, 'This is it, Sis, this is where I came from,' and she said 'Yes.'

My heart felt as big as the country I was looking at when I saw those two hills right in front of us, and the creek that ran down from the centre of them right beside us. I knew for certain that I had found the place that I was taken away from so long ago. We were at a bend in the road that gave me the whole view of it. As we drove on to the old homestead, everything was exactly as I remembered it, including the ridges of red rock nearby and the big black rocks that I used to play on with the other kids. Everything that I had carried in my memory all those years was there. Even the areas where my people camped on different parts of the property were in the places that I remembered them to be. I knew, without a doubt, that this was the home I had been longing for. It seemed as though every bird, tree, plant and all of the earth were saying, 'Welcome home, son.' I cried with joy and sadness as even more memories flooded my mind and heart. I walked away from the car and my family so that I could be by myself while I thanked God for bringing me back to my country.

When I got back to the car Junie said, 'Now we've got to go to Areyonga to look for your mother and the rest of your family.' But it was a long time before I could manage another trip to Alice so that Junie and I could go there. It didn't happen until I was hired as Director of the Aboriginal Legal Aid Service in Alice Springs in the late '70s. It would have been good if I could have stayed in the Alice Springs area to meet everyone in my family as soon as I met the first group. But the reality of the situation was that during all of those years of searching, I had a job, a house and kids to support, and the kids were still going to school. We had all the normal expenses any family would have, plus a financial and spiritual commitment to helping others. We had to use the few resources that we had left over to make these trips, first from Darwin, later from Adelaide, and then again from Darwin, as my working life took me to different places.

Living in Alice Springs enabled me to find more of my relatives because I could travel out to where they lived on weekends. Areyonga was another Aboriginal community set up by the government with a ration depot and a mission church run by the Lutherans. Most of my mother's family had moved there. When we drove in, Junie was able to communicate with the family there because she still spoke the Yankunytjatjara language. She said, 'Bob's here to meet family.' So they all came out to meet me. Junie is the daughter of my mother's sister, so according to Aboriginal tradition she is my sister. At Areyonga I met another sister and a couple of brothers and the minister who my mother used to work for. The minister told me that my mother was dead and that she had been crippled towards the end of her life. He also told me that my Aboriginal father Joe had looked after her right up to the very end.

The first time I went to Areyonga, I had a strange feeling come over me while the minister was talking to me about my mother. The minister was standing in a doorway and suddenly that doorway became my mother's grave. I saw myself standing at the end of her grave as they were burying her. This was a very clear vision and I've never forgotten it. Until that time my mother was still alive to me and I was expecting to meet her. My niece Daphne then took me to my mother's grave and we stayed there for a while. At the end of the day I asked my wife to drive home. I must have cried all the way from Areyonga to Alice Springs. While I cried I composed a twenty-verse song called 'The Highway of Tears'. Now that I knew my mother had passed on, I kept wondering if we could have passed each other on the street when I first came to Alice Springs.

The minister showed me the houses they had lived in. The cottage where they last had lived was a really good house. He told me that when they first got to Areyonga they camped, but because my mother was a good worker she was quickly moved into one of the clay brick cottages. Later on the government went crazy putting up aluminium houses for Aboriginal workers. This kind of house is freezing in winter and like an oven in summer, but these were the next line of houses for Aboriginal people to live in on this reservation. So from the bush shelter they moved to a nice brick house and then to a tin shed. They lived like this until the church turned over the whole area to the Aborigines and then they moved back into their brick cottage that had been housing the white staff while they lived in the shed.

When Aboriginal land rights became law in the Northern Territory, some of the churches, like the Uniting Methodist Church that I belonged to, handed the property they had been using back to the people very quickly. Other churches really dragged their feet because they didn't want to give it back. They thought it belonged to them. This was especially true of the Lutherans, who were the slowest of all the church groups in Australia to give the land back. But land rights meant that the land they were using belonged to Aboriginal people and they had no choice but to return the land to its rightful owners. The old missions then became communities for the Aborigines who had been living there.

About this time, the churches began training Aboriginal ministers, who were willing and able to do the religious work as long as the church continued to employ them and pay them to run church programs for the community. Some of these ministers were my family members. They were brilliant men and were able to do everything the white ministers had done except they did it in the language of the people. Recently some of these ministers, drawn from the Catholic, Anglican, Lutheran and Uniting Church groups, have begun to explore the idea of 'Rainbow Spirit Theology'.[2] They have also concluded that many Aboriginal people today affirm the positive message of the Gospel brought by the missionaries, but see the rejection of our traditional culture as unnecessary and destructive. Because the Christian message was imposed from above and, like the strangler fig tree does in nature, choked the life out of our rich spiritual tradition, it also choked life out of our people themselves.

Areyonga was only one of the places where my Yankunytjatjara family was living, so I continued to look elsewhere for other family members. I was told by my relatives at Areyonga, 'The rest of your family is at Uluru.' So that's where Junie took me on our next trip out together. Sure enough, I found my younger brother Dixon at Mutitjulu. He lived at the camping area designated for Aboriginal people near Uluru. He introduced me to my other brothers, their wives and children and my grandfather. Once I had made the connection with these family members I visited them often. I'd take visitors out to see Uluru and then go to see my family. My grandfather, Nipper Winmati, introduced me to the land of my ancestors and told me many of the stories of our traditional land. Some of my uncles gave me a tour around Uluru and Kata Tjuta and told me the stories of these sites. I discovered that I was of the Mala totem. Mala are the small wallabies who live around Uluru.

As Robert Layton[3] discovered, when he was researching owner-ship of Uluru in relation to the Aboriginal people's claim for that site under native title, although different groups had rights to dif-ferent parts, there were no clear and rigid boundaries, as is the case with white law about land rights.

When Layton talked with my grandfather, Nipper Winmati, and the other senior elder of Uluru, Paddy Uluru, he discovered a pattern of overlapping rights, but also a sense of Uluru (the Rock) as a unity. Many of the ownership areas (Layton used the English idea of 'estates' to translate these into Western concepts) are clus-tered along the ranges where there are rock holes and soaks, and therefore there is a source of water in this very arid desert region. We Yankunytjatjara, from the eastern side of Uluru, and the Pitjan-tjatjara, from the western side of Uluru, think of *ngura* as not only our immediate camp, but also the whole of our area where we have rights (our estate). We use the term *ngura kaputu* to refer to the area over which we have hunting and foraging rights, and this can extend beyond our so-called 'estate' area.

When we visit neighbouring estates, we need to make contact with the people with rights there, or we have to know the legends and the location of sacred sites in that area. Our estate contains several ancestral tracks associated with many sacred sites, which record the travel of the ancestral beings, and which we learn about through the *inma*, the song cycles of the Dreaming tracks. To be an owner of a place, we have to learn all of this through the path of ceremonial knowledge which begins in our youth, and then our responsibility is to pass this on as we become ceremonial elders. For instance at Uluru there are *inma* associated with the *Mala* and *Kuniya*, while at Atila there are the *Wati Nyinnga* (Ice Men) and

Kungarangkalpa (Seven Sisters). In our tradition we never married a woman from the same land-owning group, so our children would always begin life with a connection to two estates. In my case, my mother's side gave me access to her people's estates through my grandfather, Nipper Winmati. However, because my father was a white man, and I am what is considered under white law as an illegitimate son, I didn't have strong legal rights to Angas Downs as a cattle station. But because this was on my tribal land, from my mother's side, I have strong Aboriginal ownership rights over this country. So in the case of the extended Liddle family, these two ways of relating to country have become rather mixed up.

When I recently met up with Milton Liddle's son, Bobby (from the legitimate side of the family under white law), we visited the old homestead site on the station. His stories go back to a life inside that house, but for me, my stories go back to the Aboriginal camp on the riverbank across from that house. Yet we both feel this strong connection to the country. This land is so arid that it has not survived as a viable cattle station. Now the only industry is tourism, and here there is a powerful and complicated relationship between modern commercial rights to land for the purposes of erecting buildings and running a business, and traditional rights to land associated with ancestral Dreaming, which the tourists want to hear about. So unless you have the traditional rights to the *inma*, just having a legal right to land excised as a cattle station will not be sufficient to enter this new industry of cultural tourism.

Traditionally, senior ceremonial elders often developed knowledge of the *inma* of the whole area, including estates not part of their own totem. For instance the story of the Seven Sisters passes along a Dreaming track which stretches from near Ernabella, through Yankunytjatjara land (which includes Angas Downs) across Luritja land, the Kings Canyon area, then in a westerly direction to the Walpiri country. This is women's *inma*, and forms part of their ceremonial path of knowledge. My tribal sister, Bessie, is one of the holders of the Seven Sisters story, but it is also well known because it is told through the paintings they have on the Ghan, the train which travels from Alice Springs to Adelaide. It is also the subject of many paintings.

The Seven Sisters now dwell in the sky and form the Pleiades cluster of stars. But back in the ancestral creation time of the *tjukurrpa*, these seven sisters were travelling together across country, making camp at different places and living off bush tucker. A man heard their noise and decided to investigate, and found these seven beautiful sisters. So he followed them. However he was no ordinary man, but a clever man with magic powers. He had the power to appear in the form of whatever a person most desired. Because he was single, he decided he should have one for his wife, and in the story this is shown with great humour. He manages to fool all the sisters except the eldest, because he can change himself into whatever a person likes. So, for example, the youngest sister was fooled because she thought he was just some flowers. Later in the dance each sister, starting with the youngest, would approach him with their container of 'food', but he would refuse to eat their 'food', because he only wanted 'food' from the eldest sister. He was looking for a wife who could see him for who he really was. But she refused him because she would not abandon her sisters. So they escaped to the sky. And now, every night in the sky you can see these seven sisters together, and you can see that magic man still chasing them.

This story of the Seven Sisters is a women's story. You can see how, as young girls learn this story, they also learn about how to relate to men. But especially they learn about how to deal with the way our minds fool us. And we all know how easy this is when it comes to sex and love!

The ritual knowledge associated with *inma* is sacred secret and I may not talk about it publicly through this book, unless it has already been made public knowledge, like the story of the Seven Sisters. As my grandfather Nipper Winmati recorded it, my line is associated with the following places: Mutitjulu, Kalaiya Tjunta, Wila Alpuru, Kuniya Piti, Taputji, Inintitjara, Kantju, Mala Wipu,

Walu Katjuta, Mutjuranpa, Lungkata Waru, Pularinya, Patji, Kapi Yularanya Pulka and Kapi Yularanya Tjukutjuku.

All this I learned from Nipper Winmati. Finally I had come home to claim my *ngura*, to revive my deep connection to my country and its *tjukurrpa*. Today I am a *tjilpi* (elder) for my Mutitjulu community with many responsibilities and obligations. I wish it were possible for me to spend more time there, particularly with my sisters and aunties. It is a strange experience, these days, to come here and see the thousands of non-Aboriginal people who visit Uluru and Kata Tjuta every day. At first people seemed to come to see them as giant geological formations in the desert, and felt a great compulsion to climb to the top. But increasingly people come here in search of a connection with Aboriginal spirituality. Since Uluru was handed back to my community in 1985, we have worked together with the Northern Territory Parks and Wildlife Department to make this possible. We have a cultural centre near Uluru, which enables people to learn about the *tjukurrpa* stories linked to Uluru, and there are National Parks guides who take people around the site, some of whom are our Mutitjulu people.

To help protect the area, it was decided to build accommodation for the tourists some distance away at a place called Yulara. Here there are luxury hotels, apartments, hostels and a camping ground. It is becoming like a small city; all because of Uluru. However you will not see many Aboriginal people working there. We do not really feel comfortable working as waiters, cleaners and sales assistants for the tourists on our land. We are happy to share these sacred sites, but the whole white way of organising things is foreign to us.

It took some time to develop feelings of connectedness with all of these new family members of mine among the Yankunytjatjara. At first I had no feelings at all, it was like meeting strangers. It was the continuous coming together that brought family feelings back to me and strengthened the ties. When I was living in Alice during the late '70s and early '80s I got to know many members of my biological family better because I was able to visit them on a regular basis. During this time my sister Junie helped to raise my youngest children and all of us had a close relationship with her. I eventually moved back to Darwin and just stopped over in Alice Springs to visit family when we were travelling between Darwin and Adelaide.

As large as this part of my family is, it's only a small part of the big picture. I am related to so many others through our kinship system that sometimes it seems like there are relatives around me wherever I go. In addition to the Liddles and my Yankunytjatjara and Pitjantjatjara relatives, I also have my extended family from the mission, the Iwaidja, the Gumatj, and the Gunwinku up in Oenpelli, as well as the Walpiri people to the north-west of Alice Springs and the Arrernte people of Alice Springs, through their skin system. In our culture, each of these groups relates me to others because all of their brothers, sisters, aunties, uncles, and grannies are now my relatives as well. This not only includes their biological relatives, it also includes their ceremonial, totem and kinship relationships as well.

When I married Amy I became related to her Anmatyerre family at Aileron, and because our culture does not recognise divorce, Amy and her family will always be an important part of my family for the rest of my life. In our culture we just continue to add family members and no one is ever eliminated.

When I went to college in Adelaide one of my Arnhem Land elders said to me, 'You're doing well, my son, but be careful that we don't lose you. You can get lost to the system and become just a high-flying lecturer at the university. You can be a teacher on a high income, marry outside of your own, and end up raising your children away from family.' So what I did to remain close to my people, to my culture and to my spirituality, was go back home every year and take my children to visit their grandparents. Most of their grandparents have gone now, and all but one of my children live in cities, Darwin, Adelaide, Canberra and Alice Springs, but at least they can reflect back on the times they spent with their grandparents and the stories they were told about their country, both in Arnhem Land and in the Central Desert.

An organisation called Link-Up was started to bring people of the Stolen Generations back together with their Aboriginal families. Coral Edwards, the Aboriginal woman who started this organisation, told me she did so because she saw the film *Brown Skin Baby* and felt she had to do something to help. She had also been taken away from her family as a child. Link-Up is now a national organisation, with local agencies in towns all over Australia helping stolen Aboriginal people get back together with their families.

Not many obvious changes occurred in my life as a result of the film. I just continued doing what I was doing at the time. But as more and more people became concerned about the system, many positive changes began to happen for Aboriginal people all around me. The government was finally being challenged. Many letters were being written to them and to me.

When I eventually met up with my family, they told me Bill Liddle was almost certainly my father, and was well regarded by my people because he accepted our ways, and continued to stay there and care for my people for a very long time. When he was an old man, he went to live with one of my sisters at Alice Springs, until he died. In Aboriginal culture all the children, whatever their colour, are accepted and taken within the Aboriginal group as precious gifts, and loved by everyone. So my being mixed race was never an issue amongst my people, other than that they had to hide me from the police.

Although my mothers herded Bill Liddle's sheep from one area to another to protect them from the dingoes, my Aboriginal family moved, usually in groups of about twelve, but never more than fifty people, across our traditional land through a number of neighbour-ing properties, pursuing our traditional way of life. Once a year the sheep were shorn and the wool was taken south on a big wagon, pulled by camels. Eventually my father discovered that the dingoes ate so many of his sheep that he wasn't making enough money, so he decided to switch to cattle. When this happened my mother and her sisters started working in his house. My people formed a close relationship with Bill Liddle because he was good to them, but many white people were very prejudiced against white men such as my father who formed these close associations with Aboriginal people.

I think it is important to distinguish between those white men who just used and abused Aboriginal women, and retained their racist attitude to Aboriginal people, and others who, like Bill Liddle, sought to relate to Aboriginal people in a way which integrated Aboriginal and European ways.

Who Am I? What Am I?

The mission changed my life
By just making me have one wife.
The welfare gives me food.
To do nothing must be good.

Who am I? What am I?
What will happen until I die?

My father had a will,
When hungry he'd go and kill.
If I sit and wait
'll be eating off a plate.

Who am I? What am I?
What will happen until I die?

Some say if you be white
Living will be all right.
When sober I be sad
When drunk I'm very glad.

Who am I? What am I?
What will happen until I die?

Might be I get a job,
For grog I make a few bob.
As far as I can see
It's the only thing left for me.

Who am I? What am I?
What will happen until I die?

New Horizons

Adelaide was a huge city compared to Darwin. When I first arrived there in about 1969, I thought it was strange that Aborigines only seemed to come out after dark. When I met some friends who had moved to Adelaide from the Croker Island reservation, I asked them why they were 'sunset Aborigines'. They told me they only went out when the sun went down to avoid being picked on by the police. It didn't take long before I had a first-hand experience of how Aborigines were discriminated against in the south. Many businesses would just refuse to serve us.

I encountered this in a big way when I tried to buy a house. Even though a white friend of mine went with me when I applied for a loan, I was told outright by several bank managers that they did not lend money for mortgages to Aborigines. It made no difference that I had a job, a family, a college degree and owned a house in Darwin at the time.

Maybe because of this rampant discrimination, the mixed-blood Aborigines who came from mission schools and foster homes in the south had a different attitude about themselves than their 'coloured' counterparts up north. I found that here they strongly identified as Aboriginal. They were proud of their heritage and wanted to learn more about it. At the college in Adelaide I enrolled in a Residential

Workers course for welfare officers. In Darwin I had taken the required courses to become a social worker, and this three-year course was to give me the additional education and training I needed to work in institutions where young Aboriginal people were being held for committing crimes. At that time I thought this was the best direction I could go in, to help my people.

In Australia, Aboriginal people make up a disproportionately large percentage of the prison population. Usually they first come into contact with the law through vagrancy, use of abusive language, petty theft and resisting arrest. This unacceptable rate of imprisonment further increases the impact of institutionalisation on Aboriginal people, reinforcing the lessons they have learned from life on reservations.[1]

One of the courses I took was Australian History. It opened my eyes to the terrible ways Aboriginal people had been treated throughout the country, right from the first day of colonisation. I met fellow students who had been raised on some of the other reservations and we compared notes about how we had grown up. The main similarity was that the church was the authority and had the backing of the government in every situation. No matter what the circumstances, we were always in the wrong. Until 1967 we were a subject people, under the arbitrary rule of the missionaries, who had little regard for our beliefs and practices and were determined to impose their own beliefs and way of life. In this they were supported by the government and its police force. Harsh physical punishment and deprivation could be handed out, and this was never regarded as criminal assault or deprivation of liberty, which would have applied in the case of non-Aboriginal people. Being locked up inside buildings and separated from family and country is a very harsh punishment for Aboriginal people and results in severe depression and suicidal tendencies. It is not surprising that there is a very high rate of suicide among Aboriginal people while being held in detention, particularly while in remand awaiting trial because they are unable to afford bail.

Part of my program was residential placement. I was sent to live in the institutions that housed offenders for weeks at a time. To get back and forth I needed a car, so I got a little two cylinder Gogo-mobile that had a roadrunner painted on its door. My kids were ashamed of it, but it ran for a week on a teaspoon of petrol. I had good rapport with the inmates and because of this I frequently ignored some of the institutional rules. When I would take someone to town for medical treatment, for example, I would let them sit in the front seat of my car instead of locking them in the back. I would also have them do little errands. They always came back and I didn't see any harm done. When the other workers saw me driving back to the institution with the inmates in the front seat, they told me that it wasn't allowed. My feeling was that it was my job to demon-strate a trusting attitude and treat the inmates as ordinary people, rather than as criminals. Perhaps this came from having grown up in an institution myself. It would have made a big difference to me, if I had been trusted then.

One of the institutions I worked at was for girl inmates only. These girls were so man-hungry that, whenever the matrons were not around, they would corner me and the other male residential worker and try to get us to make love to them. Some would hold onto our hands, while others would kiss us and touch our bodies. They were quite big girls and they attacked us in large groups. Roger and I were both Aboriginal men and these girls were all white, so if we were caught in this predicament, we would have been held responsible and our careers would have been destroyed even though the girls were the perpetrators every time. We had to be extremely careful not to offend them, which was hard to do when they were so sexually aggressive.

This compromising situation was a typical one for Aboriginal people. No matter how right we were in any situation, the colour of our skin made us wrong. Even if we had a senior position of author-ity, a white worker in a junior position could all too easily destroy our reputation and get us fired from our job. We had to be constantly on guard so that we didn't offend anyone with white skin. This kind of tension produces an outer behaviour of subservience, while underneath there is a simmering rage that can easily be triggered, particularly when we are among our own people where it is safer to express our real feelings. Perhaps this is why there is so much conflict in Aboriginal families and communities today.

After doing two years of residential placement, I realised that I was intentionally locking myself into yet another institution, and I began questioning whether I wanted this to be my life's work. I didn't like it because it was too much like my life on the reservation. During the final months of my three-year training, an English friend of mine named John Marley approached me about setting up an Aboriginal community college with him. John was a white man who worked with Aboriginal elders in Adelaide. He had already organised night classes at a local college building for people coming in from reservations who were interested in the arts. I became involved in this program as a singer and performer.

These night classes were just the beginning of our work together. The next step was to give classes at two Aboriginal reservations located outside Adelaide. The classes were well received and the people enjoyed the singing so much that we recruited a lot of other performers to join the program. These activities led to the establishment of the Aboriginal Community College in Adelaide. As far as I am aware, this was the first college in Australia to have a strong cultural curriculum. Aboriginal culture was like a stream that ran through everything that was taught at the school. I was one of the staff and Harold Thomas was the other cultural staff person. I designed and facilitated a unit of study called the 'Aboriginal Culture Awareness Program'.

We had to fight for funding. Those Aborigines who were already well educated and had good positions in the white system were not initially supportive of our philosophy, designed to give adult Aborigines a second chance at an education. They said it was a waste of time and money to put adult Aborigines back into school because they were too old to learn. However, we believed that many good people had dropped out of school because of pregnancy, prejudice, and the lack of understanding that white teachers had of Aboriginal learning strategies, rather than through lack of interest or capacity to learn. We proved our critics to be totally wrong.

Our students ranged in age from sixteen to sixty. The older ones wanted to learn technical skills such as how to repair windmills, pumps and engines, because they lived far from where these services were available and had to maintain their own equipment. Some were beginning to buy cars and they wanted to know how to keep them going. Others were interested in learning about navigation so they could set up fishing ventures. English and mathematics were compulsory. We wanted all of our students to learn to communicate effectively and to manage money.

To enhance the cultural programming, I went with my wife and another staff member, Joan Binion, to live on the Lardil reservation on Mornington Island in Queensland, for a while. We learned their dances and songs, and how to make the implements their ancestors used. I also brought the Lardil people to Adelaide to do cultural workshops at the college, and the Walpiri people from Central Australia with their dances, paintings and implements, and some of my family from eastern Arnhem Land to share their traditional ways. There were no resources to draw upon to use as examples in our classrooms, so I had to find ways of acquiring traditional implements to make teaching kits. The best boomerangs came from the Lardil people, and the tools they taught us to make were a lot more authentic than anything being marketed for tourists today.

We decided to expand our teachings to other classrooms outside of the college. To do this we needed our students to start sharing what they were learning about their culture with others. I encouraged them to become teachers. To qualify they had to do research and learn to speak the English language well. I made sure that these Aboriginal students became good public speakers so they could go out and do presentations about their culture for non-Aboriginal people, whenever they had the opportunity to do so. I also led workshops to train white classroom teachers so they could teach their students about Aboriginal culture. When the students were ready to start teaching, the Aboriginal Cultural Awareness Program was no longer limited to the college. It became a Community Education Program. In this program I would take two students with me into the local schools to introduce our artefacts and talk about how they were made and what they were used for. We brought our dances, singing and the whole program into the public schools. We even taught about local bush tucker.

Big things grow from little things, if they are good. This was a very good little thing, so it grew very big. In some of the southern Australian states it is now compulsory for every student to take 'Aboriginal Cultural Studies'. I worked at the Community College in Adelaide until the end of the 1970s. While I was there I also began setting up Aboriginal learning centres in other colleges and universities. I wanted as many Aboriginal people as possible to get higher degrees, so they would have the strength and power of education.

People from all over Australia were now working hard to make government policy changes at both federal and state levels, as they became more aware of the wrongs that were still being done to Aborigines in Australia. Back in 1965 my nephew, Charles Perkins, led a 'Freedom Ride' through western New South Wales to protest against discrimination.[2] In 1966, Gurindji stockmen had begun a nine-year strike against a British cattle station owner in the Northern Territory.[3] The strike began because of the terrible conditions these stockmen and their families endured, but eventually became a land claim for Gurindji traditional land. Most Aboriginal people didn't know that we no longer had rights to our land until white people started telling us, 'you don't own the land'. Our old people just couldn't believe that a man could put a flag down on the coast of Sydney or somewhere and take ownership of all the land that Aboriginal people had cared for since the time of creation.

They had always believed that no one could own the land because the land is our mother and it owns us.

In 1967 there was a national referendum to have discriminatory clauses deleted from the Australian Commonwealth Constitution and, much to our surprise, ninety per cent of all Australians voted in favour of Aboriginal and Torres Strait people having equal rights as citizens.[4] Australia has always prided itself on being a country where everyone has a 'fair go', and when confronted with the reality of our status, most people could not see any justification for this. For the first time since the arrival of Captain Cook in 1770, we were considered citizens of our own country.

Now that we had the rights of citizenship it was time to strengthen our political impact. Many of the students who enrolled in our Aboriginal curriculum decided to join me in the political arena. Once university students get into an issue they will publicly make enough noise to attract worldwide attention, and that is what they did for us. The students began to bring a lot of media attention to the situations we were campaigning against in New South Wales, Victoria and South Australia. The situation in Queensland and Western Australia took longer to come under the national spotlight. Queensland seems to have a legacy of resentment and hostility towards Aboriginal people. It was in Queensland that Torres Strait Island people and those from nearby Vanuatu, Fiji and the Solomon Islands had been kidnapped to work as slaves in the sugar plantations in the late 1800s.[5] It did not surprise us that it was a Queensland electorate which elected Pauline Hanson as a member of federal parliament, or that in her maiden speech she attacked government programs targeted to redress the many social and economic injustices we face.[6]

During the college's second year of operation, I was invited by a group of white school teachers to spend evenings and weekends with them going through books used in government schools. This was to determine which ones were discriminatory towards Aboriginal people and needed to be taken out of circulation. I was also involved in culture celebrations sponsored by NAIDOC (National Aboriginal and Islander Day Observance Committee) that were held in schools and other places in the community to help raise public awareness.[7] To support our cause, Harold Thomas, my colleague at the Community College, designed a black, red and yellow flag. The black represents the Aboriginal people, the red represents the earth, red ochre and our spiritual relationship to the land, and yellow represents the sun, the unifying factor that gives life.[8]

In 1971 my southern friends who were fighting for Aboriginal rights decided that our voices needed to be heard by Parliament. To accomplish this, a tent was set up on the lawn of Parliament House in Canberra. This tent became the Aboriginal Embassy; it was also known as the Tent Embassy.[9] People from all over the world saw Aborigines on TV demonstrating openly, and the police brutality that occurred when the government tried to stop us. The black, red and yellow flag became a symbol that united Aboriginal language groups throughout Australia when it flew over our Aboriginal Embassy.

I went with a busload of students from the Community College and other interested people from Adelaide to participate in this demonstration. We formed a big circle and did street marches around the area. Whenever possible I sang my songs. We were now able to tell the world that our country had been stolen from us and the government had no intention of compensating us for it, or even giving us true equal status. There were some really tough fights when the police tried to pull our embassy down and the circle of Aboriginal people fought to stop them. Unfortunately, the northern tribes, where the European presence was not so strong, were still resistant to involving themselves in social struggles because they really believed they still owned their land. They told us that fighting to get something we already owned was ridiculous.

Aboriginal culture is very egalitarian and communal. Our 'nations' (language/culture groups) are quite small, and each has its own particular customs and identity through relationship to country. It is only in our relation to non-Aboriginal society that we seem to be one people, Aborigines. And we in turn have many differences from Torres Strait Islander people. I suppose it is a bit like Europe. We talk about Europeans, but French people see themselves as quite different from the English and German people.

So it has been hard for our first generation of well educated Aboriginal and Torres Strait Islander people, who were called on by the white system to try to represent our interests in national and state politics and in the government administrative system. Charlie Perkins, from Alice Springs, eventually rose up the ranks to become the head of the Department of Aboriginal Affairs in Canberra. Despite his history of activism, a lot of our people felt he must now be on the government's side because he worked for them. Soon, however, Charlie's example was followed by other Aboriginal people who started raising public awareness through their own areas of expertise. Aboriginal poets, actors and writers began to be noticed.

When the Labor Party won office in 1972, the state governments were all controlled by conservative political parties, so the new federal government bypassed them and directly funded a whole range of community organisations, including Aboriginal ones, as agents of social change in many areas of social policy. Recognising the failure of services that had been run by white people for Aboriginal people, new Aboriginal health services, legal services, community organisations and education services were established in this way. These provided an enormous opportunity for our people to now become involved in the wider community, and to begin to find new ways for practising the sacred principle of kanyini.

Organisations were even set up to look at the material that had been written about us in books and at the conditions we were living under. The periodical, Identity, was funded so that we could produce a good quality publication that told the true story of what had happened to our people. Many Aboriginal people, including myself, contributed stories and articles. New curriculum material was produced for schools, and slowly white Australians began to have the opportunity to find out about their own history with us.

The Whitlam Labor government wasn't in office long, but in the short time they were in power they did a lot of good for Aboriginal people. In general, I would have to say that Labor governments have been more sensitive to the needs of our people, and more embracing of ideas of cultural diversity which allow our culture to co-exist with the dominant white culture.

For me, these were exciting new times of political involvement and social action. However my wife, Amy, was not interested in politics and this created more and more tension in our family life. In many ways she was still very much a 'mission girl' and she wanted a different lifestyle from the one I was living. We decided to separate. Our oldest daughter was already in college in Sydney and the boys were grown up and ready to go off on their own. I moved out of the house and Alan and Johnny went to live with relatives in Alice Springs. Our youngest daughter, Anita, stayed with her mother. After Amy and I were separated for a while we agreed to get a divorce.

I had a terrible time finding a flat. I had to have someone white, pretending to be my wife, go and look at the flat and sign the contract with the owner before I appeared. This was the only way I could get a unit to live in. This is the sort of continuing racism that eats away at our self-confidence. It takes a strong sense of humour for a lecturer to hide behind his white students in order to find a place to live in his own country, and not get bitter and twisted about it.

Where we came from

Chorus
You know the sun and the moon
and the stars up in the sky.
You see the mountains
and the flowers and the trees.
You see the river and the sea,
Feel the wind that blows the breeze,
that is where and from them all,
You come from.

Late at night, just after tea,
my baby boy came up to me.
With his eyes shining bright,
he said to me, Daddy, I want to know
about some things that bother me.
Daddy, where did I come from?

Chorus

Well, my son, all I can say
are the things once said to me
by your grandpa and your grandma, so long ago.
In the past when things were men
and men were things, long, long ago,
these are the words that, when I asked,
were said to me.

Chorus

Our ancestors in the past
walked this land and made the Law,
saying all living things are all the same.
We may be different in many ways,
but we should live in harmony
with all things and each other all our days.

Chorus

Walytja

kinship and family

Walytja, our system of family relationships, is the thing that holds Aboriginal society together. We live it out in our relationship to our immediate family members, but also to our wider kinship connections associated with our totemic links, to the people with whom we have done ceremony, and to the people with whom we share country. It is also important to realise that we don't just limit this to people: we use the *walytja* way of thinking to relate to everything in our environment.

Although sometimes the responsibilities of *walytja* can seem overwhelming, especially when your family members are experiencing difficulties with money, accommodation, relationships and health, nevertheless I think it is our *walytja* system which has enabled Aboriginal people to survive white racism, and to retain the essentials of our Aboriginality. You can see this especially with Aboriginal people from the south-east of Australia, where the original languages and many of the Dreamings were lost. They still have a very powerful sense of their Aboriginality, and through this they extend great hospitality to people like myself who come from other parts of Australia. We Aboriginal people draw a great deal of strength from this.

I met my second wife, Lorraine, through the Community

College in Adelaide. She was one of my students who enrolled in the Community College during its second year. She was a really good worker and we began spending a lot of time together setting up the Aboriginal Community Education program. She liked me because I was a northerner and had strong knowledge of the traditional way of life. I was different from all the men she had known. She had a husband but they were not getting along very well. They had agreed to separate, but he would still turn up every month or so to see his son and they were having lots of hassles.

One day I said, 'I'm beginning to like you, I think I'll ask your husband if it's all right for us to be together.' She didn't know what I was talking about, so I said, 'In the Top End, we don't just spend time with a woman without the husband saying it's okay. I've got to ask your husband if your relationship with him is finished and I've got to ask him if it's all right with him for us two to be together.' She said 'What! You guys are mad!' But I said, 'No, that's the way it is. We don't hide things.'

So when her husband came home one weekend, I went out for a visit and met the whole family. Her father-in-law and other relatives were there with her husband. I told her, 'I want to talk to your husband,' and she said, 'No, don't do that.' 'I'm going to,' I replied, 'if he wants to fight me he can fight me. If he tells me that he still loves you, I've got to walk away. You've told me that he doesn't want you and I've got to ask him if that's true, face to face. We will go down to the beach where there's open space and we can be alone.'

I went over to her husband and said, 'I have a matter to raise with you regarding your wife.' So we walked down to the beach and I said, 'Look, Willy, your wife told me you two were finished and I'm interested in being with her, if you don't want to be with her any more.' He said, 'That's okay. Yeah, we are finished, we've been finished for a couple of years. I just come back and check on my son.' I told him, 'I'll be taking your wife away if she wants to come with me and, according to my ways, I will be responsible for your wellbeing as well.' 'What?' he said, in complete amazement. 'Yes,'

I told him, 'That's our Law. You will be in a brother relationship to me and I've got to look after you, as well as look after this wife of yours.' They were from the south and didn't know the ways of people in the north. He then said, 'Well, I'm not interested in keeping her. If you want her, you take her.'

When I told Lorraine that he said I could have her, she wouldn't have anything to do with me. She saw my behaviour as treating her just as something two men could hand over between them, and she could not understand my northern culture of respect that required me to act this way. She thought I was mad. But it wasn't too long before she got over her anger and came to live with me.

I introduced her to Amy and my children. Under my Law, Amy was still my 'wife', and I would continue to have responsibilities towards her, and whenever I am in Darwin, where she is now living, I still try to visit her and make sure she is okay. Divorce for us does not create a hard line of separation. After Lorraine and I had been together for about a year, I took her to meet my family in the Top End. Shortly after that visit, I got a call from one of my brothers in Arnhem Land. He told me that the welfare department was forcing his daughter to give her baby to them for adoption. She was young and they were accusing her of neglecting the child. I discussed the situation with Lorraine and we agreed that I should go up there to see what I could do. While I was on the plane I figured out a plan.

The baby had been placed in a foster home but the birth mother was still allowed to visit her. I told my brother's daughter to tell them she wanted to take the baby for the day to introduce it to its other father who was visiting from Adelaide. When she brought the baby to me, I was waiting with a return ticket and was ready to board the plane. I took that beautiful baby into my arms and headed home. When the welfare department found out about this they were furious. They contacted the authorities in Adelaide and they came to my house to get the baby. I refused to give it to them. Lorraine, her son Shane and I moved a lot that year. The welfare department kept coming after us and we kept moving. Somehow we managed to raise that beautiful little girl until her mother was married and able to take care of her.

On semester breaks, we travelled from Adelaide to Darwin to visit family. I still had my house up there and had leased it out to friends who were looking after it. It was a place where many family members would go for holidays. During one of our Christmas visits there were about a dozen or so people staying at my house, so Lorraine and I decided to stay at a friend's house because it was empty. A couple of nights after we arrived in town my house, along with most of the other buildings in Darwin, was demolished by Cyclone Tracy.

All during that night the wind was humming like a big diesel engine, and we could hear loud banging noises as the other houses in the neighbourhood were being busted up. We couldn't see anything. Luckily the house we were staying in was protected by a row of mangrove trees. Houses sheltered by mangrove trees survived the storm with very little damage, but those built on piers all around us were flattened. I kept moving the kids to the furthest point from where the wind was hitting the house. I put them under a bed, with a stack of mattresses and cupboards on top of the bed, so they would be protected from all the debris if the house fell in.

When we woke up the next morning the walls of the house were shaking and ready to crumble but they were still standing. The wind was starting to lessen because Tracy had spent nearly all its energy and was travelling east. My kids had no idea why their father kept moving them around during the night. They thought it was just a rainstorm. A couple of louvres in the roof had come loose and rain had come into the house. We had put up a Christmas tree the day before, and the tree was wet and so were the presents under it. The first thing my daughter Dorothea said was, 'Daddy, who made my presents get wet?' I took her outside and showed her the other places around us that had been totally demolished. In some cases you could see a toilet and a bathtub; the wind had taken everything else. We saw bits of swimming pools on top of telephone wires, power poles twisted into knots, and debris everywhere. It was as though a bomb had dropped on Darwin.

My first concern was for my older children who had their own cars and were out that night. I took a very slow drive to our own house where I knew they would go. The roof of our house was gone and one side of the house was leaning over all of the rooms. One fellow was still in bed fast asleep and I had to wake him up. Most of the people who were staying upstairs and in the caravan had taken shelter for the night in the bathroom of a unit that was located under the house. They were all right. The only house in my area that wasn't damaged was painted purple. I've often wondered if the colour of the house was significant in its survival.

The roof of my house was in a neighbour's yard three lots away and their roof was somewhere else. I was lucky to find that all my children were unharmed. We salvaged what food we could and checked around with other members of the family to see what they wanted to do about Christmas. We agreed that we would go to Rapid Creek and cook a meal together over an open fire and let the kids have a swim. A lot of other people had the same idea.

After the Christmas barbecue my family decided to stay together, and we camped in the yard where our damaged house stood. Some of our relatives had cooked their Christmas meal the day before Tracy's appearance, so we shared it with them when we went to visit. When we got the radio going, we heard that we were being told to tune to the radio all the time to listen for directions. Everyone in Darwin had to be evacuated as quickly as possible so the Army could come in to start sorting out and fixing the damage that had been done. I rounded up Alan and Johnny and their cars and we travelled back to Adelaide together.

The cyclone experience had been so difficult for Lorraine that when we returned home she didn't want to have much to do with me. She went to her house at the beach and I went to my flat and the boys went to stay with their mother. Lorraine was so distraught that members of her family came to stay with her and for a while she and her former husband tried to bridge the break in their relationship. When she finally accepted that it just wasn't going to work out with him, she started moving back and forth between her house and my flat. I didn't know when she going to show up or when she would be leaving. I was older, twice her age, and even though I was good to her, her white foster parents and her friends were not happy about our relationship.

Lorraine's reaction to the cyclone and her attempts to reconcile with her husband were very stressful for me. I wanted to support her in what was right for her, but suppressing my emotions to do this was very difficult. I continued my work at the college while she went back and forth between my flat and her house. When she decided that she wanted to be with me, she went into hospital to reverse a procedure she had done previously so that she could have a child. When I knew that we were finally going to be together, I decided to buy a house for us to live in as a family. I didn't want a big house, just something small and comfortable with trees around it, and I found what I was looking for in a place called Windsor Gardens. Discrimination was still a problem, but by this time the Department of Aboriginal Affairs had set up the Aboriginal and Torres Strait Islander Housing Association, which was guaranteeing mortgage loans for Aborigines who could afford to buy a house. I was one of the first Aborigines to buy a house under this program.

After we moved into the house, I became ill. I was listless and could barely muster enough energy to get around. It seemed as though all my body parts were shutting down, one at a time. I kept going to the doctor but nothing he gave me made any difference to my condition. One weekend when Lorraine was staying with me, I got up from the bed sometime during the night and sat in the lounge to commune with the energy of Jesus. During my meditation, three Aboriginal men came and sat with me and we conversed together. When dawn arrived, I returned to bed and Lorraine asked, 'Who were you talking to?' I replied, 'I don't know who they were or where they came from, but three men were visiting with me in the lounge.' I went to sleep and could not remember the conversation I had with those men, but there was no doubt in my mind that they appeared in my flat and then disappeared.

One day when the doctor examined me, he was very disturbed. He said, 'There is nothing more I can do for you. You have scarlet fever and it seems as though your body has decided it no longer wants to live. I know that Aborigines like to die in their home country, so why don't you get your affairs in order and go home.'

Lorraine packed me and her son Shane into the car and drove us to Darwin. From Darwin we took a plane over to Croker Island. When we got to my brother's place the only thing I could do was lie on a blanket under a big tamarind tree. My brother Jim and his family were staying at one of the old campsites where the Macassans[1] had processed trepang almost a century before Captain Cook came to Australia. Trepang is a sea slug that is considered a delicacy in China, and the Macassans travelled a long way across the Java and Timor seas to collect and process them for their Chinese customers. The places where they camped now have tamarind trees growing there, because these trees grew from the beans that the Macassans brought with them as food.

The camp was located on the south-western side of the island. It was a beautiful beach area; we could see the coast of Australia about ten kilometres away. There was a small bay and my brother's sons would go out there with a throw net or spear and get whatever fish we needed. They also had a vehicle, so if we wanted magpie geese they would just jump in the Land Rover and drive to the same swamplands where my *Boonyi* Mick had taught me how to hunt for these geese as a boy. Jim's wife and Lorraine prepared all the fresh food that I could eat. They fed me local bush tucker, geese, seafood, wild pigs and the fresh and saltwater turtles that I had loved as a boy.

My older brothers Dick and Lazarus came from the mission to visit me as often as they could. At this time Lazarus was the minister there and Dick was one of the elder traditional owners of the island.

I don't remember much about my sickness except that I never believed that I was as sick as the doctor said I was. I do remember how weak I was, and that I couldn't do anything. I enjoyed the beauty of the land I was lying on and looking at every day, and I was happy to have Lorraine and my brother Jim and his family looking after me. I felt loved and cared for as I slept and prayed on my blanket under the tree.

After several weeks I was able to sit up and I began to take short walks along the beach. When I was alone I read books. As I got stronger I was able to go for a swim when I took my daily walk. Lorraine learned how to spot crocodiles so she could watch out for them while I swam. The crocodiles weren't interested in people in those days, so unless we had a dog with us (one of their favourite foods), they would just stay in the water and leave us alone.

My brothers started taking me to different sacred sites on the island, and we talked about how we were going to record the history of the island so that the stories of these sites could be preserved for the younger generation. Unfortunately I wasn't there long enough to accomplish this.

As I got stronger I started going hunting. The more I walked and hunted, the stronger I became. At some point the illness just decided to leave. I was still taking heaps of medicine but noticed that I began to feel better if I didn't take it. It seemed as if a complete healing had taken place. I said to Lorraine, 'God has healed me. I'm well enough, so let's go home.'

When we returned to Adelaide we moved back into our house and I went to the doctor to get a certificate that said I was healthy enough to return to work. He couldn't believe I was still alive. After checking me out to make sure I was completely cured, he asked where I had been and what I had done, so that he could recommend the same treatment for his other patients. I went back to work at the college and Lorraine continued to help me with the Community Awareness Program.

In 1974, the Catholic Church was organising an international conference for indigenous people in Hong Kong, and I was invited to attend as the male Australian representative. I participated in many of the workshops that were held in the countryside and saw all of the local sights. I also met the indigenous people of Hong Kong, who told me how the colonisers of their country treated them in the same way as we had been treated in Australia. As the participants told their stories, I was surprised at how all of these stories were so similar to mine. Many indigenous groups had been forced into institutions and were not allowed to speak their language or learn about their culture. Most of us at the conference had grown up as English-speaking people.

I was frequently questioned about my dark colour, because most of the people I met had heard of the White Australian Policy and they didn't even know that Aboriginal Australians existed. I told them that I was indigenous, and the whites were migrants who had only recently come to the country. I also told them that the indigenous people of Australia were black or brown, a dark race. Everyone seemed very surprised to hear this.

The church billeted us with local people, so we could experience their lifestyle. They also wanted us to share experiences and culture with other peoples of the world. Two of us stayed with a local Chinese family. They had four children and lived in one four-metre square room in a building that housed 7000 people. They couldn't believe that I lived in a whole house with a block of land in Australia.

While I was in Hong Kong, the bus that we were riding in had a flat tyre on one of the mountain roads. As we were waiting for the driver to put a new tyre on, I was looking out the window at a big tree full of white flowers that was right in front of me. I thought, 'It's amazing how that tree looks so much like the tree in my yard in Adelaide.' I kept staring at the tree and after a while I said to my Chinese mate who was sitting beside me, 'That tree with flowers is absolutely beautiful compared to all the others, do you know what kind it is?' and he said, 'What flowers?' I replied, 'That one there,' but as we looked out the window together there were no flowers on the tree in front of us.

At the end of the day we went into Kowloon City in Hong Kong and made a stop at a local shop. As I walked past some baby clothes, I remembered the flowers and had a funny feeling that Lorraine was pregnant. Three days later, when we were able to phone home, I asked my wife if she was pregnant. She said, 'Don't be stupid. I am not.' Four weeks after I got home she said, 'I'm pregnant. How did you know?' I told her the story about the tree and said, 'It was the tree from this yard that sent me the message in Hong Kong. It appeared to me full of flowers, and I had that knowing feeling that something was going on at home.'

Our people believe that spirits use things like birds, animals, trees and other things as messengers. People can also give messages without even realising they are telling you what you need to hear. They just say whatever comes into their mind at the time. One of my brothers received a message about his wife's pregnancy from a wallaby when he was out hunting. When he came back to the family that night he shared his experience. 'I was hunting with my spear and *woomera* when I saw some wallabies nearby. And I thought, Now I've got to get as close as I can so I can kill one of them to take back to the family. But as I got closer to them, one of them hopped towards me instead of going away from me, and stopped only a few yards from where I was standing. I quickly put my *woomera* at the end of my spear ready to throw at the wallaby, knowing it was so close there was no way that I could miss it. Then it hopped right towards me again and stopped.

'I thought, What's wrong with this one? He must be blind. That wallaby just stopped a few yards in front of me, and even though I had my spear and *woomera* ready I just couldn't throw it. There was something strange about its eyes as it looked right at me and there was no way I could launch my spear. I decided to stop hunting and just walked home. I knew he was trying to convey some kind of message but I didn't know what it was.' The people had noticed that he had come home empty-handed, and when they heard his story someone from the group said, 'Ah, yes. Your wife is pregnant.' At that time neither he nor his wife knew she was pregnant, but in a few weeks' time she found out that she was.

About the fifth month of Lorraine's pregnancy, her body started swelling up and the doctor said she had toxaemia. From then on, he had her come to see him every week. At the end of the sixth month, she went to see him for a routine check-up and he took her directly to the hospital emergency room. I received a phone call and rushed down there just to be told, 'Wait here.' I don't know what happened at the clinic, but the doctor decided that she needed to have the baby by caesarean section right away. While she was in surgery, one of the young doctors came out and said, 'Mr Randall, we may not have the results that you want. You'll either have a mother without a baby or a baby without a mother.' He said to me, 'They are fighting each other and one is going to kill the other.'

I was so used to bad news that I just accepted what he said with a kind of numb resignation. I see good news and bad news as two strong powers that run alongside of each other. I waited and waited, and then a nurse came out holding the tiniest baby I had ever seen. It was still messed up with blood so they rushed her to where they could clean her up and put her into a humidicrib. She weighed only three pounds, and her whole body could fit into my two hands.

Lorraine was asleep for about five days, and during that time it was touch and go. I'd go and sit next to her while she slept. It was Christmas time, so one day I got permission to bring in my guitar and sing Christmas songs to her. I don't know whether she heard them or not. After that she started to come around and she told me what happened. She said, 'I died. I saw myself leaving my body and I saw all those doctors working on a body but didn't know it was mine. I looked and could see a long tunnel with the light of a Jesus figure standing at the end of it. I had a beautiful feeling as I was being drawn towards that light. As I got closer to it, Jesus said, "Stop." He crossed his arms and then said, "You've got some more

My mother, Thungawa, at Areyonga, Northern
Territory, with her husband Joe.

This picture, taken at Middleton Ponds in 1929, was given to me by my
nephew, Doug Abbott. The fair-skinned girl in the middle told me that
I am one of the babies being held, but I do not know which one.

On Croker Island.
From left: Jim
Wauchope, me,
John Hunter,
Tony Newcastle,
Alec Ross.

Croker Island.
The ex-Army building
used as our classroom.

The house that was built
for the superintendent
and minister.

The teacher's wife
sitting in the doorway
of one of the cottages
we lived in.

Arnhem Land: Uncle Timothy Yarmid, baby Henry and Boonyi Mick
Yarmid, who taught me to be a successful hunter. I owe these men a great
deal and I apologise if reproducing their photographs here gives offence
to any members of their family.

Uncle Tim in a
croc-hunting canoe.

Edna Bailey with Pegleg, the croc I shot for killing my Timor pony.

Florie, Dolly, Gladys, Dorothy and June in their home-made swimming
costumes. On Croker Island, the girls outnumbered the boys by
about five to one.

The results of a successful day's hunting of huge-bellied honey ants
(tjala) at Mutitjulu, Uluru.

Witchetty grubs (maku) in the root system of an acacia bush
at Mutitjulu, Uluru.

Holding my favourite water
bird, the magpie goose,
Oenpelli, Arnhem Land.
Each dry season the family
goes hunting for these
popular birds.

As an executive with Pan Continental,
photographed on the 33rd floor of a
Sydney building.

Gum tree (kamiku) grandmother, Alice Springs

In my office at the Institute of Aboriginal
Development, Alice Springs, 1994

My Buddhist friend Lopong puts up prayer flags at
Honeymoon Gap, Alice Springs.

With Hazel MacKinnon in my country.

Reunion of stolen generation members at Alice Springs, 1998.
Left to right: Ethel, Sonya, Amy, Junie, me, Alfie

work to do. Look behind you."' She said that my hand came out to her and she took it. Shortly after Lorraine told me this story of her experience the doctor said, 'We lost your wife two or three times that night, and each time we were able to bring her back.'

Lorraine remained in the hospital for two weeks after the surgery, but the baby had to stay there much longer. After I came home from work, we would go visit the baby together and Lorraine would take with her a daily supply of breast milk. During this time my son Alan came for a visit with his girlfriend, Andrea, a beautiful girl who looked like a model. On Saturday morning, three of her high society girlfriends came to have tea with her. All of them looked like they had just stepped out of a fashion magazine, with their make-up and beautiful clothes. Lorraine had been brought up as a white girl and knew what quality was, so we had fancy china and everything was matched up for a nice presentation. One of the girls said, 'Have you got any milk?' and Andrea went to the fridge and poured some milk from the bottle into the milk pitcher and served it to her friends. They continued talking and gossiping while they drank their tea. Meanwhile Lorraine was in the shower all this time, and when she came out everyone had finished their tea. She went to the refrigerator and the first thing she said was 'Where's my milk?' Andrea had used her breast milk for the tea. All Lorraine could say was, 'What did it taste like?' They didn't even know the difference. Poor Lorraine had to get more milk out of her breasts to feed the baby, and the usual amount was not there when she delivered the milk to the nurses at the hospital. When she told them what happened they all had a good laugh.

Eventually we were able to bring the baby home. Lorraine always carried her around in a little *coolamon* lined with kangaroo fur to protect her because she was so small. We cut diapers into quarters and borrowed doll clothes from a friend's daughter because regular baby clothes were just too big.

About a month before the baby was born, I was awakened about two o'clock one morning with the thought, 'The name of the child is Itumathungawa.' The name kept repeating in my head and wouldn't leave, so I got out of bed and wrote it in my diary on that date. The baby had come so early and Lorraine was so ill that we didn't even talk about the baby's name until she came home from the hospital. When she asked me what I wanted to call the baby, I remembered that I had written something in my diary and went back a couple of months to find the name I had written. There it was, 'The baby's name is Itumathungawa.' I said, 'Iti means small, the middle part means honey ant, and the end part was my mother's name. If you put it together it means little sweet mother.' Later on I was thinking that I was given a name that told us how that girl was going to be born, because to get the honey ant you have to break the earth and dig deep into the ground. The spirit had told us about the caesarean but, because of living in the city, I just didn't relate to it until after the event. That really made me realise how close the spirit is to us in the physical.

After her near-death experience, Lorraine became a lot quieter. When I first met her she was a really lively person who liked to party every weekend, but after the baby was born she would go out a lot less frequently. Our relationship became a lot closer, and she saw our precious baby daughter as her special gift to me. Prior to the baby's birth she would often go out without me, because I didn't drink or gamble. On one occasion she went to the racetrack and just disappeared for two weeks. I was frantic, but no one who knew would tell me where she was. I was sure our relationship was over, when she surprisingly showed up again. I had no choice but to accept her behaviour because we were not married, but I was always hoping that she would decide to stay with me. When the baby came, she became committed to our relationship, and we became more like husband and wife than just two people living together.

After Lorraine and the baby were strong, when another semester break came I took them both back to Croker Island. It is our custom that, when there is a marriage breakdown or change of partner, the family needs to know all about it so they can adjust to it. In accordance with this custom, I needed to take Lorraine and the baby to the place where Amy had grown up. Sometimes the relatives of the first partner feel offended because of the break-up, but having a baby to introduce to them usually helps to erase some of those bad feelings. That's exactly what happened when the women saw our baby. The women took Lorraine and the baby into their circle and separated us, so that I would have time to spend with the men. An unending number of relatives came to our cottage to hold and play with the baby and take her for walks. Lorraine hardly had any time alone with me or the baby while we were there. Without realising it, Lorraine had been taken into the kinship system and was treated in the traditional ways of the people who we were visiting. In this way she got to meet two of my brothers who were now in the position of being her other husbands. All Aboriginal wives are cared for by their husband's brothers, but these relationships are not necessarily physical.

One weekend the family took us into the bush for a picnic day on the other side of the island. I went out hunting with the men, and when we brought back pigs and geese we left them there for the women to prepare. The women went fishing and came back with seafood. They prepared everything and then set it out on paperbark and served it to the men. Lorraine had to stay with the women and the men stayed together. This was how she learned about the traditional lifestyle that I grew up with. Some parts she liked and some she didn't. It was very different from the way she was raised by her white foster parents in Adelaide.

I asked one of my brothers to pick Itumathungawa's second name. Without hesitation he said, 'Gujarley' which means 'fire' in Iwaidja. He sure picked up on her personality.

When our holiday was over we returned to Adelaide. A lot of people started coming to stay with us. This included my foster daughter, Pilawuk, who was doing her nurse's training, and my son Johnny's partner Linda, who gave birth to her first child while she stayed with us. I was delighted to have Linda and my new grandson

Michael with us, even though Johnny wasn't able to be there with her. Pilawuk made our life a bit crazy because she would only put fifty cents worth of fuel in her little motorbike and was always running out of fuel when she visited friends in other parts of the city. I was constantly getting calls to pick up Pilawuk and the bike and bring them home.

When Ituma was about six months old, Auckland University sent a brochure to the college asking if any Aborigines there would like to participate in an archaeological dig they were planning to do in Arnhem Land. The purpose of the dig was to determine the time frame in which Aboriginal people had lived in the East Alligator River basin area. I had a natural interest in this sort of thing, and thought it would be invaluable to help me find sites in South Australia that were important to the Aboriginal people of that area.

Lorraine and I volunteered and joined a group of about twenty people from New Zealand and different areas of Australia. When it was time to leave, I loaded up the car and drove north with a guy from Darwin who was living in Adelaide at the time. Lorraine was supposed to fly up with Shane and our baby Ituma, because travelling on such a rough road would have been very hard on her with such a young baby to care for. When I went into Darwin to meet them at the plane, they weren't on it. I called her foster parents and was told, 'Our daughter has decided not to come.' When Lorraine got on the phone, I asked her what was going on and she said, 'Oh, I don't think I want to come up. It's too far from my people and my parents don't want me to come.' So I said, 'Okay, I'll see you soon,' and immediately booked a ticket to Adelaide. I went straight to her parent's house. Her parents were really shocked to see me, and when I said, 'I've come to pick up Lorraine and the children,' they replied, 'Oh, she's not coming.' I told them I wanted to hear that from her.

When she came out, we went for a drive and I asked her to tell me what was going on. She gave me lots of reasons why she didn't want to come and I said to her, 'We are together and it would be good if we stayed together. I would like for you to understand my ways. You are a city girl and I am an Aboriginal from a reservation in Arnhem Land. This dig will give you a chance to live with my Aboriginal family and understand our ways. I've booked a ticket for us to fly out tomorrow morning, so I'll be sleeping with you here tonight.' She responded, 'You can't sleep with me. I'm in my parents' house.' She didn't think it was proper for us to sleep together, even though we had been living as husband and wife all this time and she had my baby.

My daughter was crying in a cot. I was horrified. I couldn't imagine why anyone would have a baby sleeping in a cot separate from its mother. This was one of the many differences we had to deal with. Everybody got excited about the whole situation, but the next morning Lorraine, Shane and the baby accompanied me when I flew back to Darwin and got my car to drive to the camp at the East Alligator River. We were there for about four months. During that time we just took the children along as we did the sifting and sorting that the job required. The dig was located at a large escarpment where the Jabiru storks and cockatoos had fought during creation time. It was covered with big galleries full of rock art. At one point we started to come across a lot of bones, so we shifted our search further away from the cliff where we didn't find so many bones.

We dug down three or four metres to where the readings tested out to be about 20 000 years old. At that depth we were finding only rocks and basic stone tools. We found turtle skeletons and many different kinds of fish bones all the way down. The non-Aboriginal people were very much in awe of the rock art paintings. When one of the traditional owners, Bill Neidjie[2] came by, one of these students asked him how the paintings were done. 'Ah, real easy,' he said, as he picked up some ochre and covered one up to draw over it, 'we just do it like this.' It was a big lesson in cultural differences for those students. Aborigines have a different way of valuing things. He valued what was being done in the present, while the students valued those paintings because they came from the past. I thought this was hilarious because they were waiting for his words of wisdom and got something quite different from what they were expecting.

My two sons came and worked with us for short periods. We also met some people from the Pan Continental mining company who were living in the area. One time when we were out shopping at the border store, we met the guy who was in charge of their camp. He was telling everybody that he was looking for a local Aboriginal person who could work as a liaison officer. He spoke to us about the position and it sounded interesting to me because I was leaning towards moving back to the area that I considered home. I applied for the position, and after we had returned to Adelaide I received the news that the job was mine. I was now in my late thirties and this was a chance to return to the Top End again.

Walya Ngamardiki came from the sea.
She walked across the islands and places in the sea, which are now sacred.
She walked across the land until she met Warika.
She sent the spirit children out to different parts of the country asking them to
speak different languages. She left them food and gave the laws of living.

Everything we see today is descended from Walya Ngamardiki.
She turned into a rock, and if you speak to her in a special way that rock will
move as she speaks back to you.

As others like Walya Ngamardiki moved across the land they also made different
groups of people that belong to certain places.

They too made all of the things in nature and put them in special places.
You might know them as the Rainbow Serpent or the Lightning Man.

They are the ones who created traditional owners and caretakers of the land.
The trees are spirits that look after sacred sites.

If the trees are damaged and the spirits leave, the people associated with them will
die.
That is why it is important to honour all living things and warn them when you
approach.

Creation story from western Arnhem Land

Top End

When I went to work for the Pan Continental Mining Company as liaison officer, there weren't many job opportunities for Aboriginal people on the Arnhem Land reservation. I thought that as long as big companies were setting their businesses up in the area, it would be a good idea for me to negotiate some employment there for my people. These jobs paid good salaries, not the meagre amounts the people were getting from the missions.

I knew that my Aboriginal brothers were not accustomed to working the white man's way and was challenged to compensate for that. Many white people talk about Aborigines as being irresponsible because they don't show up for work or appointments when they are expected to. Aborigines have a different value system. We put responsibility to family first. If there's a funeral, we go. If there's a ceremony, we go. If a family member needs help or a granny wants to see us, we go. We may be gone a couple of weeks. To us, honouring the tradition, which includes honouring the relationship system of that tradition, is far more important than turning up for any job or meeting. We are brought up not to offend our family.

We learned a long time ago that if we asked permission from the white bosses to do these things, the answer would be no. So that is why we got into the habit of leaving without giving notice. The term 'going walkabout' resulted from this cultural clash.

Our high level of family caring continues to cause problems for many Aboriginals, who are attempting to maintain the traditional cultural ways in today's world. Some of them are evicted from their homes because a big mob of family may show up for the weekend and they spend the rent money on food to feed them.

Because I knew Aboriginal cultural ways and could also understand the needs of my white employers, I was able to work out a system for the mining company that allowed their Aboriginal employees the flexibility they needed and the job could still get done. I did this by developing a job sharing system. Instead of the company insisting that Aboriginal employees work a strict nine to five day, I arranged that they could work when they wanted, but they would only get paid for the actual hours they were on the job. I knew they would work hard for long hours when they had something they wanted to buy, or until they were called away for family business. So the agreement I made with them was that they would be responsible for replacing themselves, when they couldn't come to work. In this way they could work when they wanted to, and if they wanted to stop working because they had earned enough money to buy their Toyota, the company would get another hard worker as their replacement.

I employed Aboriginal workers whenever possible for temporary, casual or full-time employment. I also was the overseer of scientists, mechanics, drillers and other workers. I made sure they had good accommodation, meals and travel capabilities to and from Darwin. In addition to these duties I also looked after the many visitors who came from all over the world.

Uranium mining was becoming political because of its use in the making of nuclear bombs, such as those that had been dropped in Japan. Many politicians came up to have a first-hand experience of this place that was becoming such a hot potato. Our mob didn't understand what this was all about, but those who were close to the church became very anti-mining and were opposed to traditional owners agreeing to this use of their land.

As well, Kakadu is a very special area in Australia. The land has been set aside as a large national park, adjacent to Arnhem Land itself, which remains Aboriginal traditional land under the land rights legislation of the Fraser government back in 1976. Kakadu itself covers 20 000 square kilometres of floodplains, billabongs, woodlands and the spectacular escarpment of rock plateau which crosses the landscape and is home to sacred sites and ancient rock art. The rock paintings of Kakadu are the longest unbroken tradition of art in the world, dating back possibly more than 30 000 years.

The ore deposit site is at Jabiru, right near the border with Arnhem Land on the East Alligator River. There were, therefore, many competing considerations. From the Aboriginal side, there were questions of caring for land and sacred sites, and questions of economic opportunity in order to become more independent of government welfare. By the time I arrived on the scene it was already known that the richest deposit of uranium and gold was at the Gecko Dreaming site.[1] This wasn't a very big area, but the deposit turned out to be one of the richest in the world. Pan Continental wanted me to locate the traditional owners of this area and talk to them about whether or not they were agreeable to having their land mined. There are a lot of traditional owners, but there is always one head owner who makes these decisions. It can be very difficult to identify that person if you don't know the system.

When big companies started to become interested in mining Aboriginal land, an Aboriginal organisation called the First Aboriginal Mining Company of Arnhem Land (FAMCO) was set up by a missionary on Croker Island, so that Aborigines could negotiate directly with these companies. Through FAMCO, traditional landowners had the opportunity to create partnerships with mining companies for the exploration and mining of any worthwhile ore that was found. This organisation wanted Aborigines to become independent of the government welfare system and I felt good about my position as a mining company liaison officer for the same reason. I had lived on welfare for a significant part of my life and knew how terrible it was to be owned by the government and have them control everything in your life. I also saw mining as an opportunity for local Aborigines to make improvements in their communities, such as better housing and services. I enjoyed working with FAMCO and met many of the traditional owners through this organisation.

What most people don't realise is that these traditional owners are highly intelligent men and women, who have been trained since childhood for their responsibilities. Many of them are spiritual leaders. That means that they have a special connection to the spirit world and the spirits guide them when they are making decisions that effect their communities.

One of the first things I did for Pan Continental was to make a list of all the traditional owners of the land which the mining company had leased. When I located these owners, they told me the degree of special significance for each sacred site in their area. We explored the area together during the wet and dry seasons and then made a colour-coded map of this information for the company. The most sacred areas were marked in red, and I recommended that the company not even consider planning to do anything at these places. The orange areas were important and in a safety zone, but there was some room for negotiation with the traditional owners on the use of these sites, so I told them who they would need to negotiate with. The green areas were really safe but could be very close to a very dangerous area, so I recommended that the company always consult with the traditional owners first, just to make sure they didn't get too close to one of these sacred areas.

This was a wonderful opportunity for me. It enabled me to reconnect with my Arnhem Land family and to get to know the senior ceremonial men of these parts. They shared with me the creation stories of their country, their *tjukurrpa*. Here too the Rainbow Serpent occupies a special place and is known as Ngalyod. She is Law for the wet season and all the renewal of life associated with that. Her anger is expressed through flash floods and drowning, reminding us to keep her Law. Most of the rock paintings also show the *Mimi* spirits, and *Namarrkun*, the Lightning Man, who carries the lightning across his shoulders and strikes thunder using the stone axes attached to his knees, elbows and head.

The government was not happy about FAMCO because they wanted to be involved in all decisions made about the land. They replaced FAMCO with their own organisation called the Northern Land Council. The government now had its say in every transaction that occurred, and it was my understanding that the percentages ultimately negotiated for Aborigines through the Northern Land Council involved far less compensation than they would have received from the partnerships that FAMCO was negotiating.

The number of areas that could be used for uranium mining, under Labor Party policy in 1983, was limited to three in the whole country, and the government didn't want Pan Continental to start their mining operation before a competing company began developing a nearby site called Jabiru. To accomplish this the Northern Land Council wanted the Aboriginal landowners to say to Pan Continental, 'No, we don't want mining.' Since I was in the position of representing the unwanted company, I was right in the middle of this controversy.

The job also had its lighter side. One of the most memorable workers who we had was a visiting scientist. He was a brilliant scientist, but seemed to have continual problems with the more practical side of life. One morning he went out on an aeroplane boat to take water tests. I made sure that he knew how to use all of the lifesaving equipment in the boat and, before he left, he told me he would not be going far. He didn't return all that afternoon, and by nightfall we were getting worried, but there was no sign of him. We found him the next morning and he was hopping mad that we hadn't rescued him sooner. He said, 'I sent up the flares just like you told me to, so why didn't you come?'. I asked, 'When did you send the flares up?' 'Around noon,' he replied. I looked at him in total disbelief. He sent up flares that could only be seen in the dark of night and expected us to see them at midday.

But this scientist wasn't the only interesting character that we had to deal with. Sometimes the old Aboriginal guides were just as amusing because they didn't understand the white system. One of them was an old man who we called Uncle Jimmy. He helped me research the area when I was doing the sacred site coding. One night we came in late and I offered him a bed to sleep in that was in a room with one of the white workers. In the morning the white man got up and began his morning routine. Jimmy watched him shave and decided that it looked like a good thing to do. When the man put the razor down Uncle Jimmy picked it up, put the man's cream on his face with the shaving brush, and shaved off his beard. The white man just watched as he did this but didn't say anything.

Then the white man brushed his teeth. When he was done, Uncle Jimmy picked up his toothbrush, put on some paste, and brushed his teeth just like he saw the other man do. The white man watched with great discomfort, but didn't know what to do because Uncle Jimmy had such a commanding presence. Finally he said, 'You can have the whole lot!' Uncle Jimmy just nodded as he used the man's towel to wipe his face.

Sometimes cultural differences showed up that made it hard for everyone, but part of my job was to arrange programs that helped to create a bridge of understanding. One of the most successful ones was a cultural sharing program I set up, where Aboriginal women spent time with the wives of white mining company employees. The Aboriginal women took the company wives out in the bush to collect pandanus leaves and then taught them how to strip, colour and weave these leaves into baskets and mats. They also taught them how to fish and cook the fish on an open fire. The company wives took the Aboriginal women to their houses and taught them about their Western ways. They learned how to vacuum, to use a washing machine and to cook on a gas stove. The Aboriginal women created a dance to the rhythm of the washing machine and then taught this dance to the white women. The women also spent time together with all of their children in family-type get-togethers. My wife, Lorraine, became the administrator of this program.

All the controversy and red tape between the government, the Land Council and the mining companies prevented Pan Continental from getting permission to begin their project, so I was transferred to Sydney to be trained in personnel management. We found a nice house and I worked in an office on Circular Quay, while Lorraine stayed home with the children. It was real city living. After a year of this we both got tired of waiting for something to happen, so I left the company and we moved back to Darwin.

Lorraine was bored with the life of a middle-class housewife, so she got a job with the Welfare Department while I did odd jobs and went back to school. This time I studied archaeology and geology. It was during this period of our lives that our son Tjugingji was born. TJ, as he became known, always had a very special relationship with his mother. Lorraine used to cradle him in her arms, saying, 'My little chocolate baby'. By this time my two older daughters, Dorothea and Anita, were also living in Darwin and they both had young babies to care for. Lorraine, Dorothea and Anita would frequently nurse each other's children, and it wasn't unusual to see one of them with a baby at each breast. This was the way I was raised by my mothers in Central Australia. Aboriginal babies are constantly being handled and nursed by other people. An infant belongs to everybody and everybody is responsible for that child's welfare.

After seeing an advertisement for a position as Director of the Legal Aid office in Alice Springs, I decided to apply because it would give me the opportunity of living closer to my traditional country. Conditioned by my city experiences as a good corporate executive, I dressed for this interview in a business suit with a freshly pressed white shirt and a tie, and carried my briefcase. I went into the Department of Aboriginal Affairs office early, and while I waited for the appointed meeting time, I said to the secretary, 'I'm Bob Randall and I've come to be interviewed for the Director of Legal Aid position. Will you let me know who the people are who are coming in to interview me?' She said, 'Okay, I'll nod my head when they come in, to let you know.'

So I'm sitting there when the first guy comes in with his shirt hanging out of his trousers and he was wearing thongs. She nodded and said, 'That's one of them.' I took off my jacket. Then another one came in dressed in a similar way. She nodded. I took off my tie. Then a really well-dressed girl came in and she nodded again. A sensibly dressed old man followed and there was another nod. Each time the secretary nodded I would feel more and more uncomfortable in my corporate suit. The next one that came in had on a dirty shirt, jeans and thongs and she nodded again. That's when I rolled up my sleeves and crumpled my shirt. It was obvious that I was just too flash.

The interview was conducted by all of the elected Central Australian Aboriginal Legal Aid Service (CAALAS) members, because I was applying for the director's position. When I finally went into the room, I discovered that some of the panel were relatives of mine. My brother Milton was one of them. They were all very businesslike in the meeting and told me they would let me know, but very soon after I got back to Darwin I had a call telling me I had the job.

Lorraine was able to transfer to the Alice Springs Welfare office, so we headed back to Alice together. When we stopped for petrol in Ti Tree, we found out there had just been a big murder there. A policeman had shot two of my own family members after an argument, one fatally. When I went into the office for my first day of work, this murder was the first item on the agenda, and I remember thinking to myself 'Wow! what a big thing to get for my first case.'

I met with the staff and lawyers of the Legal Aid office and the senior lawyer said that we needed to discuss the killing and lay murder charges against the policeman involved. The story the police were telling was that he had acted in self-defence, but from what we knew and what our people were telling us, these people were shot in the back. So we decided to advertise for a good lawyer who could pursue a murder charge against the police officer involved in the killing.

We decided to advertise outside Australia because we couldn't be sure that an Australian lawyer would be entirely free of racist attitudes, and we were quite used to being treated as lesser beings under white Australian law. It was just my personal feeling, and the others said the same thing, that a lawyer raised in Australia, under the prevailing racial attitudes of the time, might not fight the case as we would want them to. So eventually we decided on a legal team from England, Henry Spooner and his wife.

So we got the Spooners in and we gave them the case, to lay murder charges against this policeman who shot our people. The policeman was stood down during the trial, and I really thought that we would win and get a murder conviction against this officer. But I was told that the police were threatening to go out on strike if the case went against them, because they really believed it was all right to shoot our people. I was amazed, because it reminded me of the Coniston massacre in which the killing of our people was justified; and how many times have they said that when killing our people?[2]

I was really proud of our two lawyers, and I thought that they did a really good job. I don't think anyone will ever succeed on getting a charge proven against police who murder our people in this country. As in the case of John Pat in Western Australia, they seem to have a licence to kill.[3]

As part of the legal system, I now learned a great deal about what was going on amongst my people and the wealthy white cattle station owners. Aboriginal people were destroying themselves and their families with alcohol, and the white men were doing the same, but were a lot less open about it. I was shocked when I found out about the incest and child abuse that took place in the white culture. I had no idea such things existed.

As the director of a major Aboriginal organisation, I was soon part of everything that went on that affected Aborigines. I travelled a lot because part of my job was to set up a legal aid office in Tennant Creek. I did a lot of negotiation with department heads of other organisations and represented the people whenever called upon. I was also involved as a guest speaker in Aboriginal Cultural Awareness Programs that were given for the local police at the Institute for Aboriginal Development (IAD). I became very active in the church, as despite my success in worldly life, I was more and more drawn to explore the spiritual path. That's how I made friends with an African-American who worked at Pine Gap, an American base located outside Alice Springs. He was a Baptist minister who came from Hawaii. He wanted me to go to the United States to become a Baptist minister too. I did send an application to Harvard University, and was accepted, but my wife didn't want to be the wife of a minister. She thought it would restrict her social life.

One of my major projects for the Department of Legal Aid was to push for 'customary law' to be accepted as part of the Australian punishment system.[4] In traditional Aboriginal society, there were no police to enforce the law, although in Central Australia we did have the tradition of the *kadaitcha*, the ritual executioner. They wore special shoes made of marsupial fur, string and emu feathers to disguise their tracks. Such a person is requested by a senior man to take the life of another, as payback for a serious breach of law, and a great deal of magic surrounded the practices of the *kadaitcha*. Fear of this alone acted as a great deterrent for the breaking of traditional law. For example, the types of offences recognised by the Walpiri people of Central Australia have been identified as including, in order of severity: unauthorised homicide, sacrilege, unauthorised sorcery, incest, abduction or enticement of women, different types of adultery, unauthorised physical assault, usurpation of ritual privileges or duties and personal insult. Other offences of omission included physical neglect of certain relatives, refusal to make required gifts and refusal to educate certain relatives.

Different forms of payback were an important part of traditional law, and varied between different groups. The white system of law is quite difficult for our people to understand: if a man has caused a death, which in white law might result in his spending time in jail, our system would have required immediate punishment for which he would have automatically presented himself. So after serving his punishment in the white system, he might be still required to meet his punishment under traditional law. Some traditional forms of punishment included spearing (of the leg, for men), physical beating with the *kutra* (for women by women) and death, where a life was lost. It also included many different forms of sorcery, including pointing of the bone, whereby psychic powers are used to cause illness and possibly death to another. White medicine on the whole has proved very ineffective in dealing with people who become ill through these means. We wanted 'customary law' to be used in the court system, so that punishment could be immediate, and payback would not be visited on another member of his family in order to meet customary law requirements.

I was also called upon to help lawyers when they discovered that their Aboriginal clients, who had participated in the 'making of the man' ceremony, in our ceremonial path of knowledge, would not lie. If saying 'not guilty' was lying, they just wouldn't say it. They would always say, 'Yes, I did it.' When a mature Aboriginal man says, 'I didn't do it,' you can be sure he didn't. If he did do it, he would be the first to tell you he did and be ready to face his punishment. Not to do this would be to deny his manhood status. That's the way Aboriginal Law goes. We have to offer ourselves to a family when we commit crimes against a member of that family.

Speaking the truth didn't give these men a chance in the Australian legal system, where everyone is expected to say 'not guilty' whether they committed the crime or not, in order to exploit the concept of 'reasonable doubt'. Our lawyers couldn't defend these men. I told the lawyers to ask their clients, 'Have you been through business?' They will say yes or no. Once you know that they have, don't take them to court, just represent them in a legal sense.

Living in Alice Springs gave me the opportunity to get to know my birth family better and, when I wasn't working, I spent a lot of time with them. At that time, I was also invited to attend another conference for indigenous people. This one was in New Zealand. After this conference, I stayed over for a few days to spend time with the Maoris. Somehow I got drawn into their politics. A Maori politician asked me to join him while he was campaigning for the Maori Party to break away from the Labor Party.[5] I agreed and we travelled around New Zealand together visiting other Maoris at their maraes.

They told me about a hot water spring near one of the maraes where we were camping for the night, so I said, 'Let's go over there, I'd love to have a swim.' So we went early the next morning and it was locked. I said, 'We've come all this way, let's break in. We can jump over the fence or squeeze through the small chain.'

Amazingly, it was an hour before the police came and we had already finished our swimming and were ready to leave. As we were walking out the police pulled up and said, 'Why are you people causing trouble?' And I said, 'We're in the process of leaving. We've had our swim. We came here to swim and we have. Now we're leaving.' The Maoris asked me how come I was prepared to stand up to the white man and I said, 'I've learned a lot over there in Australia. You have to stand up for yourself to get somewhere.'

When I returned home, I discovered that the problems I had been seeing amongst Aboriginal people in my job were also showing up in my family, and I became so upset about this that I decided to leave Alice Springs, and resign from my job as director of Legal Aid Services. Partying and fighting were just not part of my world, and I was continually being dragged into these situations. I didn't know these extremes of happiness and hate, and I found them very hard to be around. My close association with the church and my interest in a spiritual approach to life, as well as my involvement in sports and education, had protected me from this kind of world. Lorraine and I packed up the kids and we went back to Darwin.

Although I was now in my forties, one of the first things I did when we were settled was to enrol in college again. This time I studied ancient history and anthropology. Lorraine kept moving up in her job and was doing very well financially. We now had three young children to look after, so we agreed that as long as I wasn't the income earner, I would combine my studies with taking care of the children. What I enjoyed most were the get-togethers that the parents of the pre-school children would have. There were a couple of men involved, but it was mainly young mothers.

I'd tell Lorraine when these days were coming up and she'd just say, 'Have a good day.' She didn't realise that there would be twelve to twenty women there and only two men. We men had a really good time in the company of all these gorgeous young mothers. One day I said to Lorraine, 'Why don't you come to the pool today and have lunch with us?' She came and saw all the beautiful women and said, 'That's what you go there for.' I said, 'Yes, that's part of the program. I don't know what you mothers complain about if this is what you do with your time. It's really pleasant to stay home and look after the children.' On weekends I would take some of these mothers out to see country. I'd tell Lorraine, 'I'm taking some of the people in the club out bush.' I loved seeing the look on her face when I said that.

I will always offer whatever skills I have for the benefit of the group or society that I am in. Sharing resources is as natural to me as breathing. I think most Aboriginal people are like that. This way of living used to be our Law, as taught to us through the path of ceremonial knowledge, so we grew up believing that it was the right thing to do. We learned to share whatever we have with family members in our kinship system. This is *kanyini*. Depending on the closeness of the relationship, some people will need permission to use things like a car, household items, clothes, and so on, while some don't even have to ask. To me *kanyini* is a lot more than just sharing what I have with those close to me. My spiritual practice is to consider all living things to be my family, so actions of unconditional love for everyone and everything have become my *kanyini*. It is applied to every relationship I have, whether that relationship is with a person, an animal, a tree or a rock. This has become the guiding philosophy of my life.

Red Sun, Black Moon

Red Sun, keep shining overhead,
on the bodies of my people lying dead.
I can't see so clearly through my eyes,
my mouth dry, I make no sound as I cry.

My people lived so happily long ago,
such deep sorrow part of life we didn't know.
Living our life with others, day by day,
doing all the things we liked, in simple ways.

Then came men with other skin from afar,
we made room by moving back, as brothers are.
We didn't mean to give up all we had,
but it seemed our way of life was too bad.

Bang! bang! bang! sound of gun,
all my people camped around began to run.
Men on horses ran among us, making dead,
all my people were screaming, as they fled.

Black Moon, keep shining overhead,
On past memories of my people, lying dead.
I can't see just what the future holds,
But I hope it won't be my people, lying cold.

Sorry Business

In our Yankunytjatjara culture, once someone has died, we do not speak their name for many, many years afterwards. We believe that when we die, we return to *tjukurrpa*, the Dreaming, to the spirit world of the ancestral beings, before we return again into our realm on this Earth. Sometimes our spirits have difficulty leaving this world. They may have strong attachment because of their connection to their family members, or because of a sense of anger and grievance about the situation that led to their death. We believe that speaking their name will encourage their spirits to hang around and prevent them from passing into the *tjukurrpa*. So, for this reason, people's names, objects, and even place names are replaced with the term *kunmanara* among my people, the Yankunytjatjara, our neighbours the Pitjantjatjara and the Walpiri, further north. This is the reason why, when someone died, we painted our bodies in white clay, and we used smoke to prevent the dead spirit finding its way back into our realm. We also abandoned the camp where the death occurred.

Traditionally, widows were not allowed to talk to their sisters-in-law or brothers-in-law until well after the mourning period, often many months or even years. When you look at the way Aboriginal people live physically, it might seem very simple. But the social laws about how people interact with one another can seem very complicated to outsiders. For us it is not so difficult, because we learn these rules as a natural part of growing up with our families. It is these kinship rules that organise Aboriginal culture.

At Galiwin'ku (Elcho Island) in Arnhem Land I had spent many months living with my traditional family, with whom I had hunted, and through this became involved in ceremony. I got to know Bapa Willie, my father, because he was the captain of the supply boats that brought supplies from Darwin to all the missions. I became close friends with his son, Dunjatee, who from the age of twelve was a brother to me. Bapa Willie adopted me as his son. This also happened with my friend, Jacob, at Gumbullunya (Oenpelli), whose mother adopted me as a son, which made us brothers. Thus my kinship connections were extended in Arnhem Land and through this, today, I can call this my country.

When my father Bapa Willie died, I travelled from Canberra, where I was then living, for the funeral that combined both modern Christian and traditional ways. Because Bapa Willie was a senior ceremonial man, many people came to his funeral from right across Arnhem Land and from Darwin. When I arrived on the plane, together with other people from Darwin, we were met by the mourners who were painted with white clay on their face and exposed parts of their body. This also included the people working at the airport. The whole township of Galiwin'ku was wearing the sign of mourning, the white clay.

We were taken to the sorry house, the house where he had lived and where he now lay in his coffin. The wails of the women and men were very powerful, flooding me with memories of our times together and all that we had shared. We clasped our arms around one another and shared our grief at the loss of this great man, who had grown so many of us up, and who had shared with us his deep knowledge of our culture. As an older man, I was now in the role of an older brother with responsibilities for supporting the ceremony. Outside, dancing was being performed, telling the many stories of our ancestors. The dancers' bodies were painted with traditional designs in white clay; the men carried the ceremonial spears; and the drone of the didgeridoo and the clap sticks, accompanying the songs, was continuous. They sent a deep sonorous vibration connecting the mourners, the earth and our ancestors. This continued for about five days, from morning until late into the night. My younger brother, Djiniyini, who was also the local Uniting Church minister, was involved as the ceremonial song and dance leader.

At the end of this traditional mourning, we drove the body to the church, with the ceremonial dancers leading the procession to the church. At the church, we put on our Western clothes over our white mourning paint and entered into the Christian ceremony, where Djiniyini now took the lead as the Christian minister. After this, I drove the funeral car to the Christian cemetery, to the site that Bapa Willie had chosen, overlooking the Arufura Sea, across which he had sailed all his life. There were smoking buckets on all the roads leading away from the grave and these were lit to create clouds of smoke, so that his spirit would not try to stay, but would travel on into the Dreaming, which in Arnhem Land is known as *wangarr*.

Recently, when one of my brothers died from a heart attack while in Alice Springs hospital, I attended the mourning that took place at a sorry camp on the eastern edge of Areyonga, where he had been living. Meanwhile the house where he had been staying in Alice Springs itself was immediately vacated by all the family members, who then headed out to organise the sorry camp at Areyonga. All the family members gathered, drawn from Alice Springs as well as many places around. The mourners gathered for many days, close family members forming the inner circle, while more distant relatives sat at some distance around. Here the wailing was quieter, with a sharing of deep grief coming over us. The bell from the small Lutheran Church in the community announced when the body had arrived from Alice Springs for burial. My other brother and I, as the senior members, led the mourners to the church. Church stewards sought to prevent our traditional practice of hitting ourselves with the *kutra*, the traditional fighting stick, to draw blood. After filing around the coffin, we all sat for the ceremony. But no church is ever big enough to hold the many mourners who gather for such a funeral among Aboriginal people. As part of this death all things associated with my brother were smoked in the traditional way. For someone who has worked in an office in recent times, this practice can also include their workplace.

Traditionally, in Central Australia, when someone dies we immediately vacate the place where the death occurs. The pattern of mourning is determined by our kinship system and relationship to the deceased, with close relatives forming the inner circle. Members of that person's totemic group sing his sacred songs daily until the *inma* cycle has been completed. This is done to help the person return to the *tjukurrpa*, the sacred spirit world of the Dreaming, and to let go of his relatives and attachment to country. The mourners, in empathy with the dead person and full of grief for the loss of a member who formed an intimate part of their *walytja*, their web of kinship interconnectedness, would hit themselves with sharp sticks and rocks in order to draw blood.

Aboriginal people are particularly concerned to prevent the dead person staying around as a spirit-ghost, which might cause future trouble. Such stories abound. My brother Jim tells the story of such a spirit-ghost in Arnhem Land where he lives. Jim and the other timber workers were sitting around the fire with one of our old Aboriginal elders, *Boonyi* Mungeno (Bob) after a hard day's work. Suddenly, Jim's dog, Bluey, a blue heeler cattle dog, pricked up his ears and began looking to the east. A low growl came from the dog and the hairs on his back started to bristle. Bluey rose and rushed out at someone near the ironwood tree at the edge of the glowing firelight. He kept circling the tree, growling all the time, as though he was trying to frighten something away. Jim and Ron went for their rifles and joined Bluey to investigate what was there. They called out, 'Who's there? Come out where we can see you,' thinking it might be someone who needed their help.

Then Bluey jumped back as if someone had thrown something at him and gave a yelp, and scuttled back to the camp where Jim was standing, while keeping his eye on the area around the ironwood tree. After a while the dog settled, but his eyes continued to follow something that was moving away from where the commotion had occurred, in a westerly direction, until after twenty minutes the dog completely settled down. Jim asked *Boonyi*, 'What was that, old man?'. *Boonyi* had not moved from his position with his back to the fire. He calmly answered, 'That old lady from Goulburn Island, she bin finish.' Jim asked, 'Who?' and *Boonyi* replied, 'That one they call Rosie. She bin die and she bin walking, visiting places along this country where we at. She just stopped to let us know because she was attracted by the fire.' He named a hill, right out on the horizon across the bay on Cobourg Peninsula, as the destination where she said she was heading. A week later the boat pulled in to pick up some logs to take to Croker Island mission, after it had finished delivering supplies to the other missions along the coast of Arnhem Land. Soon after it anchored, the dinghy came in with the crew and the food they wanted to prepare on the beach for their meal. They told Jim and his group, 'Remember that old lady, Rosie from Goulburn Island? She died last Sunday evening.' Jim said, 'We know. Old *Boonyi* Bob told us. Her ghost came to our camp and spoke to the old man.'

Even recently, when I met my nephew, a mining consultant who lives in Melbourne, at my favourite rock hole at Angas Downs, he asked, 'Did you hear the old woman come to collect water?' Bobbie's father grew up at Angas Downs. He related the story of a woman who had died in childbirth near that area, and that her ghost had continued to haunt the area. People had often heard her hitting her buckets at the rock hole in search of water. For this reason Bobbie had never camped at the rock hole over night. He was afraid of her spirit visiting his camp.

For most Aboriginal people, life is a cycle like the arc of a rainbow. We are drawn to our parents as spirit beings, and take a human life with them. When we die, we pass once again back into the spirit realm. That is why small children and grandparents have such a natural affinity. They are closest to their awareness as spirit beings, one because they have just come from the spirit world, and the other because they are about to pass into this world once again. As middle-aged adults we are furthermost away, caught up in the concerns and responsibilities of our earthly existence. It is through the path of ceremonial knowledge, when we enter into the world of the ancestral beings of the *tjukurrpa*, that we can again experience our closeness to this spirit world. It is through our songs, dances and ceremonies that we learn to be sensitive to this way of knowing. With this sensitivity we are able to open our senses and experience our relationship to everything around us, to talk with the trees, the earth, and the many creatures that make up our extended family in the great cycle of life and death. Traditionally we were not afraid to die: it was just a natural part of life. For us death was a matter of helping the spirit let go of its attachments in this world and pass into the spirit world of the ancestral beings.

There are still strong protocols surrounding people engaged in 'sorry business'. People are expected to take time off work to be with their relatives to express their grief, and people often become silent and withdrawn. This takes precedent over all other commitments, including work. For example, while organisations in white society might grant their workers two days' compassionate leave, Aboriginal organisations grant much longer leave to enable their workers to meet their kinship obligations between the time of death and the actual burial. This is usually between one and two weeks, and may include the period of time associated with any post mortem. Aboriginal organisations are also very sensitive to our need to mourn. For this reason I have always preferred to work for an Aboriginal organisation, like the Institute for Aboriginal Development, where I worked until I retired.

Traditionally, in some Aboriginal cultures, during mourning which might go on for many years, close family members may

174

remain silent, conversing only with sign language. Others might not cut their hair, or make other gestures about not being quite ready to resume their life, which has been torn apart by the death of such a close family member. In our culture we are very sensitive and respectful of the need for this, and no time limits are placed on people.

Today, in Aboriginal society, much of our sorry business is associated with the effects of cultural loss and dislocation, inflamed by the devastating effects of alcohol and other drug addictions that have come to our world from white society. Additionally there is the daily toll of racial discrimination against us, and the knowledge that we are now a minority people in this land where we have lived for many millennia. In certain parts of Australia this burden is so heavy that it is unbearable. We seem to spend our whole lives in sorry business.

Many white people are appalled by the level of alcoholism amongst Aboriginal people. With us, it is very visible because it happens on the streets or in public parks, rather than in the privacy of the home. However, alcoholism is actually just as endemic in white society, though it is more hidden. There are many more secret and closet drinkers in white society, because so many people live alone or in very small families. We live in large extended family systems and so alcoholism soon leads to noisy partying.

For us, alcoholism has been more devastating than for white society. It has unleashed the anger and fear we have hidden within ourselves as a result of our recent history. This anger and fear have torn apart the fabric of Aboriginal family life. Money meant to feed family members, especially children, is spent on alcohol. Children, once the centre of love and attention, are often neglected. Sexual jealousies and insecurity lead to endemic and often serious violence. I remember the case of two of my aunties. They were wonderful women, elders in my community. Eventually they gave in to the 'grog culture'. They were exhausted by arguing against it. During an argument between them, one picked up an old piece of iron lying nearby and struck the other a blow, which killed her. What would once have been a minor dispute became a violent murder. It is hard to bear the pain of these situations when you know the people involved. You know they are not murderers and you know the unbearable remorse that they will feel once the reality of what has happened hits them.

Aboriginal culture, traditionally, did not use any forms of intoxicating drugs, so we do not have any traditional Law to deal with these new things which attack our minds and spirits. Now we are surrounded by loss and grief on a daily basis as close family members die premature deaths from suicide, accidents and preventable diseases. Recently I attended the funeral of one of my grandsons in Darwin. He was a promising young man, a football star with the world before him. But unknown to his family, he harboured dark thoughts of failure and confusion that broke his spirit. It is very difficult for our people to live happily in modern white society, constantly bombarded by the images of material and social success that are so difficult for us to attain.

Many of us, stranded in unemployment, turn to television for distraction. Often we do not even realise the subtle messages that are flooding into our minds, though the images before us are nearly always of white people, rich, successful, powerful and happy. The cleverness of the advertisements entertain and amuse us, but they also leave us with this constant sense of lack, and of envy and dissatisfaction. Then we turn to alcohol and other drugs such as marijuana and petrol sniffing to help us deal with these deep feelings of anxiety and depression.

Those of us who were taken from our families were described by Mick Dodson, the Aboriginal and Torres Strait Islander Social Justice Commissioner, as 'ruined souls', never really fitting into either black or white culture, lurching from 'a tragic history to a tragic future'. Despite the obvious success of many from the Stolen Generations in the modern world, the hurt and anger still live right beneath the surface for most of us. Too often, instead of showing it to the outside world, we direct it at ourselves and the ones we love the most. This self-abuse continues the cycle of hurt, because it is often the cause of our children being taken away from us by welfare agencies who are required, under state child protection laws, to intervene in families where children are at risk of neglect or abuse. Given the extent of abuse which resulted from white colonisation and dispossession, and the removal and institutionalisation of so many mixed-race children, there is probably not one Aboriginal family in Australia which is not directly affected. All over Australia, we Aboriginal people are now looking for a way to cut this cycle of our suffering.

In white society it is also the custom to celebrate success or special occasions with alcohol. For those few of us who were successful in white society, we were quickly introduced into this world of celebration. So initially for these reasons, alcohol was always associated with happiness. We did not know that the way this drug works on our minds is actually as a depressant. I only came to understand this through my work with health workers. It seems at first to make one happy and sociable. Slowly the dangerous side of this drug has shown its face right across Aboriginal culture. One of the earliest cases of this tragedy was the famous early Aboriginal painter, Albert Namatjira. As part of his success as a painter in the white world, he was given the privilege of drinking alcohol with other white people, both fellow artists and patrons of the arts. Under Aboriginal Law, everything to which he had access had to be shared with his relatives, even though sharing alcohol with other Aborigines, at that time, was against the white man's law. His success put him in an impossible situation and eventually cost him his life. He died soon after being released from jail.

I became suspicious of alcohol very early in my life because of the effect I saw it had on my family from the mission. I was frightened of it. A lot of people thought they could handle it easily but it was just too powerful. Many have now died of alcohol-related problems, even some who were younger than I am.

Part of my work was with health workers who were seeking to help our people deal with alcohol-related health problems. Many Aboriginal and non-Aboriginal people worked together through the HALT (Healthy Aboriginal Life Team) project. Some of the things which Aboriginal people said to HALT workers about their relationship to alcohol show its seduction. They say it helps them connect with the feelings of fulfilment attached to hunting and ceremony. In the euphoria of their addiction they could feel again the companionship, noise, excitement and sense of belonging to an exclusive group, as long as they could stay within the fog of alcohol. Some women reported that alcohol gave them the confidence to become a story teller, or to recover a sense of companionship with their menfolk, whose drinking had caused them to become alienated.[1]

With the white colonisation of Aboriginal culture, and the devastating psychological consequences of the policy of removing Aboriginal children from their families and institutionalising them, our responsibility for our own spirit was taken away from us. We could no longer practise the sacred principle of *kanyini*. Many of us later thought that alcohol would make us strong, because it gave us a false sense of courage. Where once we were timid and frightened in the face of white culture, now we found we could speak up. Where we might have been afraid of the power of the police, now we found the courage to shout abuse and threaten them with our fists. We were unable to follow the old ways of caring for family so we thought, 'Ah, here's something to fix us. This medicine, this grog (alcohol) is good.' Grog then became the remedy for all our weak feelings and when we shared it with family members we thought we had found another way to care for each other. But we were tricked.

One interesting project with which I have been involved is the Sugarman Project. Back in the early 1990s, a Sydney Jungian psychologist, Craig San Roque, came to live in Alice Springs, to study traditional healing practices with our Aboriginal elders. He became involved with the HALT workers and through this met the artist,

Andrew Spencer Japaljarri, who had been trying to use art to find a way to talk about alcohol and other health problems. Because we base our culture and our Law in the *tjukurrpa*, we have found alcohol very difficult to deal with. We had no story for it, so we could not 'understand' it. Our knowledge system encodes everything in song, dance, paintings and ceremony and all is linked back to the *tjukurrpa*, to the stories of the adventures of our ancestral beings, which carried the hidden psychological truths which underpin our Laws. Our Laws are not just something that ordinary people make up. So without a story from the *tjukurrpa*, we could not enter into this process of making laws about alcohol.

Japaljarri talked with Craig about this and asked Craig if there was a European story about how such a powerful force, such as alcohol, had come into white culture. Craig had had a long-term interest in Greek mythology as a means of understanding some of the deep currents of white culture. He had already done some work with the tensions between the myth of Dionysius (the Greek god of wine and sensuality) and Apollo (the Greek god of reason). So he decided to explore this some more from the perspective of alcohol. He discovered that Dionysius was regarded as a god of wine and intoxication, so he wrote up the story of Dionysius' life in a style similar to the way our ancestral stories are told. He told this story to Japaljarri and his family, and they searched for a name for Dionysius in Aboriginal culture.

Sweet things were rare and precious in Central Desert culture. Our only sources of sweetness were from honeycomb, the honey ant, the sweet secretions on branches of the mulga tree called *kurku*, and the nectar of the yellow flowers of the corkwood tree (*witjinti*), which we call *kulingpa*, that could be soaked in water to produce sweet water. Initially alcohol had come into our lives as this sort of precious thing, so its nickname was sugar. So we identified Dionysius, the Greek god of wine and intoxication, as 'Sugarman', the Australian white man who sold alcohol to Aboriginal people, the flagon runner and peddler of booze.

Craig then worked with a number of us in Alice Springs who were involved in the performing arts. I became involved because of my connections with the HALT program, and because I got involved in many performances and concerts through my songs. We all got together and tried to create a performance about Sugarman, one that would combine song, dance and painting. We wanted it to be a healing event of participation that would be taken up by different communities and explored and adapted further. The first performance of Sugarman was held at Injatnama, a community that had been established as a rehabilitation healing centre by Elvira and Barry Cook. This community used open space and country to help people heal, where traditional white methods had shut people up in small rooms. This was very crushing to the spirits of Aboriginal people and didn't help them get away from alcohol at all.

This first Sugarman ceremony traced the really tortured family history of Sugarman (Dionysius) whose father is Lightning Man (Zeus). Baby Dionysius (Sugarboy) was born into a world of family violence which immediately began to undermine his spirit, his *kurunpa*. We know about Lightning Man as he is a very popular figure in Arnhem Land mythology, with strong connections to the Rainbow Serpent. In this story we also brought in the Crow People (the God Kronos who tried to destroy Sugarboy physically and mentally), and showed how Sugarboy became trapped by dreams. When he uses alcohol to deal with this, his dreams turn to madness. In this way, through the ceremony, participants discover that if you step into Sugarman, as an ancestral story, you understand how inevitably you will be swallowed up by madness. Sugarman is the story about how not to get seduced by false courage, false happiness and false friendship. This is how *tjukurrpa* works. *Tjukurrpa* stories are *inma*, cycles of story songs that call up the spirit of the ancestors, so that the past comes to meet the present and show you the way.

The madness of Sugarman affects all four dimensions of our being. It attacks our mind and its clarity. We are depressed and befogged, overcome by all kinds of emotions we can no longer control. It fills our bodies dangerously with sugar. Many Aboriginal people, like myself, have adult onset diabetes. We must avoid sugar in our diet or it will kill us. We also often suffer from high blood pressure and are very susceptible to kidney failure. Alcohol is poison to our bodies, weakened as they are by all these things. It also kills our brain cells and attacks our liver. We betray our path of ceremonial knowledge and its commitments to secrecy, thus poisoning our link to country and *tjukurrpa*. This is the deepest spiritual wound of all, striking right at the heart of our culture. So we continue to die young. Few of us live into our sixties, let alone into our seventies and eighties.

There was another Sugarman ceremony at Injatnama in 1999. This time it was run by the Aboriginal community and had a very different flavour. It will be interesting to see whether this story is taken up, and so becomes available to our people, in the way in which our traditional stories are. Only time will tell. It would help if it became part of the education system, so that our children grow up with it. But I know it will be hard to compete with stories of television and cinema.

I remember when alcohol was first introduced for Aboriginal people in 1967. I was in Darwin at the time and everyone wanted to try it. I had a taste but I didn't like it. Others didn't like it either, but they thought there must be something good about it, otherwise why would so many of our white mates be drinking it? We actually made ourselves drink it because of the social interaction it allowed us. And then things went crazy. Aboriginal people started yelling out the names of the dead and breaking tradition. They started talking loudly about secret parts of the ceremonies. A great divide came between those of us who were caught in the seduction of the madness of alcohol and didn't even realise we were behaving in such an embarrassing and sacrilegious way, and those of us who remained outside its influence. This has been so hard on family life among Aboriginal people. Our Law of sharing is so strong that those who are trapped in alcohol's seduction seek actively to share it with

181

everyone, irrespective of their age or health. This conflict has reached deeply into all our families, even my own.

When I saw the power of it, I talked with some of my elders in Central Australia about what I saw happening to our people. They said, 'It's not our problem. We don't get any money from grog. We don't make grog. Grog is not in our *tjukurrpa*. It belongs to white man. White man has got to do something for Aboriginal people when things happen because of grog.' These old men just refused to accept it as their responsibility, even in telling our mob not to drink, because they didn't see that as their role.

In fact it has often been Aboriginal women elders, the grandmothers, who have taken a leading role, acting from their traditional Law of responsibility for peace and harmony in the family and the care of young children. It is the grandmothers who have led the way to creating communities which have been declared alcohol-free, and where it is now illegal to take alcohol. Many communities have created night patrols that seek to head off trouble amongst people who have been drinking, taking them to a safe place to sleep off their intoxication.

We are only two per cent of Australia's population, yet we comprise nineteen per cent of the prison population. The really dreadful truth is that, for some of our people, prison becomes safer and more manageable than real life. We are most vulnerable to suicide when we are first taken, before we learn how to submit to the imprisonment not only of our body but of our spirit and mind, and the acute pain of our loss of connection to country.

I have had my own share of this grief. One morning shortly after the Christmas of 1992, when we were working in Canberra, my wife Lorraine got dressed and left for work as usual. We kissed goodbye at the car and I said 'See you for dinner tonight.' I got home from work about four o'clock and was settling in when the phone rang. One of the workers at the Social Security office said, 'Your wife took ill and we are trying to get her to the hospital. Meet us there.' I got Shane, her son from her first marriage, and Ituma, our first born, into the car and we went to the hospital and waited. Some time later the ambulance pulled in and when I saw Lorraine on the stretcher and the paramedics working on her with the heart machine I knew that I had lost her. They rushed her into the emergency room and tried to bring her back, but she was gone. I will never forget the sound of my daughter shrieking when the doctor said, 'We were unable to save her.' While I was by now in my mid-fifties, she was only thirty-nine years old, enjoying a successful and rewarding professional life. Our children were only ten and twelve years old, and she loved them deeply. Unlike our Yankunytjatjara culture, her people do not have the practice of not mentioning her name, so here in my story I use her name, Lorraine.

The kids and I held each other and cried. We were stunned with disbelief. Because I was so much older than Lorraine, we had always assumed that it would be me who would die first, from diabetes. She had been with me when I had scarlet fever and nearly died. She had made preparations for my death because to her I was the old and sick one. It never occurred to either of us that it would be the other way around. However, Lorraine was never a really well person. She had terrible asthma and high blood pressure and had a habit of gaining a lot of weight quickly and then dieting to take it off. I ran every day and exercised a lot but she couldn't do it with me. She had a different constitution. We had often talked about her having an operation on her heart, but her answer was always, 'Not yet, I'll do it soon.'

We had a memorial service for her at our church, but I would not agree to have her coffin there. The church wasn't big enough for all the people who came. After the service I flew her body to Adelaide so she could be buried in her home country. I drove across and met the family there. Some of my relatives came down from Alice Springs. The night before her funeral I said to the kids, 'We are going to bury Mum tomorrow. Would you like to talk to her while she's still in state, lying in her coffin?' They each went in separately and then we went in together. I felt so peaceful with her body while

I was talking to her. I knew her spirit was there. It was like she was telling me, 'It's okay and I'm okay. Don't worry. Just do what needs to be done.'

I would have preferred to have her buried in a traditional way, but it wasn't possible in Port Pierce because this was a real 'up-town' reservation, which had lost its connection to traditional culture. I didn't want to freak* the ministers out by having us appear in mourning with the traditional white clay. However, I was able to get the family to wear red and white armbands as a symbol of death and we wrapped bands of the same colours around the coffin and the cars that drove to the cemetery. I also managed to have buckets of smoke near the grave site.

When we got back to Canberra I wanted to do a ceremony in the place where she died. When I went to her office she was still there. I could smell the spirit. Her desk was the same as if she was still there. I spoke to her as I placed a huge vase of white flowers and a vase of red flowers on her desk, 'Baby, you are no longer here, but I'm here with the sacred colours. I will leave these with you.' Heather, one of the relatives who was with me, said Lorraine laughed and said, 'Don't be silly, I'm still here.' She had a particular laugh that everyone could identify as hers, and Heather heard that laugh. The Aboriginal office workers wouldn't go near Lorraine's area. They would go to parts of the office that were furthest away. The only ones that went near her desk were the non-Aboriginals, because they couldn't feel anything.

Her spirit found it hard to leave us and she could be felt around the house for quite a while. We had people come in to help convince her that it was time to leave. We also had counsellors come to help us deal with her death, but I don't think they came often enough. Our youngest son, Tjugingji (TJ) was away on holiday when Lorraine died, and the last letter she had written was to him, telling him how much she wanted him to come home. It was really hard meeting him at the airport and telling him that his Mum was dead. One of the hardest things for me to bear was to see my youngest children suffer the same fate as I did, to lose their mother, to no longer have her loving arms around them and hear her laughter.

I was very lonely and soon became extremely depressed. At the time I would have given anything to leave this world myself. I called my Gumatj brothers on Elcho Island and shared my feelings with them. I spoke to the whole family and as we spoke on the phone, they were all touching a little wooden animal. They told me they were going to sing what I needed into the animal and would send it to me. I was to put it in the room where I spent the most time. When I received it I did what they said and the feeling in the house changed. Whenever I travelled I took the wooden animal with me, but I continued to feel very much alone. I was forever listening for my wife's footsteps. They never came.

Lorraine

Chorus
Together we lived and together we loved,
Our life was a dream that could never end.
Time had to come when we just had to part.
I must walk alone and let go of your hand.

Oh my darling I write you through the words of this song,
To let go of me now can never be wrong.
I have always loved you as we walked on our land
I must walk alone now and let go of your hand.

Like the snow from the mountain to the river they go,
Joining up with others on the road towards home,
Till in the sunrise we will all meet again
In an ocean of love, we will be one again.

I remember the time where we first held our hands
As we both wrote our names on the tree and the sand.
Our love for each other will always be there
In that heart shape of time, darling leave right there.

Oh my darling, I miss you as I still walk our land,
For part of my life you still hold in your hand.
I long for the day we will both meet again
In our home made of love, where forever we'll stay.

I must turn around and in love walk away.
You have gone from this life to a home far away
Where our spirit will rest till it's my turn to leave
This land of our love where alone I still grieve.

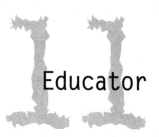

Educator

With Lorraine's death the familiar world of Canberra, university and students began to feel very blank and lifeless. I was very lonely. For the first few weeks after her death there were a lot of people around, but after the funeral they left us alone to get our lives back together. When her son, Shane, went to Adelaide for her funeral he decided to stay there, and this made another hole in our family unit. Ituma, although only twelve years of age, stepped into her mother's role in the house and looked after me and TJ. It was as though she became her mother. I made an arrangement with someone to live with us as a live-in nanny, but Ituma increasingly took care of all the meals and did the laundry. I see my wife in both of our children and am grateful for the happy memories I have of our time together. Lorraine made such a big contribution towards improving the conditions of our people that the Department of Social Security established a scholarship fund in her name. I continued to live in Canberra for several more years, trying to bring up my children and give them the opportunities that Canberra offered.

My life as an educator is intimately tied up with memories of my second wife, Lorraine, but it also continued after her sudden and shocking death. Remember, we met in Adelaide through the founding of the Aboriginal Community College. In 1985, just after

I turned fifty years old, we returned to the world of education when we moved to Canberra. She had a job with the Aboriginal Education Consultative Group, while I worked at the Canberra College of Advanced Education setting up an Aboriginal and Islander centre with a 'Museum Studies Course'. The purpose of the course was to teach Aboriginal people how to manage, protect, preserve and look after historical objects that were important to them and to set up museums for local artefacts in their homeland areas. It was my job to find students who would stick with being away from home to undertake the studies and who had high enough grades from previous schooling to handle the college-level classes that would be offered. To help build enrolment, the college wanted also to set up a bridging component whereby Aboriginal students could get a year or two of basic education in instances where they hadn't had a high rate of success in the normal schools. These bridging courses have proved very important, not only for Aboriginal people, but for the many adults, particularly women with children, who wanted to gain tertiary level education.

We began with six students and it was my job to look after them. I arranged transport, found them suitable accommodation and made sure that their social and academic needs were met, while they were in Canberra. The group gradually grew to twenty students. Canberra is quite different from anything we Aboriginal people are used to, but there was so much open space incorporated into this design, and the city is surrounded by mountains, so we found it a very attractive place to live. We also met many old friends there, whom we had met in the Northern Territory and in Adelaide, and through my work in the 1970s addressing social issues.

When we started planning the National Aboriginal Day of Celebration (NAIDOC) programs, I discovered that the Ngungawal people, the Aborigines from the Canberra area, were holding back from taking any leadership roles. Having come from a traditional society in the Northern Territory, I knew that the protocol was for these people to be the up-front spokespersons and planners of the events that were taking place in their traditional country. As I got to know them, I worked quite hard to get them to learn about their traditional lifestyle and revive their interest in Aboriginal culture.

So, in addition to setting up courses at the college and looking after the students, I began also doing a lot of cultural awareness programs in the public school system and at other colleges. At one of these schools I met some children, Michelle and Paulie House, who were very interested in learning about the traditional Aboriginal lifestyle. They told their mother Matilda about this Aboriginal teacher who spoke with such confidence and knowledge about the old ways, and then introduced me to her. She proved to be an elder of the Ngungawal people and I was able to get her permission to send Paulie up to Arnhem Land to spend time with my people in the East Alligator River region. This enabled him to get a feel for country from a traditional Aboriginal perspective. While he was in Arnhem Land, Paulie developed a keen interest in the didgeridoo, the Aboriginal wind instrument that is now known throughout the world. He became a very good player. He is now a strong teacher of Aboriginal culture through music and dance. It is through music and dance that we have had most success in reviving our culture, both in terms of reaching out to non-Aboriginal people, and in terms of reaching out to our own people, particularly those who live in cities. Our own traditional culture also used these methods. All our learning involved the telling of stories, singing of songs and dancing, as well as the acquisition of technical skills and practical knowledge.

At this time Lorraine had left the world of education and moved to a senior position in the Department of Social Security, dealing with the needs of Aboriginal people. She introduced cultural awareness programs for non-Aboriginal staff, and when people we knew from Arnhem Land were in town she would introduce them to non-Aboriginal people who had never met a traditional person before in their lives. One of the major contributions she made was to help bureaucrats understand the Aboriginal family system, what we in the Central Desert call *walytja*. In this system grandmothers, aunties and other 'mothers' often look after children instead of their birth mothers. When she began working for Social Security, the money allocated for the care of Aboriginal children was only ever paid to the birth mother, and in a lot of situations the money was being used to buy drugs and alcohol, instead of being used to look after the children as intended.

The majority of Aboriginal people are in the lowest income group in Australia. Because of racial discrimination and poor education, most are unemployed and many are single parents with lots of children. In our system children move from an aunty to a grandmother and then to another mother at any time, according to need. The unemployment pension for one person is just not enough to raise an extended family, and my Lorraine knew that many people were close to starvation because they could not get access to the money intended for the children for whom they were caring. Under her guidance the government brought in a new policy that directed the children's money to the actual caregivers.

Our family also became involved in cultural activities. We started a cultural dance group for children six years and older, called the Glow Worms, and they were taught how to perform traditional dances. Gumatj teachers from the eastern end of Arnhem Land would come to Canberra to do special performances associated with national events, and while they were in town, my daughter Dorothea would make sure that they spent time teaching their dances to our kids. The Glow Worms began dancing at various social functions and soon they were in great demand. Every year they participated in the huge NAIDOC cultural celebrations in Sydney and were the youngest performers there.

My interest in promoting cultural awareness saw me take up a position as a consultant with the Department of Aboriginal Affairs, to meet the increasing international interest in Aboriginal culture. This expanded my understanding of other cultures and brought me into contact with many international media people. However,

I quickly became frustrated with the life of a consultant and its inse-
curities of income. This was not helped by Lorraine's demanding role
as national head of the Aboriginal Division of the Department of
Social Security. So I applied for a teaching position at the University
of Wollongong, a coastal town just south of Sydney and about two
and half hours' drive from Canberra. I figured we could alternate our
weekends together between Canberra and Wollongong.

I spent that first week finding out about my duties at the university, looking at offices, meeting staff and learning a little about the
Aboriginal Cultural Centre's history. I was told that I was the last
chance for the continuance of the unit. The college administration
felt that too much money had been wasted. My role was to salvage
the centre.

I had already set up this type of program at the Canberra
College of Advanced Education and at the Community College in
Adelaide, so it was the history of these two successes that got me
the position. At the time, setting up this kind of a centre in a college
or university was still a new idea. I knew that I could do what they
wanted and that this was an opportunity for me to earn the level of
salary that I felt I deserved. I made a commitment to myself that it
was going to work, and that I would not be forced to rely on
Lorraine's earnings.

I continued to be involved in political life. Australia was celebrating its bicentenary in 1988, 200 years after Captain Cook had
landed and declared this whole country as the property of the King
of England. For us this was celebrating the day of invasion and we
converged on Sydney to stage a day of protest. Representatives from
many of the Aboriginal nations (language groups) paraded in the
streets, dressed as they would for a traditional ceremony, on the day
when Queen Elizabeth was arriving from England on her private
yacht. Our protest extended to the waterside to let her know that
our people did not welcome this celebration of their suffering and
conquest. Media coverage of our protest allowed us to communicate
to the world about the way we had been treated by the colonisers,

continuing to this day. Another benefit was the growing feeling of unity across the many different Aboriginal nations amongst those of us marching, and with the many non-Aboriginal people who joined us in the demonstrations.

I had a brief break from my routine at the University of Wollongong, when I travelled overseas accompanying a group of Aboriginal cricketers to England to retrace the steps of the touring Aboriginal team which was the first cricket team that represented Australia in England. I was responsible for the cultural part of the tour, organising dance performance, didgeridoo players and singers. A highlight of this tour was going to Wimbledon to celebrate Nelson Mandela's sixty-eighth birthday. There I met a lot of international black celebrities including Whoopi Goldberg and Whitney Houston. These famous people were easy to talk with and we had good rapport because we were all black and had experienced similar racial discrimination.

Back at home in my university job, I began to notice that I was suffering from unpredictable mood swings and fits of anger. I was to learn later that this was a sure sign of adult onset diabetes, a condition that is endemic among Aboriginal people. This was not before I had a major conflict with a colleague in my office, which resulted in my leaving this job and returning to Canberra. There I took on more consulting work as a cultural ambassador for the Department of Aboriginal Affairs, which took me to some of our neighbouring Pacific nations. This opened my eyes to the similarities between indigenous people across the Pacific. For instance, the people I met at Rarotonga in New Zealand also had big families and a family system similar to ours, so we got along well together.

This was also apparent when I had the opportunity to visit the United States to represent the Australian government in a big murder trial. The accused was an Aboriginal person who had been adopted and taken to America, where he experienced a lot of racial discrimination and cultural alienation because he found black

American culture as foreign to him as white American culture. He had confessed to a brutal murder, and his defence lawyers wanted to explore the effects of his being a member of the Stolen Generations.[1] This trial was very stressful for me, and I took time off to visit other parts of America. I was able to meet with a group of Blackfeet Indians, who wore really long braided hair. One of them took me to spend a day with his family, and I found them to be similar to urban Aborigines. They had moved off the reservation and were living in houses close by. They told me that growing up as an indigenous person in America was similar to my experiences in Australia. I was, however, surprised to learn that everything on their reservation was tax-free, and that they could run any business that they liked from there.

The government decided I was a good cultural ambassador and wanted me to go to Mexico and Japan, but I was just too tired and was missing my family. Instead I accepted a full-time position with the Australian National University (ANU), to create a similar program to the one that I had run in Wollongong. It was during my physical examination for the job that I discovered that I had diabetes. Diabetes is a very common disease amongst our people. Changing our diet from 'bush tucker' that is high in natural roughage to the standard ration of refined white flour, sugar and tea have had a devastating effect on our health. While people living on their traditional land might still supplement this diet with hunting, those of us who lived in town had adopted a diet that was high in both sugar and fat. We sure do love soft drinks.

Ever since this happened, I have had to monitor my diet very carefully and avoid refined sugar. Like most diabetics, I also have to pay particular attention to any cuts to my feet, particularly around the nail area. We diabetics lose some sensitivity in the nerve endings in our feet. Failure to notice wounds and treat them can result in infection, which rapidly turns into septicaemia and gangrene. I later lost my sister Junie in this way.

With my diabetes now under medical control, I embraced my

new challenge at the Australian National University. Dr H.C. (Nugget) Coombs, the Chancellor of the university, was a long-term friend of Aboriginal people and I had met him many times over the years, particularly in the Northern Territory. I approached him to help me get cooperation from faculty deans and professors to allow my students to study their courses. He taught me how to wine and dine these people to build rapport, before approaching them directly with my request. You wouldn't believe how difficult it was to secure their cooperation. My first task was to organise more suitable premises than those allocated to me at the very edge of the campus. I found an old abandoned computer room and visualised how I could put a wall in to make a student room and an adminis-tration room for myself. My request to use this space was success-ful, and I fixed it up and bought furniture, and it became the new Aboriginal and Islander Centre.

This centre started with six students and I was surprised to discover that some of them were from Darwin and were related to me. I had known them there and also knew their families. I encouraged these students to take the courses they needed to get a degree so that they would be qualified to make a difference in the future. The program quickly grew to reach my goal of twenty students and today it is still one of the most successful Aboriginal programs in retaining students. There were two guidelines that I adopted to which I attribute this success. First, I would not accept a student who hadn't reached the year twelve level academically or through work experience, and second, if I advertised a position, I would not discriminate against non-Aboriginal people. These policies got me into a lot of trouble with my people, because they believed that they should be admitted or get the job just because they were Aboriginal, especially if they were family to others who were already there. There was a lot of pressure on me to do it their way, but I insisted that everyone I worked with be qualified, and I didn't budge from this position. I hired white academic advisers because no qualified blacks applied, and in another situation

I employed a Mexican over Aboriginal applicants. I got a lot of backlash for this from my students.

When the centre had a staff of four people we started producing brochures and other advertising materials, and during every Christmas and semester break I would visit Aboriginal organisations all over the country, seeking to recruit good students to come to Canberra to pursue degree studies.

Back at the ANU Aboriginal and Islander Centre, there were a lot of changes taking place. The success of the program was attracting many people who wanted to play a significant role. It felt competitive, and I just wasn't in a state to deal with this. I decided to resign and take some time out for myself. When I was ready to work again I got another position with the New South Wales Education Department at Queanbeyan.

I was still grieving for Lorraine and was in the midst of making this major career change when Shane came back home asking for his share of his mother's estate. She had died without a will, and everything had reverted to me. I hadn't given any thought to what would comprise her estate. We both consulted a lawyer, and as soon as it was determined what was due to Shane, I gave him the cash and he returned to his job and family in Adelaide.

Dealing with these things just increased my loneliness because I had no companion to discuss them with. I decided to join a singles' club. I took a lot of women out but didn't meet anyone I felt would be right for a long-term relationship. While attending a conference on mental health, I met a woman who was working as a tutor at a university where I used to work. When I first noticed her I just saw her back as she was looking at the books and posters we had on display. She was little, with long hair hanging down her back, and I wondered what she looked like from the front.

I was giving the opening presentation and while I was speaking I noticed her again in the audience. When I finished my talk. I introduced myself and asked, 'How are you? What's your name? I see you are here for the conference. Where do you work? Do you have a husband looking after you?' I could tell from her shocked expression that she thought that was an unusual question to ask at a first meeting, but she answered 'No'. One day on an impulse, I called her up and invited her to lunch. Although Robyn was a white woman, I think I felt comfortable with her because she was working with my people. I didn't see her often in the beginning because I was travelling quite a bit at the time. But once I began meeting her friends and found out that she was an actress and a singer like myself, I was even more interested in spending time with her because of our common interests.

In the beginning I was only interested in a friendship, but as I got to know her we became close and I took her home to meet the children. They liked her and it was comfortable to have her spend time with the whole family. At one point Robyn needed to find a new place to live, and after talking it over with the children, I invited her to come and live with us. Robyn became part of our family. When she introduced us to vegetarian cooking we thought it was a bit funny that she didn't like meat, but that didn't worry us. She made good meals for us and ate her vegetables when we ate our meat. She did like seafood, so we would occasionally enjoy eating the same thing.

When we sang together it was magical. Robyn has a beautiful voice and added nice harmonies to my songs. I admired her artistic abilities and appreciated her willingness to do the things I wanted to do, even when it meant changing plans she had already made. I enjoyed the way she looked, the way she laughed, and the fact that she didn't smoke or drink. She cared for the kids in a very special way, and because of that she was easily included in the family kinship system.

Meanwhile, I was teaching cultural awareness programs as a consultant, going from job to job without any stability. I trained teachers to be cultural teachers and coordinated programs on how to make and throw comeback boomerangs, how to make music sticks, how to play the didgeridoo and how to do traditional dances. These were then taught to children throughout New South Wales. I also spent time working with Aboriginal people in the outlying communities. I really enjoyed doing these things, but each time a contract ended or the money ran out to pay me, I had to go looking for my next job. I kept busy and could have struggled through, but I was tired and still hadn't completely recovered from the loss of my wife, so I decided to pay a visit to Alice Springs.

During this visit I stopped in at the Institute for Aboriginal Development (IAD) where some of my relatives were working, and they told me there was a position coming up in the cultural teaching area. It wasn't long after I returned to Canberra that I heard from them, and soon after applying I received a phone call to tell me that the job was mine.

TJ was still in junior high school when I moved back to Alice Springs to take up the position as teacher of cultural awareness at the Institute, and I stayed there till my retirement in 1999. When I was hired by the IAD, Ituma was in the process of completing her college education and her boyfriend had moved into our house to live with her. They were both dancers and were performing with a very popular dance group. Ituma stayed on in Canberra and completed her college course, then moved to Perth to take up further studies in creative arts.

I needed to return to my country in order to handle the grief of the loss of my beloved wife, and to feel the warmth of my connection to my extended family, which stretched around Alice Springs, from Uluru to Tennant Creek. The red ochres of the ancient rock and sand of the Central Desert embraced me once again, the pain of my lost mother and my lost wife merging into one. I opened my senses to the grandmother and grandfather trees, especially the she oaks and old river gums. They give so much, yet they never ask for anything. The birds visited me, especially the colourful little lorikeets to which I would give bread in water, dribbled with honey. My eyes searched for the tracks of the little lizards and other creatures of the desert who come out at night to forage. The swift flight of the kangaroos and wallabies filled me with their joy. Slowly, slowly, I began to heal and rebuild my life.

The Institute for Aboriginal Development is a community-based educational institution set up by Jim Downing of the Uniting Church and Yami Lester[2] on behalf of Aboriginal people. The purposes of the institute are to assist in Aboriginal community development and to create a bridge between Aboriginal and non-Aboriginal people. Many courses are offered to non-Aboriginal people who work with our people, so they can learn about our ways, our protocol and our belief systems. When the Institute was first formed, Aboriginal people were taught how to look after themselves hygienically so they didn't get sick. This health unit became so big that a separate college grew out of it.

Today, IAD offers literacy, vocational and college level courses as well as cross-cultural and indigenous culture courses. There is a department that provides interpretation services and does language research. Another department publishes books about Aboriginal people, Aboriginal languages and Aboriginal culture. There is also an arts program to teach art styles and art stories and an extensive library containing books and tapes about Aboriginal history and culture that are available to anyone who participates in an IAD program. All IAD programs have a strong indigenous cultural emphasis, so frequently there are young and old people in the same class which enhances this component.

Robyn had said she was interested in moving with us to Alice Springs, but I didn't want her to rush into such a big change unless she checked it out first and knew it was right for her. About a month after TJ and I had settled in our new home, Robyn came out for a visit and she really liked the country. She also met some of my extended family and they liked her and made her feel comfortable. She decided to make the move. She hitched a trailer onto her car and drove to Adelaide. I took a bus there to meet her so I could accompany her on the long hot stretch between Adelaide and Alice Springs. Some of the family still laugh about the big trailer Robyn was pulling behind her little car when we drove into Alice Springs. When Robyn arrived, TJ and I moved to a larger house so the three of us could live together.

TJ attended school and began playing sports again. It wasn't long before he was winning awards in rugby because he was such a good player. He also enjoyed being with his big extended family, but unfortunately his relatives liked to party and it was easy for TJ to get caught up in that lifestyle. This ended up causing him a lot of problems. Robyn and I began singing together at charity shows and everyone we sang for seemed to like what they heard.

One of the best things Robyn brought into my life was her interest in spirituality beyond the Christian tradition. The aspect of spirituality that she introduced me to was quite different from the gloom and doom of the Christian teachings that I had been brought up with on the mission. Robyn had a sense of appreciation for the smallest things in life that even I myself would miss. She could bring out details of the beauty in little things in her artwork. Very early during our first visit to Alice, I took her for a drive on the western route along the Macdonnell Ranges, and at one point she asked me to stop; she got out and just sat on the ground. I was surprised at how sensitive she was compared to the other white people I had driven on the same route. I was impressed that she set aside a period at the end of each day for meditation and would never let that go. I tried to learn to meditate but I just wasn't successful at it. That lack of success directed me back to my own spiritual ways and the beliefs that came from my own people. It helped me to clarify my spiritual beliefs.

Robyn believed in women's rights and got involved in other teachings that I didn't understand, but I'm used to women doing 'women's business' and men doing 'men's business'. Anything she did in this way I just considered 'women's business' and it didn't worry me. The only aspect of women's rights which I never did understand was its encouragement of a simmering anger and grudge against all men. I never could understand how you could be spiritual, on the one hand, and hang on to a sense of anger and grievance on the other.

From late 1994 until mid–1999 when I retired, I taught Aboriginal cultural awareness programs for IAD. These programs addressed living off the land, traditional culture, artefacts, songs, dance, bush tucker, tracking and hunting, and kinship relationships. I also taught the history of Aboriginal people and used my story songs to emphasise the impact of what we experienced at the hands of the colonisers. This always evoked an emotional response.

Sometimes I was asked to work with a group out in the bush so I could provide longer and more in-depth programs. I enjoyed doing this because it was different from the daily routine and I got to know a lot of interesting people this way. I was also often called upon to travel with groups as their cultural presenter. One of the groups that I have had a long-standing relationship with is the Healing Touch organisation. They train medical professionals all over the world to do their unique method of energy healing. As the trainers travel from place to place to teach, they bring with them other members of the organisation who are interested in learning about the healing methods of indigenous cultures. They regularly do an exchange of healing techniques with the Maori healers in New Zealand and the Aboriginal healers (*ngangkaries*) whom I introduced to them.

I quickly became involved with this group in a personal way because I could see that their natural way of healing is very much like the way our healers scan the body for heat and cold and then massage affected areas to relieve symptoms. I have also conducted programs for the employees of the Correctional Service, who work in the prisons, because the majority of jail inmates in Alice Springs are Aboriginal people. And through IAD, I have given regular presentations for the Health Department, whose staff are mostly white people, but whose patients are largely Aboriginal people. I was also involved in teacher training in the public schools, so that teachers can have more effective communication with their Aboriginal students.

Since the Coalition government of John Howard took office in Canberra in 1996, money for Aboriginal organisations has become progressively scarce. One of the sad things about IAD is that the Northern Territory government doesn't effectively support this really important educational program. Since the 1970s, IAD has made a major contribution to society by educating both Aboriginal and non-Aboriginal people about our culture. It is important that this organisation continue to operate because it fulfils a very important function in the process of reconciliation.

I have always preferred working for Aboriginal organisations, and I have consistently maintained that the Australian government has an agenda that is bad for Aboriginal people. I believe that their system develops dependency because they have never trusted us to manage our own affairs, and they still don't. There is now an organisation called Aboriginal and Torres Strait Islander Commission (ATSIC) that is supposedly run by Aboriginal people, but the top person who controls the funding of this organisation is the white Minister for Aboriginal Affairs. Not all ministers have had good relationships with our community.

I'm not saying that our people are better at doing things, and I recognise that many of our organisations lack the sort of administrative and accounting skills that the very strict rules of accountability for the expenditure of government funds requires. I recognise that there are good and bad in every society and every culture. However, some of our communities have demonstrated that they can manage their own affairs very well. More and more of our people are being educated at institutions like IAD, so they understand the effects of cultural differences and can work effectively in any situation. Only when we are given unfettered opportunities for total self-management will I feel that our culture is getting the respect it deserves.

Robyn and I had been together for about four years when she told me she wanted to move into her own place so that we could sort things out in our relationship. I had to realise that it is actually very difficult for a non-Aboriginal person to take on the full extent of extended family obligations which characterise Aboriginal family life. I wasn't sure what Robyn meant by this, but accepted her desire to have her own place. In our way of thinking she will always still be 'wife' to me because she has become part of my wider family. Before our separation we toured America with the Healing Touch organisation. Rose Pere, a Maori woman from New Zealand, was also on the tour with her husband and daughter. Rose and I had previously worked together at a conference in New Zealand and had become good friends because of the similar way we relate to land and to people. A man from South Africa, a Cherokee elder from Tennessee, and about thirty or so members of Healing Touch from New Zealand and Australia who practised different forms of holistic healing were also on the tour.

We went to many cities and towns throughout America and Canada, giving workshops wherever we went. Robyn and I joined the group in Atlanta, Georgia. That first morning everyone on the tour gathered together in a circle. There didn't seem to be much feeling there so I suggested that we all move into a spiral, forming it from the outside and then tightening it as tight as we could before breaking it up at the outer edge. This helped bring us all together and we used this exercise in some of our other group sessions. We went from Atlanta to Tennessee and then travelled by bus and plane to other locations. I was surprised at how large the Healing Touch organisation was. As I talked to the people I met, they all seemed to share the philosophy that doing things for others was the reason we are on earth. They were looking for ways to strengthen their ability to give to other people.

I was surprised at how interested the American people were in indigenous cultures. Boulder was one of the places where we stayed for a longer time, because we gave a full week of presentations there. It was summer and we were so busy that we didn't have much time to explore the natural environment. From Boulder, our group flew to Vancouver, British Columbia, in Canada. When we got off the plane I saw a sign advertising an Aborigines' Day, and it was happening the weekend we were there. I thought it would be like our NAIDOC Celebration Day, so I was very excited about attending. It turned out that this was a celebration of the local indigenous Canadians. We missed the main activities, but Robyn and I attended one gathering that was mostly singing and dancing. There was a woman telling her story through poems and talking, and her story was the same as the story of our Stolen Generations. After that there was a very powerful circle dance where at least six men beat on a huge drum and women joined them in the singing of chants. Everyone came together in the dance.

During this tour I met Aruna Byers, an American women from Boulder who was interested in promoting indigenous teachings. She asked if I would be interested in visiting Boulder again to give workshops and talk about Aboriginal culture in local schools. Six months after returning to Alice Springs, I decided to take up Aruna's offer. I was interested to see if her organisation was like the Institute for Aboriginal Development in Alice Springs, in the way it worked with native American people. I was very tired when I first arrived in Boulder and for the first week all I wanted to do was sleep. As the fog started to lift, though, I began doing promotional things and met many friendly people. They arranged for me to do several public workshops and visit a lot of elementary schools where the students were studying about Australian Aboriginal culture. I also spent a day at the University of Colorado in Fort Collins where I met quite a few indigenous Americans. I felt that same kind of connectedness with them that I have experienced with indigenous people in other parts of the world. They invited me to participate in a pow-wow gathering, so towards the end of my visit Aruna and I did just that.

Aruna volunteered to assist me with writing a book. We began this work while I was in America, staying at her house. When I got back to Australia, I was successful in gaining a grant from the Australia Council for 'new works' by Aboriginal writers. Aruna came out to Australia and I was able to pay her to continue her work with the book. Over six months, during which time she had to make several overseas visits, Aruna was able to produce a draft of my story. This involved many hours of taping and transcribing, reading documents and visiting my country in Arnhem Land. Without her help this book would never have been written.

After Aruna left, the more I thought about it, the more I realised that this first draft lacked an important element. It did not really enable me to share the Aboriginal spiritual philosophy which has informed my life and allowed me to survive the legacy of being a member of the Stolen Generations. One of the wonderful things about the spiritual path is that, when we are faced with this sort of challenge, the right person will often appear to help. In 1999, while participating in the Aboriginal Philosophy Farm program at Linga Longa near Port Macquarie, I met Barbara Lepani. We had many conversations about Aboriginal spirituality, and as a result of this I asked her to help me with my book. I found a literary agent who confirmed my feelings that I should re-write the manuscript, weaving the story of Aboriginal spirituality like a snake through my life's journey. When my agent used this image of the snake, I knew without a doubt that I wanted to work with her; we both asked Barbara to help me, and she agreed.

Wave Love to the Wind

All the clouds are going by
Way up there across the sky
And the wind is moving on
All the trees wave to the wind.

Chorus
Wave, wave to the wind,
Wave, wave love to the wind.

All the birds are flying by,
Flying by from tree to tree.
Pretty flowers everywhere
They all wave love to the wind.

All the bees and butterflies
Dancing there across the skies,
And the wind is moving on,
They all wave love to the wind.

Little children, you're so tired,
Now it's time to go to sleep.
Go to sleep and dream of love,
Wake up waving to the wind.

Wave, wave love to the wind.
The wind of love is everywhere.
Wave, wave love to the wind.
The wind of love is everywhere.

Healing and Wellbeing

Traditionally, Aboriginal people were strong, lean and agile. We walked long distances across country, and we learned to control our hunger and thirst in order to fit in with the conditions of the land and the seasons. Our family structure was very strong as this was our basic survival unit. We felt secure in the vast landscape of Australia, whether that was the desert, where I come from, the tropics, where I grew up, or down in the south where I wrote my story. We lived without clothes, our bodies naked to the elements. Even in Tasmania where snow and ice cover the hills in winter, our people lived this way. We did not die of pneumonia, we did not get influenza or suffer head colds.

Probably it is true that when we were small babies, if we weren't strong, we may not have survived. But barring accidents with fire, or breaking our limbs when moving across country, our only other source of danger was fighting with one another, or being exposed to poisonous snakes and spiders and, in saltwater country, the crocodiles and sharks. We had our own healing methods, using both the spiritual powers of special healers, which my people call *ngangkaries*, and the many natural herbs from which we could make ointments and poultices. Our women held the Law of child bearing, and they supported one another in the mysteries and difficulties of this experience.

I can remember my own life as a child among the Yankunytjat-jara. Living this life out in the open, and curled up with my mothers around the campfire at night, did not feel like poverty. All my senses were so alive. Each day, my mothers would take me to examine the small trails in the sand left by little creatures in the night. They would interpret their tracks to me, talking about them as members of our family. Where two trails came together, they would exclaim, 'Look there, that little fellow got into a fight with that big one. Him finished now. Him tucker for that other one. Ah! poor little lizard.' So each morning, examining the ground for tracks would be an exciting adventure. At the same time I learned how to detect the tracks of those lizards which I, as a small boy, could catch. And so that became even more exciting.

Not only was I taught to really open my eyes this way, but I was also taught how to hear. My mothers would help me tell the differ-ence between various noises in the grass or among the leaves, and identify these with different animals, birds or insects. Each day we moved across the country, so our life was very active. We also had to know about how to prepare the food, as some food could be poi-sonous if you did not prepare it properly. I remember there was one bush plum that looked much like another variety except that variety had thorns. Yet it was the ones with the thorns which were the safe ones to eat. Sometimes just the shade of the purple of a desert flower will tell us whether something is good or bad food, for example the wild tomato.

Later, when I was growing up on Croker Island, I continued to live this healthy life. The land itself was healthy. All the fruit came in season and the seasons came when they were expected. It was never affected by things like pollution and erosion which people worry about today. We only ever took what we needed. To live this way requires a very clear mind, and a very strong and agile body. You need a detailed knowledge of the seasons, the country and the behaviour of the animals and plants which you are seeking.

For instance, say I decided to hunt possums, those little creatures who hang around houses and feed on scraps. They are really good food. I would have to remember that the best time to hunt them was not at night when they are alert and feeding, but during the day when they are sleeping. Then I would have to know the sort of trees which have hollow logs where I can expect to find them asleep, and to find the really fresh scratch marks that tell me they are there. Then I would have to find a way of climbing up that tree to that place, and listen to find out whether there is a possum there. I would have to be really quick, because possums might be small but they have very sharp claws which can cause a lot of damage. So I would need to have someone with me, so that I could quickly grab the possum and throw it down to him. This way of living was also full of companionship.

Remember the story that I told about going hunting with one of my *boonyis* (fathers) on the weekends when I could get away from the mission? He would tell me, 'Come down as early as you can.' By that he meant at sunrise. He would be ready when I got there and, together with his wife and two daughters who were around the same age as me, we would walk twelve to sixteen kilometres away to the swamplands. We hunted with a shotgun, but in those days it was very difficult to get bullets, so we would have about four precious cartridges. We would take these, with some water and food which we would share between us. When we got to the swamplands, which are usually huge, we would choose a site where the last bit of water was still lying on the ground, before the dry season also swallowed that up. *Boonyi* knew the geese would be there, and sure enough they were there in their hundreds. We picked a spot to set up camp, and made a fire and had some billy tea. Then *Boonyi* and I set off to catch the geese, while the girls and their mother looked for bush honey or long-necked turtles.

Boonyi stalked up to the birds. At first we walked, then as we got closer we crouched, and finally we were slithering on our stomachs. The geese were floating on water which was only about a metre deep, with their necks down, feeding. *Boonyi* got some reed grass and put it on his head; I copied him and followed him. As we got closer he placed the shotgun on his back, holding it with his neck at the side. At a certain point he signalled me to stop, by cupping his hand. Then he went on, getting so close he could almost touch them. Then slowly he took the gun and sat up. The geese looked up, and then he fired the gun. He must have got about twelve geese. My job was to run and get those that were wounded but not dead, to make sure they did not get away. Then we gathered up our kill and took them back to the camp. All of us then helped to pluck them down to their tiny downy feathers. Then *Boonyi* singed these hairs over the fire, before taking the geese and slitting them open. The liver, heart, kidneys and small wing tips were put to one side to cook for a quick feed. Meanwhile the main goose was slit open and cooked.

I remember we couldn't settle down at night because the mosquitoes were so bad. So we gathered up all our possessions, together with the cooked geese, and we walked about two kilometres to the sandy beach where the ocean breeze would keep the mosquitoes away. The next morning, after some food and tea, we set off to walk back to the mission.

I learned to be a good hunter. We would go spear fishing off the reef. We were so much at home in these waters that we knew how to be with the fish. I can remember as I was about to get a crayfish, a big shark came up and nudged me, as if to say, 'Hey! I want that one, leave it alone for me.' I do not remember being afraid of the sharks. We just saw them as competitors for our catch. And it was the same with crocodiles. We knew to be alert and look around, and we knew what the feeding habits of crocodiles were, so we knew not to go into the water at sunset because this would be like offering yourself as food. I also remember hunting pigs. On one occasion I could not get the dogs because someone else was using them for another purpose, so I went without them. I discovered that my sense of smell was so good that I could track the pigs as well as the dogs could. I followed that scent and sure enough I found the pigs. I didn't even have to look for the tracks on the ground.

To live this way was to be healthy. Our spirits were also alive with the excitement of using our minds and bodies in this way to find food for ourselves and our families. We never saw the animals we hunted as enemies. We were taught to see the whole of creation as one family, and in that family there was the giving and taking of life for survival. But this giving and taking was always done with love. We loved those animals we tracked and ate. It was so gentle to be this way with country. I think the only time I was every angry when I killed was when I went hunting for that crocodile, Old Peg Leg, who took my mare. Even then I did not take out my anger on all crocodiles. I only went after the very one which I knew had taken her. This gentleness of being at one with country with all your senses alive is, for me, the basis of wellbeing. This is health.

In response to questions about *kanyini* and the nature of unconditional love, I always like to tell a story of traditional family life in Arnhem Land, as it was told to me. A family may be out hunting all day on a land area where there are lots of crabs and oysters, and all the seafood you would want to get. In the times of year when the big tides are rising, the family would plan to leave before the tide rises very quickly and covers all the land where they are. But if they were caught by the rising tide, they would make a raft out of dead tree trunks, pandanus and paper bark, and tie it all together with vine. And the system they used for crossing these expanses of water was that they would gather in a V-shaped formation. The top hunters would go in front, with the other skilled hunters ranged on each side of the raft, with their spears at the ready to ward of the crocodiles and sharks, because there would be lots of them attracted to all the food on the raft. In the middle would be the women in a group, with their babies on the raft together with the food they had collected, and they would be walking and pushing the raft along. Behind these would be the dogs, coming ahead of the old people, because they knew that the crocs when they attacked would always come in and seize their prey from the rear. In principle they might hope that the dogs would be last, but the dogs would always move faster than the old people. But the old people were always prepared to risk their own lives to ensure the safety of others. I was always really overcome by this example of unconditional love, whenever they told it to me.

The potential for becoming an Aboriginal healer, a *ngangkari*, is recognised in quite small children, and they then receive special training from the *ngangkaries* to develop these qualities. *Ngangkaries* can be men or women. While *ngangkaries* use their powers for healing, there are others, known as sorcerers, who can use these same powers to cause sickness, usually as a form of punishment for some breach of the law in relationships between people.

I remember when my first wife, Amy, was affected by a very bad knee injury and the doctors told her she would need to have an operation in Darwin. While we were visiting her family at Aileron, one of the *ngangkaries* said he would have a look at it. One of the aunties spread a rug on the ground and Amy lay down. The *ngangkari* took a handkerchief from his pocket and spread its contents out on the ground. Then he put them back into the handkerchief and returned it to his pocket. Next he passed his hands all over Amy's body, but not touching her, just feeling the energy above her body. He said he could feel areas of hot and cold on her body. Then he asked her to turn over and he began to draw out something along her spine. I saw him spitting blood into the sand which he quickly covered over. After this, her turned her over and did the same thing along the front of her body. After about fifteen minutes, he told her she would be all right.

Amy was indeed completely cured. The doctors back in Darwin said they could not believe it and wished they could refer all their patients to this *ngangkari*. Another aunty of mine told me that *ngangkaries* can make healing medicine by crushing ochre and mixing it with oil, then singing healing powers into that mixture, which they give you to rub on your body. I myself have worked with faith healing and oils with my children, using the healing touch of mind, body and spirit. Perhaps had I grown up in traditional culture I might have become a *ngangkari* myself. I remember when I was travelling with the Healing Touch organisation in America, my friend Robyn became very listless and ill. None of the other healers were able to help her. Then the thought came to my mind that I could help. In my mind I travelled back to my country, back to Mutitjulu (Maggie Springs) the home of *wanampi* (Rainbow Serpent) and called on my ancestor, the *Kuniya*, to come and help me. I asked the people around me for some red earth or something that would serve as a connection. One girl gave me a red silk scarf. I visualised this scarf as the *Kuniya*, and with my mind I drew the *Kuniya* from that waterhole at Uluru, right across the ocean, then across the land in the United States and then into Robyn to heal her mind and spirit. After about fifteen minutes she sat up and said she was hungry. She seemed completely cured of whatever it was that had been affecting her.

When white people first came to Australia in 1788, their own knowledge of healing was very crude, but they brought with them very deadly diseases which almost wiped my people out. A Methodist missionary wrote in 1826:

> . . . *Civilisation has been the scourge of the natives; disease, crime, misery and death have, hitherto, been the sure attendants of our intercourse with them. Wherever we trace the steps of white population we discover the introduction of evil, the diminution of numbers, the marks of disease, the pressure of want, the physical and moral ruin of this people . . . It is a sad truth to assert that our prosperity has hitherto been their ruin, our increase, their destruction. The history of nearly forty years seals the veracity of this declaration.*[1]

The anthropologist W.H. Stanner noted that when the colony was founded the Aborigines probably numbered at least 300 000, but by 1939 had declined to about 50 000. Five-sixths of my people were wiped out in only 150 years.[2] He noted that most of the conquest of Australia, and thus most of the obliteration of the Aboriginal peoples, took place between 1830 and 1890, the period in which economic expansionism, land hunger and pioneering were at their strongest. Pastoralists mounted punitive expeditions against my people if they resorted to killing a sheep or bullock when they were driven by starvation, which had arisen only because they had been denied access to their traditional hunting and bush tucker resources. Even women and children were killed in these raids. They just treated us like a pack of hungry dingoes (wild native dogs), not people like themselves. As I mentioned earlier, my uncle was killed in this way at Uluru by the same policeman who took me, as a child, from my family. And on that same journey to my exile from my land and family, my aunty who accompanied me was a prisoner for eating from a stolen bullock. This happened all over Australia, particularly in the early days in New South Wales and Victoria, where today there are almost no traditional languages still spoken. Numerous photographs of my people from these times show us tied up and led by neck chains, in a line behind a camel, being taken off to white men's jails.

The white farmers and pastoralists also deliberately poisoned my people by leaving food out for us that was laced with strychnine, a common agricultural poison. We had no experience with such deadly things and were easily tricked through our hunger and confusion. As well as this, when we first encountered common European diseases like influenza, pneumonia, smallpox, polio and measles we had no resistance. Today we would liken this to biological warfare.

We Aboriginal people have grown up in a climate of relentless fear and aggression. The law was the weapon used by white people to wage this war of aggression. My people were so afraid of the Queensland police that those of us from the Northern Territory would never travel through Queensland on our way from the southern states to Darwin. Aboriginal people were regularly rounded up there by the police and charged with vagrancy or being disorderly. A huge proportion of my people have been in jail, and usually their initial offence was something quite minor. This continues in the present.

So not only did we have the initial fear and confusion of being pushed off our land, but we had the even deeper fear of knowing that we were hunted. Not only by racist individuals, in violation of the formal law, but by the law enforcers themselves. Added to this fear is our experience of having our children stolen from us, and being completely powerless to stop this, or of being one of those children ourselves and experiencing the inability of our parents to protect us. Imagine our feelings of complete abandonment. It was normal practice for the government to tell such children that their parents were either dead or did not want them. To ensure that contact was difficult, it was also regular practice to remove us far from our original place. Thus, although I was born in the desert, I grew up 2000 kilometres away in Arnhem Land.

This fear still eats away at the heart of Aboriginal people. We have become strangers in our own land, yet this land is our mother. Even today, although white people have very powerful medicines and can perform very complicated surgery, there is a big debate about health and wellbeing. It is one thing to cure a disease. It is quite another matter to create wellbeing. As my people tried to explain to the politicians in Canberra:

> . . . Aboriginal children are born of women but conceived of a spiritual source whose font is the land. And to them the land has two kinds of landscapes; one is physical, which all human beings can view. The other is spiritual, which only they can see. For Aboriginal people there is only one way to own land and that is to be conceived of it. Land is parent . . . Aboriginal social existence and conflict with white society, nationally and internationally . . . is based on the unrelinquished will of Aboriginal people to maintain identity, relationship to land and refusal to accept the interference of white institutions in their lives at national and community levels.[3]

I have never trained as a health worker, but when I first went to Darwin I worked in a hospital, and I saw how white people go about healing. Although they pay a great deal of attention to cleanliness and medicines, they often seem to be insensitive to the spiritual side of healing. They do not hesitate to wake a person up who is sleeping, yet for an Aboriginal person this is quite a violent intrusion into their spirit and is especially dangerous if they are ill. For a healer to shout at a person in an aggressive tone, or to talk about them to someone else as if they are not there, is truly shocking behaviour for us.

Everybody knows that in modern Australia Aboriginal people suffer from many health problems. It is said that our health status is worse than that of many so-called Third World nations. Government health statistics show that the death rate for Aboriginal and Torres Strait Islander people, for different ages, is three times that for other Australians and much higher again for many preventable causes of death. For example: our death rate from infections of the kidney is twenty-three times higher, from tuberculosis it is sixteen times higher, from diabetes, twelve to seventeen times higher, from pneumonia, ten times higher and from alcohol-related deaths, eleven times higher. An Aboriginal person is ten times more likely to suffer from blindness, especially from trachoma and blindness as a complication of diabetes, yet both of these conditions are preventable in modern society. I am lucky. I too could have been blinded by trachoma, and for many years now I have had to live with diabetes. As a result of this pattern of ill health, life expectancy for Aboriginal men at birth is only fifty-seven years, and for our women sixty-two years, the same sort of life expectancy found in very economically disadvantaged countries. For white Australians, life expectancy is near to eighty years.

Despite many government initiatives, Aboriginal people do not benefit from the same level of health care as white Australians. Recent statistics show that on a per-person basis, expenditure on health benefits for Aboriginal people under our national health insurance system, Medicare, was only twenty-seven per cent of the average for non-Aboriginal people, and only twenty-two per cent for prescribed drugs under the Pharmaceutical Benefits Scheme.

How can this be? As countless governments in Australia have

discovered, improving Aboriginal health is not just a matter of primary health care, of giving us more doctors, nurses and medicines. Government reports indicate that they do recognise that attention needs to be given to environmental health services such as sewerage and water supply, removing waste, improving transport links and building better, less crowded, housing. However these are all physical things. Many of our health problems are also related to our lifestyle, particularly to the psychological and physical affects of white colonisation and dispossession, and these are much more difficult to overcome.

We Aboriginal people overwhelmingly live in a situation of high stress and chronic depression. We have become so used to living with this stress that we regard it as normal, yet deep inside us there is still a quiet murmur, a distant memory of another way. White people seem to enjoy stress. Yet when you get talking with them, few of them really seem to be happy. They also long for another way. In fact, you could almost say this is the predominant disease of modern society.

Not only do Aboriginal people suffer the feelings of failure and helplessness as a result of high unemployment and all the complex rules of accountability in the modern welfare system, they are also stranded in boredom. Our people are not immune to the lures of material goods. Across this country, even in the outback, you can walk into an Aboriginal house and the television will be on all day. For our people, it gives the illusion of company, of community life, and of course it is a distraction from boredom. But we are also susceptible to advertising, to feeling that want for all the wonderful electronic and other goods we see on television. We see also the lifestyle of luxury that so many white people seem to have, but we never see how we can gain access to these goods or lifestyle. This leaves us with a lingering feeling of dissatisfaction and frustration which eats away at our appreciation of what we do have.

One of the most terrible results of the welfare system is that it has deepened our sense of dependence and institutionalisation.

Once we were proud, independent hunters, filled with the sense of the grandeur of our country and its Dreaming tracks and stories of the *tjukurrpa*. Now we sit around, too many of us dependent on welfare handouts from a largely hostile government and society, and all too often we plunge into depression, prey to all sorts of negativities.

To recover our wellbeing, we have to pay attention to all four dimensions of our being: mind, body, spirit and land. To do this we must rediscover the philosophy of *kanyini*, the web of relationships based on love and responsibility which connects us to one another and all things in our world. I have noticed that people of strong faith, such as practising Christians, generally experience a much higher level of health and wellbeing. This is because they live their lives strengthened by their connection to the love of God, and the message of Jesus, that they should serve God by serving others. I have found, in my life, that to serve the needs of others is a very good recipe for one's own health.

When I worked with non-Aboriginal health workers, I used to advise them that when they consult with Aboriginal people, they have to approach the matter sideways. You cannot just ask someone about their illness. First you must ask them about country, because this is their deepest connection. Then you ask them about family, because this is the next level of connection. Only after this can you, almost casually, ask them why they have come to see you this time. Our people pay particular attention to non-verbal signals. We can feel the sort of feelings which people have towards us, whether they are kind or full of negativity, whether they are impatient or they really have time for us. In our culture, you do not look at people directly in the eye, especially with hard eyes. Hard eyes are very aggressive. When you are aggressive you show this hard eye. But when you are loving, your eyes are soft. So, if we are sick, if the people treating us show hard, abrupt actions or harsh words or hard eyes, this prevents us from getting better. Hard eyes bring in fear. The biggest barrier for all of us getting on with one another is fear.

We cannot openly love one another because of fear. This fear can come from many sources, from our experiences with our parents, or from our childhood, like the one I have shared with you in my story. But also I have come to realise that even among white people there are many with this fear. They may not have had as difficult a life as Aboriginal people, but still they carry fear. I think this is because white culture does not provide people with much personal support in terms of family. People feel very much on their own. When we retain these fears, it prevents us being open, and at ease, yet this is essential to wellbeing.

It's Time

We are laying our own foundation
For our children to build on.
Based on all our traditions
So the culture will be strong.
Getting strength from one another,
From our sisters and our brothers,
From our fathers and our mothers,
Let's be proud of who we are.

Chorus
It's time to rearrange our way of thinking.
It's time for you and I to make a stand.
Time could pass us by
If we don't get up and try,
This time let's march together while we can.

We should all become one nation
If our culture is to grow.
And we need to teach our children
What the white man doesn't know.
Each other's problems bearing,
Getting strength from always sharing,
Giving strength from always caring,
Let's remember who we are.

Chorus

Arrernte, Luritja, and Warlpiri,
Pitjantjatjara, Anmatyerre and the rest.
All tribes should come together
From all parts of this great land.
Getting strength from one another,
From our sisters and our brothers,
From our fathers and our mothers,
Let's be proud of who we are.

Kurunpa

life-force, the living energy of
relationships

Many people say what is unique about Aboriginal culture is that it is very spiritual. I think by this they mean that we do not separate out the spiritual from our world. We call this idea of spirit, *kurunpa*. By spirit we mean the life-force, the energy of all living objects, including us as people, which spreads out from all things. It is a very strong, feeling energy. Spirit does not mean, in this sense, just ghosts or spirit figures like the *mimi* spirits we have up in Arnhem Land.

Kurunpa is the living energy of the relationships between things. The life-force is in the now, that which connects us to all forms of life. You can see it and feel it. In some people it is very powerful, while in other people it can be very weak. It is usually weak in people who are very sick, particularly on a mental or spiritual level. *Kurunpa* is life. It is reality, not a mystery. Everything has got that as its base. So this unites us, whether we judge something to be good or bad. That judgement comes from us living beings in terms of how it affects us, but spirit is beyond that. From the point of view of spirit, everything exists for its own purpose, it is already perfect that way. It is only our judgement which creates the sense of good or bad, not the living energy itself.

In my childhood, in camp life, and even in Alice Springs, I

remember how scared I was even of the shadow of the medicine man. The field of energy which was around these men, their spirit, was so powerful. So we avoided even touching their shadow, which was a boundary of that energy. One of the ceremonies of passing on this spiritual energy was the way the elders would bless us with the palms of their hands, after they had gathered their own life-force through their sweat under their armpits. They would do this, then pass their hands over us, and we would feel the blessing of their life-force coming into us. I have seen people also do this with small babies. When my daughter, Ituma, was born, we took her around to visit my first wife, Amy. Amy had some family members with her, and I remember that after Amy kissed and hugged the baby, she passed it to her cousin and her cousin did this same thing. As well as gently massaging its joints, she took her life-force through the sweat under her armpits with her hands, and she then passed this over the baby. I think this is similar to the way we can use water to sanctify things. But water is not us, so it is not as powerful as actually drawing the water from our own bodies which are the containers of our life-force, our spirit.

This is the way my uncles and my grandfather blessed me, when they met me. I remember that vividly from the time I first met my grandfather, when I rediscovered my Yankunytjatjara family and country. In this way we pass on spiritual energies and protective powers, and create strong spiritual bonds between us. I never really paid great attention to this, because it was just part of the way we lived with one another. It wasn't talked about or explained. So it is only now, when I reflect on the question, that I see the full importance of this practice.

To live, you have to continually replenish your spirit. You have to feed it through other spirits in everything around you. You have a relationship of giving and taking with each of the spiritual beings that live on the same land with you. And this is done through ceremony, as a teaching tool to identify the spiritual places or home bases.

When you take from anything that is in your home base, for whatever reason, whether it is a tree branch, flowers or roots, to make tools or the foods for survival, you develop the sense of appreciation of the uniformity of the spiritual connection of giving to each other, because it is the action of caring for each other. It is the action of sharing with each other. When the ceremony is being performed you are learning how to have this appreciation for everything else that is out there. It may be really simple. You learn to identify foods to live by, how to follow tracks in order to hunt, how to listen, to see the contours of country so that you will know where the water may be. You learn what sort of food sources belong to what sort of country in the whole of the landscape, and in which seasons.

These were also spiritual teachings, not just practical. It is hard for me to separate the practical from the spiritual. I can't do it in my mind. It is all one. It makes me very confused to try to fragment it into separate ideas. It just doesn't make sense.

Many people who have worked with Aboriginal people in traditional areas have commented on our secret life, the life of ceremonial knowledge. This is our world of the *tjukurrpa* where we are brought in touch with our place in the universe, and with the things of the past, present and future that are not visible to our ordinary eye. This is the world we enter when we invoke the ancestral beings through song and dance so that it transforms our being and makes us one with country. As part of these secret ceremonies we have special paintings and designs which we paint on our bodies, and we have sacred objects (*tjurungas*) which are the Law in symbolic form. It occurs to me that these might be like the tablets of Moses. *Tjurungas* are very powerful, and are only kept by men with the highest qualities of ceremonial knowledge. To hold a *tjurunga* is like holding the very power of creation. Thus they were very important for healing and bringing us in touch with the *tjukurrpa* itself. Our ceremonies are of different types. Some are for initiation, marking our passage from boy or girl to adult. Others are associated with our relationship with our totemic group, and others are associated with rituals of increase.

As part of the *tjukurrpa*, there are special sacred sites where, traditionally, we performed increase ceremonies. Such sites would generally be at the beginning or the end of a Dreaming track, and they act as a channel for the continued release of the creative energies of the *tjukurrpa*, the Dreaming. Once I was with the elders in Arnhem Land, back in the 1960s, when the wet season had failed and everyone was worried about the long-necked turtles and the barramundi. It had already seemed, in the year before, as if they were not breeding properly. With the drought there was a danger that they might disappear, and this would spell disaster for our traditional food sources. My brothers decided we should do the ceremony for country at Obiri, the rock painting gallery in Kakadu. To do this ceremony, they took the end branches of a certain tree, and we went around the paintings on the rock that referred to the species that were in decline, and a song was sung to each, followed by wiping over it with these special branches. Other practices might involve making powder by grinding up ochre into a dust. After the singing and ceremony, this dust would be pushed into the four directions using the special new shoots of a particular tree.

Land is seen as a family member. It is like when you have a family group and you are all together and happy in that togetherness. Then one family member will go, and there will be an absence, and this will create a break in the family circle. Because of this absence, the energy in the group is lessened. For example, if there were a group of mothers who were responsible for collecting particular foods then, if just one of the mothers went away, the others have to work harder or they would eat less. So it is like this with ancestral story tracks. When you connect with the consciousness of the *tjukurrpa* through the stories, songs, dances and paintings of ceremony, then that spirit will come there and re-energise everyone who is there. Then you get the same joy as if one of our family members came back and contributed to the group wellbeing through getting enough food and being well fed.

These ancestral spirits, in the form of that consciousness, can still communicate with our elders and tell us whether we are doing the ceremonies properly. You can be with our elders when they are just talking to country this way. It is so beautiful to be around. You can see all the country, the rocks, the trees and even animals like a wallaby, just listening to this conversation, as the old man just talks to them there.

You can identify if this presence of ancestral energy, enlivening the land, is there strongly, or if it has become weak. Quite often it becomes weak through development, because it is in the natural state that the land has this spiritual power. Recently I went sailing on Sydney Harbour with my friend David Roberts. As we passed under the bridge I was suddenly conscious of two strongly contrasting forms of energy. On the northern side, where there is still plenty of natural bushland, I could feel the land joyful and alive, especially where there was lots of greenery. But on the southern side, where the city has been established, with all its highrise commercial building, I felt a terrible sadness. As I looked over to the city, it was like looking at the tombstones of a great graveyard. The land's energy had been buried. It is as if its spirit has been crushed, as if there was only one frail old family member left, instead of a whole campfire of healthy people, laughing and singing. Then I thought of all the people who come and work here, or even live here. I realised they would feel a terrible sense of lack that they could never fill. Any activity will be used to fill the absence of this relationship that once kept that country alive.

My mind went back to when I, too, had caught a ferry from Balmain to an office in this area. Although my office had wonderful views of the harbour, I had never really enjoyed being there. At the time perhaps I simply attributed this to feeling a bit bored in an office environment, compared to my previous life up in Arnhem Land, mapping sacred sites and talking with the elders. But now it occurred to me that it was probably also this deeper energy which ran right through that area.

Totem is the link between the spiritual and the physical through land. It is another line of relationship in our family system. We have totems in birds, animals, trees, places. We Yankunytjatjara people have different groups of totems. I belong to the *Mala*, the little wallaby from Uluru. *Malu*, the kangaroo, holds a very strong sacred link across our land, but I can't talk about that one because it is secret men's business.

I would have become part of the *Mala* totemic group because someone in my family would have noticed this relationship at my birth, or at some stage during my conception. It can come through how you feel the presence of something during the pregnancy. It can come through a dream, through thoughts, through the feeling of a presence, or through the behaviour of that totemic thing itself.

In Alice Springs there are two major totemic groups associated with the *alcheringa* (*tjukurrpa*) of the Arrente people. If you stand on Anzac Hill and look to the Heavitree Gap, on one side is the Caterpillar (*Yeperenye*) Dreaming, and on the other side is the Dog (*Ngoilya*) Dreaming. Anyone who is conceived or born in these areas takes on one of these totems. There are many sites as you go out around Alice Springs. They are almost like suburbs; some cover a small area and others are quite large, and these totemic groupings connect us with each other as people.

The taboos associated with the totem, in my system, applied during the breeding time which goes from mating, birthing to rearing. At this time you could not hunt or eat your totem. So you could be offered this food, but you would just say no thank you. People usually don't ask you further, they know. At other times this rule was not so strict. I also acknowledge that there are parts of my traditional culture which, in today's conditions, might serve no purpose and therefore should be let go. We have some harsh Laws, particularly around the rights of women in certain situations. I don't know why we had them, but from what I have studied in other cultures, they seem to have been quite common. For instance in the time of Jesus they had that rule about stoning to death a woman found committing adultery. But there did not seem to be any punishment for the man involved. So, Aboriginal culture, like all other cultures, should let go of any of these ideas that give men more rights than women. This is not part of our spirituality, as such.

Because I was stolen at a young age and taken away, the white system tried to being me up as Christian. At first my relationship with Christianity was confused with all my feelings about the behaviour of the missionaries on Croker Island, and the power they had over my life. At best, Christianity appeared to be just pleasant stories that I had read to me when I went to sleep. But then when I entered puberty and started to spend more time with my Iwaidja elders, I started to question things more. Like most boys, I also got into trouble from time to time for breaking rules, and we had plenty of them. One time when I had a very severe beating with a cane, I was hit behind the knee bone and was semi-paralysed. From my viewpoint I could not understand the severity of the beating. I don't remember the cause of the incident. The worst thing I can remember doing was when I was practising spear throwing with some other boys and we were using tools, rather than bush reeds. The aim was to be able to duck at the last moment to avoid the spear, and my opponent wasn't quick enough and the tool cut the side of his leg. I couldn't see why I was so severely punished, as it was a two-way game. However, it could equally have been other things like having sex with a girl, stealing fruit from the garden, or even swearing.

I was hurting physically and spiritually because I was feeling the unfairness. I went down to this beautiful tree with yellow flowers. As I sat with that tree I felt the really strong energy of that tree as if it were a mother or father, full of caring, of *kanyini*. It was so strong that I went up to it and put its leaves against my face and enjoyed a wonderful feeling of solace, of unconditional love. I started telling it all my story and then went away at peace with myself. I thought that this must be what old Sandy, the Iwaidja elder, was talking about when he was telling me how the trees are our family, and how everything is spirit. They care for us, so we must learn how to care for them. It was that incident that opened me up to the fullness of what Sandy had been telling me. I realised that there was something more to spirituality than what the missionaries were telling us.

When I started to put the teachings of Jesus on love, caring and the brotherhood of man into that context, the Christian teachings started to have a very strong meaning for me. I loved the stories about when Jesus stood up for people who were being put down by others. There is one story where the disciples are pushing the noisy children out of the way as they come to him, and Jesus tells them not to do this, and leans down and puts a child on his knee, and says, 'This one is the greatest in the kingdom of God.' I remember that when I went to public Aboriginal cultural gatherings, I would ask my children to see if they could identify the senior ceremonial leader there. They were always wrong, because they would look for the person who stood up and made announcements, or the person who had the best clothes, or the person who seemed to throw their weight around. Our elders always hide themselves in ordinariness. You have to be really observant to see who it is that people look to for advice. It is just a look and a subtle movement of the eye or hand.

Again and again, Jesus would try to teach people to question their assumptions. There is the story of the men who want to stone a woman to death for committing adultery. The men bring her before Jesus, but he just bends down, clears the earth with his hand, and writes, 'Let he who is without sin cast the first stone.' This story really affected me. It so reminded me of old Sandy, because when he taught me stories about country, he too would reach out with his hand and level the ground in order to draw things in the sand. For me he was a living expression of Jesus. I completely rejected the missionaries' viewpoint that we Christians were superior to the tribal people whose ideas were evil. I knew better.

I have always strongly believed that the spiritual path is one of action. If there is no relationship between people's ideas and the words they speak, and their actions, then it is all *gammon*, it is all without meaning. Although many of my childhood friends from the mission days have turned their backs on Christianity, I still call myself a Christian. I have always liked the sense of belonging to the wider Christian family. This gave me a way to make even white people part of my family system. I have also noticed that whenever you get involved in community life, it is often the practising Christians who do most of the work, as they put their beliefs into action. Even today it is Christian people who are the longest stayers in political struggles such as reconciliation and land rights.

When I was really confused about the relationship between Christianity and Aboriginal spirituality, I was lucky enough to come across the writings of Edgar Cayce, who was known as the sleeping prophet, who told me how God exists in all life forms. In the late 1960s, when I was working for the Mission in Darwin, I would go to the library and search for literature which talks about psychic spirituality. I found the book *There is a River*, the story of Edgar Cayce, written by Thomas Sugrue. During the 1920s and 1930s, Cayce was one of the world's most notable clairvoyants and mystics; he practised medical diagnosis by clairvoyance for forty-three years. His interest in psychic things was very close to the teachings I had received from my elders. I was so overjoyed to find a white man saying these things that his words helped me build a bridge between Christianity and Aboriginal spirituality.

Recently I was travelling on a train from the Blue Mountains down to Sydney. Just two trains before mine there had been a terrible accident when the Blue Mountains train had crashed into the back of a country train that was waiting at a signal for clearance. Five people were killed and many, many people were injured. Immediately I could feel the pain of the suffering of those people and I prayed for them and their families. This feeling of connection with the suffering of these people brought me down to the space of what we call *kunya*, the deep sorrow of sorry business that is part of our ceremonial system in Central Australia. To live this way is a commitment to being emotionally open. Many people don't understand this open loving, so I have to be careful not to overwhelm people with this attitude. Even in my Christian community, many people are cautious and guarded at first, and it is only slowly that they will open up. You can feel their fear, and you have to respect this. Fear starts from the thinking in our minds. We need to overcome this with good thoughts, which then create good feelings in our minds which we can extend out to others.

Once you have a link with nature, all nature steps in to help you. With that kind of power against one negative, you can usually transform a situation. You have to see that all happening; it is created through the mind. For instance, recently I was travelling with friends in Arnhem Land. The wife of one couple was in her early pregnancy. Although they knew this, they decided to come with us to another part of Arnhem Land, driving on roads which were badly corrugated. As we drove along these roads it was jarring, but slowing down made it worse, not better. On the way back, the husband became agitated, and because of this agitation he was becoming very aggressive. He demanded that we slow down, and finally that his wife walk back, until he realised that it was over twenty kilometres in the heat. He completely rejected our advice and experience of how to drive on those roads, accusing us of not caring about his wife.

I had been feeling his angry, frustrated thoughts for some days, and by now it was beginning to affect everyone around us. It was like a spiritual pollution. My brother on whose land we were camped could feel it, the trees could feel it, the ocean could feel it. So I explained this to his wife, because she was the link. He was very upset about this and came over to talk with me. I could see his suffering, and that this came from trying to live his wife's pregnancy for her, as if he was the one who was pregnant. I explained to him that he couldn't do this. This was women's business. All he could do was love her. Then, with my mind I reached out to the trees, the fish, the crocodiles, the turtles and the ocean and asked them to help me take his load from him. I told him he could also do this. He did not have to be alone: that only produced a terrible feeling of alienation, and all of us were then suffering. As he listened to this I could see a terrible burden was lifting from his heart, and after this conversation he was able to be much happier with everyone.

You can see how the mind affects everything. How we can cause terrible spiritual pollution with our emotions. That is why it is so important to control our emotions, to control the negatives and draw on the positives, and to stay in relationship with our environment and allow it to help us.

Because I was brought up by Christian missionaries, the only two spiritual traditions I have known anything about are Christianity and the Aboriginal spirituality, which I learned from my elders in Arnhem Land and in the Central Desert. However my eldest son, Allan, has told me that he has read about Tibetan Buddhism from the works of Chogyam Trungpa Rinpoche, a Tibetan lama who went to live in America after fleeing the Chinese invasion of Tibet. Allan said their spiritual ideas are much closer to our Aboriginal philosophy than Christianity is. I had a chance to explore this myself when I met Loppon Ngawang Dhamchoe, from the Sydney Sakya Centre, when he visited Alice Springs in late September 1998. Mutual friends told me he wanted to meet Aboriginal people and do a land blessing. So I made contact with the traditional elders, and I organised to pick him up and take him to the *Tjunpa* Dreaming (*tjukurrpa*) site. I introduced him to the grandmother tree, *Kami*, and to the grandfather tree, *Tjamu*. Both are huge white ghost gum trees, some distance from one another and giving off very different energies. Then I took him up to the natural amphitheatre with its teaching tree, up against the cliffs of the Rainbow Ridge. I also took him to the heart stone, a huge rock in the ground, a place where we go to release sadness about loved ones who have gone on. Then I took him to the three corkwood trees which form a triangle, and which we call the *tjukurrpa* place. I invited him to walk and feel where he wanted to perform his fire ceremony. Interestingly he chose the heart stone. Then, after he completed his fire offering ceremony, we walked up to a tree directly behind that, against the Rainbow Ridge, where we hung up his Buddhist flags.

After this we all had dinner together on the Rainbow walk path, just below the ridge. Later we talked about our two spiritual traditions. Loppon found many similarities between his tradition of loving kindness and compassion and our ideas of *kanyini*. When you work with *kanyini*, you learn not to retain emotions like anger any longer than is necessary. Anger can make us ill. Once that anger is in my mind it can poison my mind, my *kurunpa*. It can physically make me vulnerable to illness. My land can pick that up too and I can feel the energy questioning me and saying that there is no need for that anger. If I walk over to the trees and share why I am angry, it just lifts off. We can also learn to shift the anger. For example, in the old days, in the camp, if someone was angry he might bite something like a bag as his way of expressing this anger. Another way is to spear the image of that person on the ground, to move it from the person and let it go this way.

Loppon told me his own suffering had come from being a refugee in India, and seeing the suffering of his parents who lost their country and experienced the actions of the invading Chinese. Loppon thought his personal suffering was not as deep as mine because he did not lose the love of his own parents. But he told me, 'We often did not have enough to eat and there was always worry about survival. We were very poor and suffered from feeling a great lack in comparison with other children. Also during winter it was very cold and we did not have enough clothes so we couldn't sleep properly at night.' Loppon explained that because Tibetans are refugees they don't have the same rights as people who are ordinary citizens. Even now, although he is living in Australia which is a comfortable place to live, he still has a deep sadness because his people no longer have their own country, where they can express their own cultural values and customs freely. I thought about this. We Aboriginal people also lost our country to the invasion of the whites. But we did not flee to another country, we could not leave our land. It was all we knew; it was our mother, our heart, and link to *tjukurrpa*. However, many of us feel like strangers in our own land, particularly when we go to the towns and cities where we are a tiny minority of the population, and our values and culture have no real place.

One of the areas we immediately recognised as common to both our ways of looking at spirituality is the importance of understanding how absolutely everything is connected to everything else. From an Aboriginal viewpoint, all things around me are family members. So everything you do affects your family. For example if we look at the totem system which I discussed earlier, this expresses the strong spiritual and mental link to the land and other beings as your relatives. Through this we have our system of sacred sites which belong to the song lines of different species, and these are family members.

Aboriginal people have this idea of boomerang Law. Whatever you throw out will come back to you. If you throw out negative things from your mind, they will come back. This is a form of pollution that can affect things for quite a distance outwards. The same thing applies with the voice. An angry voice will create fear in a child, so this pollutes the love between parent and child. Voice creates its own vibration. It is the same with action. This vibration will affect the person. This is the real meaning of payback. So we have to be careful of the way we think, speak and act. This applies to how we behave to all the animals and other creatures we hunt. We are taught to think of them with love and deep respect, for they are giving up their life for us.

For example, when I was being taught how to make a spear for fishing, we went to the grove of tree saplings which are the ones to use, and some of us boys rushed in and started cutting down several saplings. Our *boonyi* said, 'What are you boys doing? Why are you cutting more than one?' When we tried to make excuses about how we needed another one just in case we lost one. He said, 'Leave them alone. Give the extra ones to those boys who have not yet cut down any. Those trees are not there for you to kill. They will willingly give up one to help you, and as you approach they send their life-force energy to their neighbour. So you end up with the shaft for the spear, but the life-energy has already been sent to the other tree.' So we collected these trees and learned how to turn the shaft into a spear.

Loppon and I then talked about the idea of secrecy on the spiritual path. As I have already explained, there are very strong Laws about secrecy in our system of ceremonial knowledge, and that is why it is so hard for me to write about it in this book which everyone can read. Traditionally one never asked why, one just listened and observed. But because of my white education, I did ask why of my elders when I was growing up in Arnhem Land. Most often they would say, 'You will know when you are older. Now it is too dangerous for you to know.' Sacred men's business can only be taught in the ceremony itself. It cannot be talked about outside this. Even today this is rigidly followed, especially in the Central Desert region. When you meet ceremonial elders, they just embody the power of our tradition. You learn by feeling this.

There is knowledge which is general and can be talked about. There is other knowledge about creation stories about which you have to be cautious, in terms of how you talk about it, and there is other knowledge which you never talk about. It is only to be experienced. I think this is for spiritual protection, because some of the energies can be powerful. Through the path of ceremonial knowledge you pass through different levels, and each of these levels teaches you how to tame your mind and emotions. That is why not all boys are able to pass through all the levels of initiation. Say of the fifty who begin, maybe only ten will go to the end.

I always say to myself, What is the purpose of learning if you cannot make things better? All knowledge should be for using, so you must ask if is it for good or bad. There is so much knowledge in our modern world, it has become like junk food.

There are more than us in the physical world we see. Some of these forces will guide us, but others can be very negative. So you can get into a line of danger. The old teachers know this, so they know how to work with these forces and when the right time has come for an individual to learn in terms of how they are with their own minds and spirits. So our elders watch very carefully for this, particularly as you go further into deeper ceremony. We look for certain behaviour indicative of developing maturity, of acting in a good way. Not in a cunning or shrewd way, but in a kind, generous way. It is the latter that leads to being chosen for ceremony.

The last area Loppon and I explored together was life after death. In our culture, everything is eternal in the sense that it never just disappears. The tree dies, it drops its seeds, it regenerates. So with people, they die, pass on, and return. When babies are born the elders look for birthmarks, the way they walk, gestures they use as they grow up and other things to decide who they had been in a previous life.

When we die the physical dissolves, but the spirit is released. Once the spirit is reborn into the physical it is restricted, but while it is spirit it can go anywhere. But we are careful to free it from attachment to this life. That is why we smoke the body and the house where that person lived, why we paint our bodies with white clay, and why we never speak that person's name. We use *kunmanara* which means 'no name'. This even applies to people with the same name, who are alive and are friends or relatives. We cannot use that name for them either for many years. We also sing songs of farewell and travel, from this life to the next one. This is all to free the spirit. So we never have pictures of our deceased relatives. We believe that if we think strongly about someone while looking at their photograph, this will drag their spirit back and this will harm both us and that spirit.

One small puzzle Loppon and I came across in our discussion was a small object which we Aboriginal people in Arnhem Land call a spindle. This is made with three sticks, one passing through the middle of the other. We use this to spin human hair into belts, but also to make special objects with which we can sing someone as a form of love magic. Loppon recognised one of these spindles in the Aboriginal museum in Darwin and thought it must be Tibetan. He explained that they call them *namkas*. They use them to spin the hair of sheep or yaks, and they are used to make objects for invoking negative spirits and asking them to take the offering and leave.

So we can see from this discussion, the many similarities and differences between Aboriginal spirituality, Christianity and Tibetan Buddhism. There is a great oneness of spirit, of *kurunpa*. Maybe there is only one truth, but different paths to that truth. This truth cannot be discovered in words, but only in action. But it has a universal language and that is love and compassion. My path is that of Aboriginal spirituality, *kanyini*, for I can and do integrate it with my Christian beliefs and life. *Kanyini* is my Aboriginal path to reconciliation and to oneness with the creative consciousness of our world.

The Trail Leads On

At times I can remember
Happenings so long ago
In my early childhood
And my growing to be a man.
There were times of sorrow,
There were times of joy,
But I just keep going on
To the end of the trail.

Life is one long road now
Of footprints I can see.
Those who walk beside me
Must look down the signs to see.
Then hand in hand together
The signs will follow on
Till we reach another hill
And see the trail lead on.

Blacks and whites together
Must live upon our land
Can listen to each other
So we can understand
That difference and things common
Need not a barrier be
We'll walk this trail together
And see the trail lead on.

We'll walk this trail together
And see the trail lead on.

Reconciliation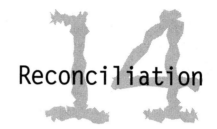

As I became interested in holistic wellbeing, I really began to appreciate the importance of the mind. We are responsible for what we allow into our minds, and for the thoughts we have in our minds about others. We have to pay attention to this in the nowness, at each moment of the present. This is the real challenge of reconciliation.

Reconciliation has two faces, the Aboriginal face and the non-Aboriginal face. From the Aboriginal perspective, it is to heal the wound of past experiences which separates us from white society. That is why it has always been linked to the need for a public apology from the Australian Government. It was the government who used the legal fiction of *terra nullius* to take our land from us without compensation. It was the government who established a policy that legalised forcibly taking Aboriginal children such as me from our families.[1] It was government policy that denied citizenship to us until the late 1960s. It was the government who set themselves up as our 'protectors', and therefore took on the responsibility for our wellbeing.

In 1998, people who had taken up the cause of reconciliation and demanding a public apology from the government organised a national Sorry Day. I was asked to participate in the event organised in Canberra, our national capital. All around the country people had been collecting Sorry Books. These were books in which ordinary people were invited to record their personal expression of regret for what had happened to Aboriginal people. Thousands of these books were collected from all over Australia. At the same time, the symbol of reconciliation became the hands. Hands were cut from coloured plastic mounted on wire spikes, each sponsored by a person, and they were all collected and planted on the lawn in front of Parliament House, to form a vast visual expression of the wish for reconciliation by the Australian people.[2] We Aboriginal people were really touched that so many ordinary white people were prepared to express their personal apology, and to see that it came from their hearts. Like us, many of them had not known about the heavy, shadowy side of our shared history, and they were finding it difficult to face that it had happened in the founding of this nation. This is the sense of regret and apology which we need to heal our pain. It is very different from the feeling of guilt, which brings with it blame and punishment, and therefore resentment. Guilt is what causes people to blame the victim, whereas regret allows us to feel empathy with them for what has happened. Guilt makes us want to deny that which is making us feel guilty, whereas regret is acknowledging it and letting it go.

I was invited to sing my song 'My Brown Skin Baby', which had become a theme song of the Stolen Generations, at the various events organised around this public expression of 'sorry', including talking at various schools and at the university. This culminated in an event at Parliament House, where a number of Aboriginal people, on behalf of our people, formally accepted the Sorry Books. It has been a very painful experience for the Aboriginal people that the Australian government, under the leadership of Prime Minister John Howard, has consistently refused to formally apologise for past wrongs done to our people as a result of government policy. He has shown a face of government which is more worried about claims for financial compensation through the courts of law, if the government does show that it accepts responsibility, than for the soul of this country's future. Prime Minister Howard, and many who agree with him, talk about the 'black armband' view of history, accusing us of wanting to drag up past wrongs instead of celebrating the nation's successes and looking to the future. While he wants to celebrate historical events like Australia's role in various wars which are publicly acknowledged on Anzac Day, he wants to deny the heavy, shadowy side of our history. We do not understand this.

When you look at countries like Germany, you can see how they have had to face the heavy side of their history during World War II, when their government was responsible for the killing of millions of people whose only 'sin' was their Jewish identity. Because this policy was aimed at the complete extermination of a people, it is called a holocaust. There are certainly some German people who are still in denial, but their government has shown strong leadership in helping the German people face their history. Denial of wrongdoing eats away at the spirit of a people, in the same way that it eats away at the soul of a person.

There are some parallels between the German government during the 1930–40s and the past actions of the government in Australia. Certainly they did not round us up and take us to camps and gas us to death. But, through their policy of removing children, and taking our land, there is a lot of evidence that they were intent on exterminating our culture, our way of life, our belief systems and our language. Those of us who personally suffered through this policy have borne the burden of deep spiritual pain and a broken spirit. The police are the agents of government, as are the courts of law. There is no doubt that we have suffered immense discrimination at the hands of these agencies of the government over the years. We are not saying that present-day Australians are personally guilty of all of these wrongs. But we are saying that they have benefited from them, at our expense, and that this is our collective history that has shaped us and our relationships with one another. This is the wound at the heart of Australia. How can we face the next millennium unless we heal this wound?

I always knew I had a white father. I could see that from the colour of my skin. I grew up believing that I was put in those institutions as my punishment for having a white father. Those Aborigines with blacker skins were not put in homes, they were not taken from their families, so what else could I think? Originally I had also doubted whether my own Aboriginal family wanted me. Why else did they not try to contact me and get me back? It was only through education that I learned that they had no say in the matter whatsoever. I discovered how they had continued to love me when I eventually found my family again. I have never felt rejection from the Aboriginal people.

The most difficult step in reconciliation for Aboriginal people is to shift their focus from feeling like victims to claiming their identity and history and becoming leaders. We begin this process with our children. To be parents we must show leadership, we must show our children how they can be proud to be Aboriginal, and at the same time live in a society where white people have the economic and political power. I found my spiritual philosophy was my greatest weapon in this struggle. I committed myself to finding the goodness in all people, and my spirituality grew as one positive proved itself, and that led to the next positive. In between there were also a lot of negatives, but I never stopped looking for the good in others. My attitude became: 'I had this terrible experience. It is my culture's experience. Let's make sure it never happens again by telling the world how it hurt, and how I am having difficulty living with that hurt.' I thought, I am going to find a way to put that hurt aside and I'm never going to hurt anyone as much as I've been hurt.

Once we change the way we think, our spirit then helps us to make the necessary changes in the way we live. But to get that help we must accept *kanyini*, love and responsibility for all things. We have to be willing to take responsibility for ourselves and for what is around us. It is very personal. I am the one who has to do it. I cannot expect anyone else to do it for me. Every one of us needs to reach out and say, 'I'm sorry, please forgive me.' If we continue to just blame others and hate them for what their ancestors did in the past, we will just end up killing ourselves. What leads to a cultural shift in a nation of people is an increase in the number of people who can shift as individuals. It starts with the individual, then the family, then the community, then the nation and finally the world as a whole.

For us to be able to reconcile with the colonisers of Australia, the white system must remove the blockages that continue to keep us powerless. One of these is welfare and unemployment benefits. What looks like assistance really isn't. It is bondage. It keeps us dependent on a system set up by the government to destroy our way of life. The very logic of that way of thinking is spiritually destructive to us. To learn to be responsible, we must have responsibility. Aboriginal people haven't had responsibility for generations, but we need to reclaim it. It might be a difficult process of learning. We will probably make many mistakes. But unless we travel this path, we cannot truly live *kanyini* and the path of reconciliation. We will not be able to live in the new millennium with dignity and hope. I do not doubt that this will be difficult, but we have to find a way through it.

Outback Australia is in the middle of a tourist boom. Thousands of people come to visit the Central Desert region and Arnhem Land every year. They are yearning to connect with Aboriginal culture, with our land and its immense spiritual power. But we take very little part in this industry. The reasons for this are complex, and not just the fault of white business and government. It goes back to attitudes to work and the relationship between work, family life and culture. The discipline of modern work culture, which white people take for granted even though they might not like it, does not come easily to Aboriginal people. Sometimes to us it seems to be a type of slavery, especially when it prevents you giving your family the care and attention they require around sorry times, or when it prevents you being able to maintain your relationship to country. That is why, as I said earlier, I always have preferred working for Aboriginal organisations. They understand the need for more flexibility around family responsibilities in the way we work. Very few Aboriginal people become workaholics. For Aboriginal people, the word 'business' means ceremony, not commercial activity to make money. We find it hard to worship money and worldly success they way white culture does. Of course we would like many of the things that this world brings, but we cannot pay that price. So for us, the struggle to find a way of living in the modern world is also a struggle to find this balance in a world which does not seem to accept the need for such a balance.

We Aboriginal people need to regain our spirit. Our spirit has always been so connected with our land that when the land was taken from us we felt we had nothing left. Too many of us have tried to blot out this pain with alcohol, or have sunk into a deep depression of nothingness. We need to recover our story of our own spiritual philosophy as a living guide to modern life. I hope my story can help people discover this.

Spirituality is the ultimate answer to reconciliation in Australia and everywhere else in the world. Loving ourselves, our families, our neighbours, our countrymen and every other living thing is the reason we are here on earth. If we follow the ripple in the pond when a stone hits the water, we can easily see that the entire pond is affected by that one little stone. If the stone represents love, and it drops somewhere in our universe, that love will send its ripple throughout the entire universe. All the people, birds, animals, insects, plants, trees and rocks will in some way be affected by it. It is the same with anger and hate. We must choose which ripples we wish to send into our universe.

Aboriginal people, by and large, recognise this spiritual dimension to reconciliation in Australia. As one of my Aboriginal brothers from Queensland said:

'We talk about problems, we talk about healing, we talk about reconciliation. But it goes much deeper. Aboriginal to Aboriginal, Aboriginal to Australians, Australians to us, Aboriginals to the land. It's a deeper problem. It's a spiritual problem.'

Postscript

completing the cycle

And so it has come, that I have completed the cycle of my life by returning to my home, which is Uluru, my mother's land, my mother's country. I have known for a very long time that this is what I would do after retirement from active work, and I told my children many times that this was what I wanted to do, to set up a outstation or homeland in my mother's country. I am able to do this under the land rights legislation of the Northern Territory.

The homelands movement has undergone many changes since it began under the Land Rights legislation of 1975. It is a lot more difficult now, because too many of our people have set up homelands and then vacated them. What has happened was that many of the elders, when they were young, were brought from their own country into the missions or communities, where they lived for many years, had employment and raised their own families, and then later decided to go back home, back to their own country. This became a strong movement in the 1970s, going back to homeland (sometimes called the outstation movement).

The old people had left their homelands initially, being brought into the missions or communities because of the availability of health facilities, education, housing and employment, with the opportunity to go out now and again to country. But now the old people sought to go back to their country, with the help of government to provide the basic requirements of a water supply, shelter and access to transport, including an airstrip if required. And the families went back to their own country, and people were so excited about it. But what happened was that they would go out and set up their homeland and the country was not familiar to the young people, and they would start to drift back to town because often there was nothing for them to do and loneliness and boredom set in. Often the young people would go back to the communities to stay with relatives, leaving the old people on their own, and many of them might not have had the ability to start the generator or get the car started if it broke down, and there were many reasons why things did not always work out.

It was okay for those who were highly regarded for their bark paintings and craft work, because there was something for them to do, and every now and again they would bring their works into the communities to sell, or buyers would go out and collect the works and pay them good money, and they would come in to buy their food, and it could work. Otherwise there was no source of income apart from social security payments. And now there are many out-stations abandoned and empty, many of them 100 kilometres or more away from the main communities, with up to a dozen homes set up, and almost everyone has gone back to the communities where their children grew up.

I was in the Blue Mountains, near Sydney, where I completed this book and I said to myself, 'Well, I need to go home now.' So I loaded up all my things and came back home, and arranged to live in a Land Council house with my brother, Gordon Williams. I told Gordon that I had come back to set up an outstation, and I talked with my family to see where the sites of country were and where I could set up a homeland. I was told that my grandfather, uncle and Aunty Barbara had already set up a place at Umbiara, and they told me the process they went through to set themselves up.

So my family told me that my place is right there at Umbiara, which is my mother's country and which is my country, the area between Kata Tjuta and Lake Amadeus, an area of hundreds of square kilometres. Umbiara is part of this land, and it is ideally located only seven kilometres from the international airport at Yulara. So now I am at the stage where I have to wait for a Land Council site clearance; they have to formally visit the site with other traditional owners and determine where the sites are. Our Law still operates in the Northern Territory Land Rights legislation, and the Law cannot be interfered with. These sacred sites come from the *tjukurrpa*, the creation story, and there are sacred lines coming from everywhere, crisscrossing the country, and these need to be known so that you do not spoil or have an effect on these energy lines, and do not upset people who have traditional knowledge of these sites.

In the end, the Land Council, and their lawyers and anthropologists, will have to clear it for us, and it is somewhat ironic that we have got to wait for white people to give us the go-ahead. And then I will have to negotiate with the various government agencies regarding housing, water and energy. This is not really a problem, but I have to work through the system to set up the outstation. Three of my aunties have said they will move out with me and they would like to set up a tourist business where they would show people around and show them how we used to live off the land in the old days. We could set up an education program and we could make wooden artefacts and grass baskets for sale.

So in completing the cycle of my life, you have to remember that the Angas Downs station, where my Aboriginal parents went to work all those years ago, is only 100 kilometres away. This is where I was born, fathered by Bill Liddle, and my parents are listed in the 'Stud Book', which registered all of the people who were listed as receiving rations. I have had access to those registers and I have seen both my parents' names recorded there as being from Ayer's Rock. Bill Liddle wrote their names down as receiving regular rations because of the work they were doing for him.

This has been valuable in helping me understand where my tribal lands were, and where my traditional land is. I was taken away from that place, and I would like to say that I have a vision of making a documentary for my children, and the vision is of me in the days before we had clothes, on the back of this old man, in the way they usually carried us, coming out of a kind of hazy image of Uluru. There is this image of the Rock, and out steps the old man with the boy on his neck, and the women and other children beside him, all materialising magically out of the rock face. This image then leads into my story, and the experiences in this book, of being taken from here and coming back home to Uluru. I have come back home and I am telling my story. This has a lot of meaning for me, and there is a sense of physical and spiritual wholeness in being able to finish my story in this way.

Epilogue

Minjilung: the one who came from the sun

A short story by Bob Randall

Today was to be a special day for the young black girl. The ceremony for the coming of motherhood would be performed in her honour at sunset. Already preparation was well under way. Everyone was helping, even the small ones, for everyone loved Theresa with her flashing eyes and quick flashing smile.

She had a special way of making everyone feel good, of changing groans or tears into laughing. She never seemed to be tired, despite her heavy belly, and she was always carrying someone else's baby or singing with the older ones or telling them stories she'd learned in the mission house. No one went hungry since Theresa had come back. If there wasn't much tucker that day, she'd go into the mission and she always came back with something for the old people and the little ones. She wasn't afraid of white people.

She'd been carrying the new life within her for a long time now, ever since the time the navy ship had come to visit the small mission station. They could only dimly remember now, it was becoming a story instead a memory. But Theresa could still remember clearly.

She could remember the young white man who had planted the

247

seed in her body. He was so tall and fair and beautiful, so finely dressed and so full of promises. He had promised her everything, a proper Christian marriage in a church, a house like the mission house and so many other things that would have made her life easy. But there was no sadness in the memory now. Her tribal husband was a good kind old man. He was very pleased when she told him a baby was coming. He was as proud of her huge hanging belly as she was. It didn't matter that another man had fertilised his wife. She was his wife and it would be his baby. He knew it would be a boy. He was always boasting about his new son. How big he was and how lively.

The dancing that night was so successful that almost as soon as the drone of the didgeridoo had died away, the rhythm of life began. The moon was sinking over the western plain, shedding its pale light on the flat clouds, making a sea in the sky. As if in a dream, Theresa touched the sleeping man beside her, 'Albert, go and get Gumou. My time to bear the baby has come now.' Old, wise Gumou came right away, bringing two other women with her.

The glowing fire was brought alive and a billy of cold tea placed beside it. The women sat down with their backs to the warmth and began all the stories about births, ancient stories and new stories about the women Theresa knew.

The moon had slid away when the sudden agonised scream rang out, waking the camp. Other women came stepping carefully through the darkness to the flickering pool of light around the fire. Old Gumou knew the girl was in trouble. The baby was too big and the girl too slim and young.

Helplessly the women watched as the relentless forces of nature wrenched the young body, forcing out the child that could no longer survive inside. The women firmly held the girl still, they spoke to her white, frightened eyes with their calm eyes. They answered the tiny yelps and they shared the pain. Drawing on their strength, Theresa worked with the natural force against her own tight, narrow body, bearing down with every ounce of conscious effort. She was bleeding terribly. Gumou ran out of rags. 'More better someone get sister from mission, I think,' she said.

The old man got up and walked swiftly away through the darkness. The medical sister was up, busily preparing trays earlier than usual, for the visiting minister was staying and she wanted that extra time to sit and chat with the rest of the staff after morning prayer. She'd had a restless night. The didgeridoo and the constant rhythm of clap sticks disturbed her, and worst of all were those terrible savage screams. She heard the timid knock on the door and ignored it until she'd tidied away.

'Oh, these stupid people,' she muttered, feeling irritated, 'they always pick the worst times to injure each other.' She opened the door.

'You, Albert! What are you doing here? Your corroboree keeps us awake all night. You know we've got an important visitor staying here. Now what do you want?'

'My wife, sister, you know Theresa, she have baby now. Gumou say you come, please,' he stared anxiously into the sister's face, but she didn't seem to see him.

'What, at this hour? Look, old man, I'm too busy. And you know what the boss will say if he sees you up here at this time. The sun isn't up yet. Now you get back to camp and you can tell Gumou not to think she can order me around. I'll come down after morning prayer. And you tell the people they better all come to morning prayer today with the visiting minister here.'

The old man didn't move. He stood staring at the ground, silently pleading. The sister sighed with exasperation. Then she turned and firmly closed the door in the old man's face.

After morning prayer, the brown mission children in their neat matching uniforms trooped into the dining room for breakfast, while the minister and the missionary staff stood around outside the church.

'No blacks at the service this morning?' the visitor asked.

'Oh, they had a sing-song last night. They're probably all

sleeping it off,' said the minister, secretly pleased. They often inter-rupted the service.

'Don't worry, I know what a difficult job it is to try and spread the word of God to these stone-age people. I can only admire you people out here,' said the visiting minister.

'You know that old Albert,' the sister chipped in, 'he had the nerve to knock on the door at five o'clock this morning to tell me to go down to the camp because young Theresa's having a baby. You know they have no pain with childbirth,' she added, suddenly afraid of seeming hard-hearted. 'It's quite amazing really. Just squat down and drop their babies. Like animals.'

The visitor was looking thoughtful. 'Theresa,' he murmured. 'Wasn't that the name of the young girl you had working in the house, Kathleen? Pretty child. Very thin, I remember.'

'That's the one,' confirmed the minister's wife, looking as if she'd just swallowed something nasty. 'We had to get rid of her. She got herself pregnant to one of those navy boys. Honestly, she couldn't be more than fifteen or sixteen. She looks simply frightful now, since she went back to the camp. You'd think they'd have the decency to cover themselves up a bit. After living with us for two years! Old Albert seems to think he's the father. Really, I sometimes wonder if these people will ever learn anything.'

'Theresa's been coming to me quite often in the last few months,' the minister revealed. 'I've been giving her fresh milk and fruit from the staff supplies. Her stomach is big enough, but her legs and arms are thinner than ever, and her face is quite sunken. No sense starving the unborn child. Though I wouldn't be surprised if she gives half the food away. You know, she hasn't lost the faith though. Quite surprising, really.'

As the first sunlight touched the earth, a ray of pink gold touched the wet, newly-born baby. 'Minjilung, we call him,' said old Gumou. 'That sun bin touch the ground when him bin born.'

After throwing some green leaves onto the fire, Gumou took the baby boy, raised him high and held him over the fire for a moment.

The baby coughed in the smoke and let out a tiny cry of defiance. Then she wrapped him in the soft cloth that she had saved for him.

Theresa lay still. Her work was over.

The calls of the brolga cut through the stillness as they began to arrive to feed on the salt flats not far or so away. Suddenly there was a large flutter of wings and one of these great birds landed not far from the hut. This was unusual. Even the dogs didn't dare make a move to chase it.

'Your wife, she finish, Albert,' said Gumou quietly. The giant bird took a few strides, then gracefully rose in the air, taking the spirit of the dead woman away towards the rising ball of gold. The sound of the brolga's music echoed everywhere. Moments later, wails of anguish rose from the people in the camp.

The missionaries were just leaving the church when the cries reached their ears.

'Must be some sort of trouble in the camp,' said the minister. 'I expect we'll soon know what's going on, if it's serious.'

Sure enough, it wasn't long before Gumou's face appeared in the doorway. The missionary staff were just finishing breakfast. They waited for Gumou to knock.

'What is it, Gumou?' asked the minister, looking up slowly. Gumou waited. She was angry. She was not going to call out her terrible news across the dining room. The minister rose and walked ceremoniously to the doorway, vaguely curious as to what message might be in that dark secretive face.

'Albert's wife, she finish when baby bin born.' Gumou's heart was full of dark anger, but the minister didn't hear it in her muttered words.

'Thank you, Gumou, for telling us.'

Gumou ground her teeth. Her eyes looked from the minister to the table where the sister sat, and back and away again. Everything she saw made her feel more and more uncomfortable, and no words came to say the curses she'd whispered over and over, all the way to the mission house. As she turned in despair and hurried away to the safety of the trees, she heard someone say, 'Poor old girl, I expect she's seen a few of her kind die like that. They just have no concept of hygiene, these people.'

The minister watched the dark shape disappear, and returned to the table.

A meeting was called by the elders of the camp. A man of strong wisdom spoke. He was always the one who spoke on important matters. 'The one who has gone must be rested blackfella way. You have all seen how her totem came and took her spirit away.'

Then someone from the group spoke. 'Last night I dreamed of brolgas. In the dream, the bark . . . in the strong branches of the jarrah tree . . . down beside the salt flat. You know the one that always has lots of fruit on it. In my dream. I also saw a brolga landing on top of it.'

'That is where the body of the gentle one who has gone must be placed,' spoke the wise one.

Preparations were made immediately, and it was a sorry group that walked with those whose duty it was to place the body in the chosen place.

The feeding brolgas, disturbed by the people, uttered calls of warning as they ran, huge wings extended, and rose gracefully, grey shapes changing in the pale sky. There, with the circling birds calling high overhead, the body was placed on a bed of saplings and bark, in the strong branches of the jarrah tree.

The old man held the baby close against his chest and felt the little heart pounding strong and fast against his own. The he turned the little body around and carefully inspected every part of him, the perfect tiny feet and hands, the smooth round head and fine black hair. It was truly a beautiful golden healthy boy. Then the old man thought of the child's mother and the terrible bargain fate had made. He thought of her laughing, beautiful face, the good feeling of having her near and of the food she brought to camp when people were hungry. He remembered the way she was not afraid of the white man.

The old man knew that all these good things would live on in the baby in his arms.

As long as Minjilung was there, the people would always be happy and well fed. Minjilung would never be afraid of anyone. The old man looked forward to the time when his son would become a man. There were harsh tests. He knew his boy would be strong and brave. He would learn the ancient secret knowledge of how every- thing is and should be and, in Minjilung and his sons, and the sons of those sons, the knowledge would go on forever.

The old man looked from the sleeping child to the leafy platform high in the jarrah tree, and his heart was so filled with pride and sorrow that he picked up his axe and cut his head and cried.

Glossary
of Aboriginal words in the text

Source: Goddard, C. (1992). *Pitjantjatjara/Yankunytjatjara to English Dictionary*, Institute for Aboriginal Development, Alice Springs. All word meanings are from Yankunytjatjara unless otherwise specified.

anangu   *n*. person, people. When used to refer to an Aboriginal person, or people, a capital letter is preferred.

angbadi   *n*. accomplished hunter, from Iwaidja, Arnhem Land.

boonyi   *n*. father, from Iwaidja, Arnhem Land.

coolamon   *n*. bowl of wood or bark for carrying water etc. This is a word adopted into the English language from the Aboriginal language, Kamilaroi. Yankunytjatjara speakers use the word *piti* to convey this meaning.

didgeridoo   *n*. Aboriginal musical instrument of long tubular shape. Aboriginal word adopted into the English language.

gammon   *n*. not real, without meaning. From nineteenth-century English.

inma   *n*. singing, song with percussive accompaniment celebrating in verse the song lines of the ancestor beings of the Dreaming. Ceremony incorporating singing and dancing.

kadaitcha   *n*. Law enforcer, ritual executioner; such people, using shoes of fur and feather to disguise their tracks, are sent by senior men to carry out pay-back for a serious crime, sneaking up on their victim and using magic or sorcery to carry out the sentence.

kami   *n*. grandmother, grand-aunt, etc., used affectionately.

kanyini *v.t.* to look after, take responsibility for, have, keep.

kulingpa *n.* nectar from the flowers of the corkwood tree (*Hakea* sp.) that are sucked directly or soaked in water to produce a sweet drink.

kuniya *n.* carpet snake, large non-venomous python; they are edible.

kunya *n.* sorrow, grief associated with death and suffering.

kunmanu *n.* substitute word used instead of the name of something, if the normal word for that thing sounds like the name of a deceased person.

kunmanara *n.* substitute name used instead of the name of a person if it is the same as, or sounds like, the name of someone recently deceased.

kurku *n.* mulga (*Acacia aneura*). A tall shrub or small tree found in many forms, and with many uses. *Kurku* is a general term, and may apply to the sweet secretion found on the red lac scale on branches of mulga.

kurunpa *n.* spirit, soul, will, self. Seen as vital to a sense of purpose.

kutra *n.* traditional fighting stick.

liru *n.* dangerous snake.

lunpa *n.* the red-backed kingfisher (*Todiramphus pyrrhopygius*) and possibly the sacred kingfisher (*Todiramphus sanctus*).

maku *n.* edible grub or caterpillar, usually found in the roots of the witchetty bush (*Acacia kempeana*).

mala *n.* the rufous hare wallaby (*Lagorchestes hirsutus*). A small hare-like wallaby once abundant in sandhill country, but now very rare.

malu *n.* the red plains kangaroo (*Macropus rufus*). An important food source and totemic animal of special importance to men. Hunting, butchering, cooking and distribution customs are strictly laid down by Law.

mamu *n*. harmful spirit being, spirit-monster, 'devil' animal.
They are generally invisible, and more dangerous at night, but can
be seen by dogs and driven off by experienced older people.

mangata *n*. quandong (*Santalum acuminatum*).

mawulari *n*. skirt woven from human or animal hair; small
apron women traditionally wore around their waists.

mimi *n*. spirit figures, Arnhem Land.

ngankari *n*. healer, traditional doctor. Traditional healers use a
range of herbal remedies and deep pressure massage. They are
able to expel *mamu* (harmful spirit beings) and *punu* (foreign bodies
such as pointed sticks or bones) from inside a person's body. These
are held to be the cause of internal pains and illness.

nyinnga *n*. ice, frost, cold time of year, winter.

ngura *n*. camp, home, place, site, locality, land, area, estate,
tract of country.

ngura kaputu *n*. a land-owning group's range, over which it
forages, is referred to as *ngura kaputu*. The area over which a group
forages is larger than its territorial country, which is referred to as
ngura (estate).

panpanpalala *n*. the crested bellbird (*Oreoica gutturalis*). Rarely
seen, but distinctive on account of its bell-like call.

pituri *n*. wild tobacco (*Duboisia hopwoodii*). The dried leaves are
powdered, mixed with the ashes of certain plants and chewed.

tjala *n*. honey ant (*Camponotus inflatus*). In their deep
underground nests, these ants store a delicious sweet syrup in their
distended abdomens. The swollen ants are eaten by holding the
head and legs pinched between the fingers, and letting the
abdomen burst in the mouth.

tjamu *n*. grandfather, great-uncle, or generally any male in your
grandparents' generation.

tjanpi   *n.* spinifex grass (*Triodia irritans* and other *Triodia* species); spinifex country.

tjilpi   *n./adj.* old man, elder. Often used to refer to or address someone, in preference to using his name, as a mark of respect.

tjukurrpa   *n.* Dreaming, Law, Creation story. There is an emerging preference for the word *Tjukurrpa* not to be given an English equivalent, since these do not capture the essence of the Aboriginal meaning.

tjurunga   *n.* secret sacred ceremonial objects, of stone or carved wood, deriving their sacredness and power from intimate association with an event of the Dreaming; they are held by senior men with requisite ceremonial knowledge.

walytja   *n./adj.* kinship, family; someone you care for, and who cares for you. Even people who come into a community as total outsiders, with no blood connections, may be fitted into the *walytja* system if they behave appropriately.

wanampi   *n.* water serpent, water snake monster, rainbow serpent. Very dangerous creatures believed to live in and guard waterholes.

wati   *n.* in a special sense, an initiated man. Used as a term among men who have a relaxed relationship. It is also used to take in Aboriginal and non-Aboriginal men from distant places.

witjinti   *n.* corkwood (*Hakea divaricata*, *Hakea suberea*). Small gnarled trees with thick, deeply fissured bark, needle-like leaves and showy yellow flowers, which are favourite sources of nectar. The flowers are sucked directly, or steeped in water to produce a sweet drink.

woomera   *n.* Aboriginal throwing stick for launching a spear, or club used as missile. Aboriginal word adopted into the English language.

yeperenye   *n.* caterpillar, from Arrente, Central Australia.

References and Notes

Foreword

1 Council for Aboriginal Reconciliation, (1999), *Draft Document for Reconciliation*.

2 Wright, J., (1991), 'Bond with the Land' in *Born of the Conquerors*, Aboriginal Studies Press, Canberra, ACT.

3 Pearson, N., (2000), *Our Right to Take Responsibility*, Goanna Print, Australia.

4 Tacey, D.J., (1995), *Edge of the Sacred: Transformation in Australia*, HarperCollins.

5 Perkins, Dr C. (2000), Quoted in the order of service document, *A Celebration of the Life of Charles Perkins*, State Funeral, Sydney Town Hall, 25 October 2000.

Chapter 1   Tjukurrpa: Our Philosophy of Life

1 The term 'Stolen Generations' refers to the thousands of Aboriginal children, over nearly two centuries, who were forcibly taken from their families to be brought up in government orphanages or church missions, under laws that controlled the lives of Aboriginal people.

2 The historian Henry Reynolds notes, 'Almost invariably the Australian settlers in the first half of the twentieth century thought of these mixed-descent children, and of the descendants of these children, whom they labelled, almost zoologically, as half-castes or crossbreeds, as quadroons and octoroons, as a growing, fearful social problem. Late nineteenth and early twentieth century thought in Australia, as elsewhere in the European cultural sphere, had been deeply corrupted by a racially based Darwinian social science.' See Reynolds, H. (1989), *Dispossession: Black Australians and White Invaders*, Allen & Unwin, Sydney.

3 The Australian Bureau of Statistics (ABS) figures for Aboriginal health
   in the period 1992–94 include the following:
   - Babies born to Aboriginal mothers are twice as likely to die at
     birth than babies born to Non-Aboriginal mothers.
   - Aboriginal people are twice as likely to be hospitalised generally.
   - Aboriginal people are three to four times more likely to be
     hospitalised for respiratory disease.
   - Aboriginal people are four to five times more likely to be
     hospitalised for infectious disease.
   - Life expectancy for all Australian males is 74.9 years and for
     females 80.6 years, while that for Indigenous women and men is
     15–20 years lower.

Chapter 2 Kanyini: The Principle of Connectedness that Underpins Aboriginal Life

1 It is conservatively estimated that before the white invasion, there
   were 300 000 people in Australia, forming 500 language groups,
   According to historian Henry Reynolds, this great language diversity
   is a manifestation of each group's identification with country and so
   is an expression of its difference from other groups, whose country
   represent different travels and exploits of the ancestral beings.
   Despite linguistic and cultural diversity, however, there appears to be
   a continent-wide philosophy, generally called the Law or Dreaming;
   see Reynolds, H. (1989), *Dispossession: Black Australians and White
   Invaders*, Allen & Unwin, Sydney.

2 See Sutton, P. (1998), *Dreamings: The Art of Aboriginal Australia*, Viking,
   Ringwood, Vic., for discussion on the concept of the Dreaming as the
   organising logic of much of the symbolism of Aboriginal art.

3 The routes taken by ancestral heroes are generally referred to in
   Aboriginal English as 'Dreaming tracks'. Uluru is the point where
   the tracks of several ancestral groups cross each other, and these
   networks of Dreaming tracks tie together desert peoples throughout
   Central Australia. This concept of Aboriginal Dreaming tracks or
   song lines was popularised in Bruce Chatwin, (1987), *The Songlines*,
   Penguin, USA.

4 For instance, T.G.H. Strehlow, a Lutheran missionary and
   anthropologist, was given a great number of *tjurungas*, in recognition

of his role as a Christian teacher, and these are now locked away in the Strehlow Collection, and are subject to continuing controversy, as they are an integral part of people's heritage (eg the Arrernte people).

5   This is why many Aboriginal people were deeply offended by Marlo Morgan's book, *Mutant Message Down Under*, especially when many non-Aboriginal people could be led to believe that this is a genuine book about Aboriginal spiritual teachings.

Chapter 3   Stolen

1   Constable Willshire was tried for the killing of two Aboriginal men who were shot at Tempe Downs in 1891, and their bodies burned on his instructions. Until this time it was rare for police officers to be asked to explain why they had shot an Aboriginal person, as the excuse of shooting in self-defence, or that the victims had been shot while resisting arrest, was accepted by the law. There was usually no attempt to corroborate the police witness's account from Aboriginal evidence. On this occasion, although damaging evidence was given by several Aboriginal witnesses, Willshire was acquitted; see Layton, R. (1986), *Uluru: An Aboriginal History of Ayers Rock*, Australian Institute of Aboriginal Studies, Canberra.

2   The Coniston Massacre took place in August 1928. The massacre followed the killing of a white dingo-trapper, Fred Brooks, in a revenge attack by a Walpiri Aboriginal man, named Bullfrog, because of Brooks's exploitation of local Aboriginal people. As a result, Constable Murray from Alice Springs, a violent man charged with administering the law in a vast territory, and the armed band he assembled, embarked on a series of punitive and indiscriminate killings of the Walpiri in their camps. The official toll was 17 dead, but the Walpiri numbered the dead as being between 60 and 70. Murray was acclaimed as a hero by local whites, and at a subsequent inquiry in Darwin was exonerated of murder. When questioned by the judge as to whether it was necessary to shoot to kill in every case, Murray uttered the infamous response, 'What use is a wounded blackfeller a hundred miles from civilisation?' See Elder, B. (1998), *Blood on the Wattle: Massacres and Maltreatment of Aboriginal Australians since 1788*, New Holland Publishers, Sydney.

3   An account of this massacre can be found in Layton, R. (1986), *Uluru: An Aboriginal History of Ayers Rock*, Australian Institute of Aboriginal Studies, Canberra.

4   The Granites is a mining area situated along the Tanami Road, 250 kilometres beyond Yuendumu, north-west of Alice Springs.

5   The *Journal of Human Evolution*, 36(6):591–612, 1999, reported that recent dating of a human skeleton excavated at Lake Mungo in the Willandra Lakes World Heritage region in southern NSW, suggests that the remains are between 57 000 and 71 000 years old. As well, the journal noted that the deceased was covered with powdered red ochre and had been cremated, indicating that this was the oldest funeral ceremony recorded in the world.

6   McPhail, *Edinburgh Ecclesiastical Journal*, Vol.1, 1846:453. Quote taken from Eckermann et al, (1992), *Binang Goonj: Bridging Cultures in Aboriginal Health*, UNE Press, pp. 14–15.

7   Wollmington, 1988:18. Quote taken from Eckermann et al, (1992), *Binang Goonj: Bridging Cultures in Aboriginal Health*, UNE Press, pp. 14–15.

8   Phrenology, or head measuring, was a contribution of modern science postulating that race could be measured scientifically, and so skull size, brain size and forehead elevation were said to be predictors of intelligence and evolution. Aboriginal people in Australia were thought to be particularly suitable for this kind of research. When Aboriginal skull size was found to be similar to that of the European, it was postulated that their brain size was smaller because of the extra thickness of their skulls. Nazi scientists' application of this type of research led to its ultimate rejection after the war; see Reynolds, H. (1987), *Frontier: Aborigines: Settlers and Land*, Allen & Unwin, Sydney.

9   Quandong, *mangata*, (*Santalum acuminatum*), is a small tree with large-stoned red-skinned fruits. The pale yellow flesh of the ripe fruit is a prized food and the fallen dried fruits can be reconstituted with water. The kernel inside the stone is mashed to an oily paste and used as a liniment. The soft wood is used for carving small snakes and similar items for sale.

10 In December 1992, the Prime Minister of Australia, Paul Keating, in a major speech to launch the International Year of the World's

Indigenous Peoples in Redfern Park in Sydney, acknowledged, on behalf of white Australia, the past crimes and injustices inflicted on Aboriginal people.

11 *The National Inquiry into the Separation of Aboriginal and Torres Strait Islander Children from their Families* was established by the Federal Attorney-General in 1995; it was conducted by the Human Rights and Equal Opportunity Commission (HREOC). Hearings took place across Australia and were conducted by HREOC President, Sir Roland Wilson, and the Aboriginal and Torres Strait Islander Commissioner, Mr Mick Dodson. The report of the findings and recommendations of the National Inquiry was published in April 1997, under the title *Bringing Them Home*.

The report declared that indigenous children had been forcibly removed from their families and communities since the very first days of the European occupation of Australia, with most indigenous families being affected in one or more generations by the removal of one or more children. The inquiry concluded that the forcible removal of indigenous children was devastating for indigenous families and communities, was a gross violation of their human rights, and was racially discriminatory. These were acts of genocide, done in the name of the community and with the authority of governments, to assimilate the children so that Aboriginal peoples and Torres Strait Islanders as distinct cultural groups would disappear.

'The Stolen Generations' is the term universally recognised in Australia to describe those who were forcibly taken and who lost contact with their families and communities, and their culture, language and identity, in many cases for ever. To date, the Federal Government of Australia has refused to acknowledge the Stolen Generations, issue an apology or provide compensation; see Elder, B. (1998), *Blood on the Wattle: Massacres and Maltreatment of Aboriginal Australians since 1788*, New Holland Publishers, Sydney.

12 On 19 February 1942, 81 Japanese planes were launched against Darwin whose harbour was full of ships. Some 243 people were killed, and hundreds more were injured. Eight ships were sunk, and many were damaged. A second raid was launched on the same day, and in all there were 64 air raids against the Darwin area and nearby airfields in the period to 12 November 1943.

Chapter 4   Croker Island

1   'Skin system' refers to the two contrasting moiety groups, or 'skin groups', in which opposite moiety people have a different 'skin'. This kinship system prescribes the relationships people may have with one another, and the two moiety groups may have any number of sub-groups that regulate whom people may marry.

Chapter 6   Ngura: My Search for Country

1   Rose, F.G.G. (1965), *The Wind of Change in Central Australia*, Akadamie Verlag, Berlin.

2   The Rainbow Spirit is a remarkably universal concept amongst Australian Aboriginal peoples, as a creative spirit of the Dreaming, though the stories which tell of the way in which the Rainbow Serpent created and shaped the land vary considerably. It is consistently a huge serpent that lives in deep, permanent water and is associated with rain. Some stories tell of the Rainbow Serpent's involvement in bringing people to live in their allotted homelands; see The Rainbow Spirit Elders, (1997), *Rainbow Spirit Theology: Towards an Australian Aboriginal Theology*, HarperCollins, Sydney.

3   Robert Layton was one of the anthropologists who played a crucial role in the Uluru land claim, which culminated in the title deeds to Uluru and Kata Tjuta being handed over to the traditional owners on 26 October 1985, under inalienable freehold title. The area remains a National Park administered by the Uluru–Kata Tjuta Aboriginal Land Trust as custodians, and the leaseback arrangement ensures that the board of management of the park has a majority of Aboriginal members; see Layton, R. (1986), *Uluru: An Aboriginal History of Ayers Rock*, Australian Institute of Aboriginal studies, Canberra.

Chapter 7   New Horizons

1   In 1987 the federal government established a Royal Commission into Aboriginal and Torres Strait Islander deaths in custody. In 1988, the terms of reference were amended to take into account underlying issues, social, legal, political and cultural, that might explain the high rates of indigenous incarceration and deaths in custody. The final

report of the Royal Commission was released in 1991 and contained 339 Recommendations dealing with the gross over-representation of Aboriginal and Torres Strait Islander people in police and prison custody.

The report confirmed that the rate of detention of indigenous people was 27 times higher for police custody and 15 times higher for prison custody than that of the general population. The final report included many recommendations designed to drastically reduce the incidence of incarceration, including decriminalisation of public drunkenness and the use of imprisonment for minor offences as a last resort.

The Royal Commission report, in consideration of the underlying issues, declared that the most significant contributing factor was the unequal and disadvantaged position of Aboriginal people in society, socially, economically and culturally. Consequently, the basic thrust of its recommendations was to eliminate discrimination and disadvantage, and facilitate empowerment and self-determination for Aboriginal and Torres Strait Islander people. See 'The Royal Commission into Aboriginal Deaths in Custody', in Newbury, P. (1999), *Aboriginal Heroes of the Resistance: from Pemulwuy to Mabo*, Action for World Development, Sydney.

The ABS 'Corrective Services' figures at June 2001 indicate that the level of indigenous representation in prison custody is over 23 times higher than that for non-indigenous people. A survey (1998) indicated that of the 197 500 indigenous people aged 13 years and over in 1994, over 20% reported being arrested (including being detained for public drunkenness) in the five years prior to the survey (i.e., 1989–1994). Of particular significance was the relatively high proportion of young men in the age group 18–24 years arrested (46%), with 32% of them having been arrested more than once over the five years (National Aboriginal and Torres Strait Islander Survey; Law and Justice Issues, 1998, Australian Bureau of Statistics). See http.www.deathsincustody.com.newnum.html.

2   The Freedom Ride departed from Sydney on 13 February 1965, a bus with Charles Perkins and 29 white students aboard, heading north-west to towns whose names were becoming bywords for segregation. This action was derived from civil rights models in America, especially the non-violent non-cooperation method used by Martin Luther King.

The Freedom Ride developed into a dramatic series of confrontations with white people in country towns, especially in Walgett and Moree. Local Aboriginal people increasingly took part in the attempts to break the colour bar in hotels, shops and swimming pools. 'The Ride' had a far-reaching impact in bringing to the metropolitan public vivid evidence of the crudity and brutality of rural white crowd behaviour; see Goodall, H. (1996), *Invasion to Embassy: Land in Aboriginal Politics in New South Wales, 1770–1972*, Allen & Unwin, Sydney.

3   In 1966, when the Arbitration Commission failed to grant award wages to Aboriginal stockmen, 200 Gurindji people, led by tribal leader Vincent Lingiari, walked off the Vesteys' station at Wave Hill, because of exploitation and intolerable living conditions. The Gurindji camped on their traditional land at Daguragu and resisted all attempts to move them, declaring that the land was morally theirs, and so highlighting their history of dispossession and exploitation. This event is regarded as the beginning of the Land Rights movement in Australia.

Eventually the Gurindji gained leasehold of 65 square kilometres of their country in 1975, purchased from Vesteys by the Whitlam government. The traditional owners have since gained freehold title through a Land Claim. Vincent Lingiari, an inspiration to black and white alike, died on 21 January 1988. The seminal photograph of Whitlam pouring dirt into Lingiari's hands remains a powerful and emotive symbol of the Land Rights struggle; see Newbury, P. (1999), *Aboriginal Heroes of the Resistance: from Pemulwuy to Mabo*, AWD, Sydney.

4   On 27 May 1967, the federal government held a national referendum with the twin proposals: that the federal government have administrative control of Aboriginal Affairs in all states, and that all Aboriginal people be given citizenship and be included in the national census. This action was the culmination of intense lobbing and agitation by key Aboriginal organisations, and a large overall 'yes' vote was recorded in all states; the promise was that Aboriginal people would now be fully included in Australian society and civic life.

5   It is not widely acknowledged in Australia that the Queensland sugar industry was 'developed' with the aid of slave labour. Pacific Islanders, collectively termed 'Kanakas', were kidnapped and forcibly taken aboard slaver vessels; this blatant exploitation was called

'blackbirding', a practice that caused terror in the Pacific Islands. From its inception in 1863, this slave trade was to last for 45 years, and by 1883 the number of Islanders in forced labour in Queensland had risen to 11 443, said to be a peak figure in the trade's history; see Fitzgerald, R. (1986), *A History of Queensland; From the Dreaming to 1915*, University of Queensland Press, St Lucia, Australia.

6   Pauline Hanson won the seat of Oxley in Queensland in 1996 as an independent after losing pre-selection for the Liberal Party because of her extreme right wing views against Aboriginal people. She became the leader of the One Nation Party, which had considerable success in Queensland state elections. The Pauline Hanson One Nation Party and its offshoots espouse radical right wing views across the spectrum of politics which, while simplistic, appeal to parts of the electorate that are disillusioned with the major parties, and feel marginalised by policies on immigration, tariff reduction, globalisation, etc.

7   NAIDOC Week is the outcome of a long history of Aboriginal and Torres Strait Islander efforts to bring issues of concern to the attention of governments and the general public. William Cooper and William Ferguson planned the first Day of Mourning held on Australia Day, 26 January 1938, marking the 150th anniversary of the First Fleet landing at Sydney Cove. In January 1940, the Sunday preceding the Australia Day holiday became the first 'Day of Mourning' Aboriginal Sunday.

In 1955, National Aborigines Day was changed to the first Sunday in July, and in 1957 it was moved to the second Sunday in July. NAIDOC Week is held to conclude on the second Sunday in July, and NAIDOC itself refers to all the events and celebrations that go on during National Aboriginal and Torres Strait Islander Week.

8   The distinctive red, yellow and black Aboriginal flag was first hoisted in Victoria Square in Adelaide on National Aboriginal Day, 12 July 1971. The flag was designed by Luritja artist Harold Thomas, from Central Australia. The flag was raised at the 1972 Tent Embassy in Canberra. It represents a powerful and uniting symbol of identity for Aboriginal people throughout Australia.

9   The Tent Embassy was established on the lawns of federal parliament in the early hours of Australia Day, 26 January 1972, as a swift

response to the announcement a day earlier by the McMahon Government that there would be no recognition of traditional ownership of land or compensation for dispossession. This announcement was in the context of the rejection of an advisory report from the Federal Office of Aboriginal Affairs that Aboriginal People should have the right to claim mining royalties on their lands and should have leasehold ownership of reserves in all states.

The establishment of the Tent Embassy also reflected the failure of the citizenship rights gained in the referendum of 1967 to lead to any gains in the land rights struggle or recognition of Aboriginal dispossession and rights to compensation. Instead there was widespread revocation of Aboriginal rights to occupy reserves and an accelerated move towards assimilation. This meant that Aboriginal people were dispersed from their communities and close proximity to country and kin, where they had been able to maintain a distinct social and cultural identity.

This was a highly symbolic and powerful protest that was significantly enhanced by the astute use of the term 'embassy'. An embassy is a place where foreign peoples are represented; it conjured up notions of the Aboriginal peoples as 'other' or 'alien' in their own land; see Newbury, P. (1999), *Aboriginal Heroes of the Resistance: from Pemulwuy to Mabo*, AWD, Sydney.

Chapter 8   Walytja: Kinship and Family

1   The Macassans were Indonesian fishermen primarily from the southern Celebes, where there existed a powerful maritime tradition. These fishermen gathered a type of sea slug, the trepang or bêche-de-mer, from shallow offshore waters and smoked their hauls on Australian soil before returning to their port of origin.

2   Bill Neidjie is the senior Lawman and traditional owner of Bunitji country. in the World Heritage area of Kakadu National Park, proclaimed in 1979. The uranium mining leases, including Ranger and Jabiluka, have been excised from this area.

Chapter 9   Top End

1   Dreaming sites are the spirit homes of different varieties of plants and
animals. and the association of site and species stems from the
Dreaming, the *tjukurrpa*. It is the crucial responsibility of local elders
to protect the site and to perform the relevant ceremonial 'increase'
rites to ensure fertility of the species. It is expected that the spirit
beings of the species concerned, as 'kin', must automatically respond
to such requests from their human custodians.

2   Although the police constable was acquitted in this case, the matter
was canvassed again in the RCIADIC in 1988, in the *Death of Jabanardi*
(At Ti Tree). This inquiry listed serious deficiencies in the police
investigation into the death and the incidents surrounding it,
including doubt as to the impartiality of the police inquiry into
potentially culpable behaviour by fellow officers. (For a full report,
see the Deaths in Custody Watch Committee (WA) Inc. web site:
http:/www.deathsincustody.com/windex.html).

3   John Pat died of head injuries in the police station cells at Roebourne
WA on the night of 28 September 1983. He was nearly seventeen
years old. Earlier that night he had been involved in a scuffle, coming
to the defence of his friend who was being hassled by off-duty police
drinking in the hotel. On being arrested and taken to the station
John Pat was further assaulted by police officers. He was placed in
an unconscious state in a cell, and was later found dead during a cell
check.

Following his death, an inquest was held and four police officers
were committed for trial on charges of manslaughter. They were all
acquitted. Serious doubt surrounded the effectiveness of the police
investigation into the death of John Pat, and the investigation of the
involvement of fellow police officers. John Pat's death was
investigated as part of the RCIADIC Report released in 1991. The
death of John Pat became for Aboriginal people across the nation
a symbol of injustice and oppression, and demonstrations on the
anniversary of his death have continually mobilised people calling
for justice.

4   Aboriginal Law, or customary Law, has proved difficult for
non-Aboriginal people to understand. The Aboriginal people of
Australia were not one people but were groups of distinct peoples

distinguished by differences in language, culture and country. Nonetheless Aboriginal Law can be described as holistic in that the Law is interwoven into the fabric of society and differs from alien systems of law in that it is non-compartmentalised, that is, religion, the law, the land and the people are one organ.

The Law is given in the story of creation that describes the territorial boundaries of the different language groups and also the local laws and customs. The creation story is a moral guide to behaviour in the social, economic, spiritual and political spheres, all of which is the Law. Both men and women played important roles in teaching and sustaining the Law, and the basis of women's authority, like that of men, rests upon ritual knowledge and expertise, rights in land and seniority.

In 1986, the Australian Law Reform Commission reported to the federal government on the matter of Aboriginal Customary Law and made various recommendations in favour of recognition, particularly in the jurisdictions of Family and Criminal law. There has been little or no implementation of these recommendations. The acceptance of Native Title by the High Court of Australia (1992) has provided for the co-existence of Aboriginal Law, and protection (albeit limited) for those laws in land rights legislation. This should herald a new era in recognition of Aboriginal Customary Law as a matter of justice for Aboriginal people.

5   The Maori people of Aotearoa (New Zealand) hold four seats in the national parliament established under the Maori Representation Act (1867), which arose out of franchise obligations in the Treaty of Waitangi, 1840.

Chapter 10 Sorry Business

1   Centre for Indigenous Development Education and Research, (1996). *Keeping Company: an intercultural conversation*, Australian Northern Territory Health Services.

Chapter 11 Educator

1   Russell Savage is currently serving a life sentence for murder in a prison in Florida, USA. There has been calls to have Russell

repatriated to Australia, to serve out his sentence here, close to his natural family. Russell's story has been told in the words and music of Archie Roach's *Munjana;* see Roach, A. (1994), *You have the Power,* Angus & Robertson, Sydney.

2   Yami Lester is *Anangu,* and has been a prominent activist for Aboriginal justice, being deeply involved in actions including the Pitjantjatjara Land Rights Act 1981, the Uluru-Kata Tjuta hand-back 1985, and the Maralinga Royal Commission in London, in 1985.

Chapter 12 Healing and Wellbeing

1   Quoted in Henry Reynolds, (1989), *Dispossession: Black Australians and White Invaders,* Allen & Unwin, Sydney, p. 2.

2   ibid., p. 17.

3   ibid., p. 90.

Chapter 14 Reconciliation

1   In 1999, Two Aboriginal claimants for compensation took their case to the Federal Court of Australia, claiming that they were unlawfully taken from their families as children. This action was vigorously opposed by the federal government. Lorna Cubillo, 62, was taken from her traditional Aboriginal country near Tennant Creek in 1947, aged about seven, and Peter Gunner (53) was taken from his traditional homelands at Utopia, outside Alice Springs, in 1956, also aged about seven. Ms Cubillo and Mr Gunner had sued the Commonwealth for the trauma, distress and continued isolation from the cultural and spiritual lives of their Aboriginal mothers.

　　In August 2000, a judge of the Federal Court rejected their claims for compensation as members of the Stolen Generations, ruling that they did not have an legal claim against the Commonwealth, even while accepting that they had suffered enormously after being separated from their families. In an appeal to the Full Bench of the Federal Court in 2001, the judges upheld the original decision.

2   The *Sea of Hands* was created in 1997 as a powerful physical statement to mobilise non-indigenous support for Native Title and

Reconciliation. Nearly 250 000 Australians have signed their names on one of the 120 000 plastic hands in the colours of the Aboriginal and the Torres Strait Islander flags to show their support for Native Title and Reconciliation. This action has been mobilised by ANTaR (Australians for Native Title and Reconciliation); see http://www.antar.org.au/SOH/html.

Place names mentioned in this book

The Centre
Atila (Mt Connor)
Haasts Bluff
Kata Tjuta
Middleton Ponds
Musgrave Ranges
Mutitjulu (Maggie Springs)
Petermann Ranges
Uluru–Kata Tjuta National Park
Uluru
Umbiara
Palmer River
Angas Downs
Tempe Downs
Middleton Ponds
Ti Tree
Alice Springs
Utopia
Rainbow Ridge
The Granites
Hermannsberg
Ailerong
Utkiya
Mulga Park Homestead
Waltanta
Paku-Paku
Yunampa
Mulyayiti (Mt Currie)
Tjunpu Dreaming site

Eyra Rock Hol
Watarrka (Kings Canyon)
Areyonga
Tennant Creek
Injatnama
Basedow Ranges
Coniston
Bob Randall's Tjukurrpa journey
Lake Amadeus
Yulara

Arnhem Land
Arafura Sea
Mornington Island
Galiwin'ku (Elcho Island)
Bathurst Island
Goulburn island
Barclay Bay
Obiri
Croker Island
Gumbulunya (Oenpelli)
Groote Eylandt
Kakadu National Park
East Alligator River
Burdham
Coopers Creek
Jabiru
Cobourg Peninsula

Other
Darwin
Aileron
Pine creek
Nightcliff
Katherine
Great Dividing Range

Sydney
Canberra
Adelaide
Wollongong
Otford
Stanwell Park
Queensland

Language groups

(for inclusion into a map of the areas covered by Aboriginal languages mentioned in the book)

Central Desert
Anmatyerre
Arrernte
Gurindji
Luritja
Pintupi
Pitjantjatjara
Walpiri
Yankunytjatjara

Arnhem Land

Gupapingu

Lardil
Gunwinku
Gumatj

Iwaidja

List of Abbreviations

ABS   Australian Bureau of Statistics

ANTaR   Australians for Native Title and Reconciliation

ANU   Australian National University

ATSIC   Aboriginal and Torres Strait Islander Commission

AWD   Action for World Development

CAALAS   Central Australian Aboriginal Legal Aid Service

CAAMA   Central Australian Aboriginal Media Association

FAMCO   First Aboriginal Mining Company

FCAATSI   Federal Council for the Advancement of Aborigines
            and Torres Strait Islanders

HALT   Healthy Aboriginal Life Team

HREOC   Human Rights and Equal Opportunity Commission

IAD   Institute for Aboriginal Development

NAIDOC   National Aboriginal and Islander Day Observance
            Committee

RCIADC   Royal Commission into Aboriginal Deaths in
            Custody